TUFF STUFF'S

Baseball Postcard

COLLECTION

Ron Menchine

Edited by Doug Scoville

Best wishes,

Ron Menchine

Tuff Stuff Books
Published by Tuff Stuff Publications, 1934 E. Parham Road, Richmond, Virginia 23228.
Tuff Stuff Books and Tuff Stuff Publications are divisions of Krause Publications Inc.

To order additional copies of this book, or to request a free catalog, please contact:
Tuff Stuff Books, P.O. Box 1050, Dubuque, Iowa 52004,
or call 1-800-334-7165.

Library of Congress Cataloging-in-Publication Data
Menchine, Ron

ISBN: 0-930625-53-6

Library of Congress Catalog Number: 99-61142

Editorial Director: Larry Canale
Editor: Doug Scoville
Proofreader: Joyce Caldwell

Design Director: Tim Roberts
Graphic Designer: Fred Wollenberg
Additional Graphic Support: Christine Schup, Abe Longmire, Randy Stepanek

Typefaces: Garamond, Gill Sans, and Bodoni

Cover Design: Tim Roberts and Christine Schup

Front cover art shows details of the following postcards (clockwise from upper left): Ty Cobb, postcard published by A.C.
Dietsche Co.; Joe DiMaggio's Restaurant, postcard published by Joe DiMaggio's Restaurant; Mark McGwire, postcard
published by Barry Colla; Babe Ruth, postcard publisher unknown; Nolan Ryan, postcard published by Barry Colla;
Mickey Mantle, postcard published by Holiday Inn.

DEDICATION

To my remarkable mother, Mildred, who at 96 is still a great inspiration.

–Ron Menchine

ACKNOWLEDGEMENTS

Like any book, this volume would not have come together without contributions from a vast group of individuals. My special thanks to:

The 1969, '70, and '71 Washington Senators, who made broadcasting major league baseball the most enjoyable experience of my life.

The late Roy Cox, longtime friend and postcard dealer extraordinaire, who taught me so much about the joy of postcard collecting.

The hundreds of baseball postcard collectors throughout America, many of whom have become close friends over the years, particularly the late Buck Barker, Bill Fitzgerald, Frank Nagy, and John Sullivan, and current collectors Doug Alford, Mel Bailey, Tom Crabtree, Jerry Hermele, Gordon Kramp, Ray Medeiros, Vic Pallos, and George Tinker.

Baseball writers Ted Patterson and Chuck McGeehan, who generously provided me with research material for this book.

Public relations directors John Blake of the Texas Rangers, Mike Swanson of the Arizona Diamondbacks, and Rick Vaughn of the Tampa Bay Devil Rays, who supplied some of the postcards for this book.

Ed Allen, author of *Baltimore Orioles Team-Issued Postcards.*

Mark Bowers, a collector from Granite Bay, California, whose outstanding checklist and price guide of baseball color postcards was a great help.

Donald R. Brown, executive director, Institute of American Deltiology in Myerstown, Pennsylvania, who lent help and advice.

Barry Colla, the photographer from Santa Clara, California, whose brilliant work from 1980 to the present has helped make player postcards such popular collectibles.

Lee Cox, the postcard dealer who introduced me to artist Sherry Kemp and sold me many of the postcards seen in this book.

Paul Dickson, author of *Dickson's Baseball Dictionary,* who never failed to provide sound advice and generous help during the preparation of this book.

Dan Even, a longtime Arizona collector whose newsletter on current baseball player postcards is useful and well done.

James R. Hartley, whose excellent book *Washington's Expansion Senators (1961–1971)* brought back some great memories.

Mickey Heise, a postcard collector and dealer whose pricing assistance was a big help.

Mike Hirsch, my collecting colleague who kindly loaned postcards from his excellent collection for illustration in this book.

Tom Holster, the president of the Washington Baseball Society, who has kept the torch of major league baseball in Washington burning brightly.

Sherry Kemp, the internationally known postcard artist who provided the artwork for the author's personal postcard.

Doug McWilliams, an outstanding photographer from Berkeley, California, whose player postcards from the 1970s are among the best ever produced.

The outstanding team at Tuff Stuff Publications who made the text sparkle and the cards look sharp, including editors Doug Scoville and Larry Canale, proofreader Joyce Caldwell, designers Fred Wollenberg and Christine Schup, and design director Tim Roberts.

Dave Sosidka, whose excellent publication *Ballparks & Ballplayers* is a must-have for all baseball postcard collectors. It's available from P.O. Box 5166, Clinton, N.J. 08809.

Henry Thomas, grandson of baseball immortal Walter Johnson and close friend whose award-winning book *Walter Johnson, The Big Train* provided much useful information.

Al Weiner, publisher of Almar Press, who launched my writing career.

Finally, Phil Wood, sports talk-show host and my longtime friend who introduced me to the good folks at *Tuff Stuff.*

–R.M.

Contents

FOREWORD

What a time to be a baseball fan. In my 23 years playing third base for the Baltimore Orioles, I don't think I saw anything that matched the excitement of baseball fans during the 1998 season. But as much fun as it was to watch Mark McGwire, Sammy Sosa, and Cal Ripken Jr. set new records for individual achievement, it was even more gratifying to see how they did it: with respect for their fellow players, the fans, and the game and its history.

Baseball has changed quite a bit since I played in the 1950s, '60s, and '70s. Strength training and conditioning have helped make today's stars perhaps the best athletes ever to play the game. But the million-dollar salaries, the fans' high expectations, and the media's unceasing attention these days have led many players to be more protective of themselves and their privacy, and to distance themselves from the public.

That's where sports memorabilia—including postcards—comes in. Memorabilia has always brought baseball fans closer to the game they love. I remember sitting in front of my locker before games, signing postcards and photos that the Orioles' office would send out to fans. Nowadays, besides signing autographs through the mail, I regularly go to sports collectors' shows. Though I'm not a collector myself, it's wonderful to see fathers and sons collecting together, and to meet fans and talk baseball. Sometimes I just have to shake my head at the hold this game has on people.

Baseball certainly has had a hold on Ron Menchine for his whole life. I first met Ron almost 40 years ago, as he was working his way into the field of radio sportscasting. He struck me as a nice fellow who knew a lot about the game. When he took over broadcasting the Washington Senators' ballgames in the 1960s, I would see him when the Senators played the Orioles.

To this day, I see Ron at least once every year. I consider him not just a professional acquaintance, but a friend. Yet until recently, I had no idea that Ron was such a passionate postcard collector. Ron keeps thousands of cards at his house north of Baltimore, just a few miles from mine. His collection includes some of the oldest baseball postcards known to exist, and it spans the entire 20th century. In the wide-ranging sampling of cards illustrated in this book, you'll find scenes depicting some of the game's great old ballparks, you'll see a host of unforgettable championship team photos, and—most of all—you'll enjoy a healthy offering of postcards featuring most of the best ballplayers in baseball history. (Ron even included a couple of cards with my picture, I'm flattered to say.)

As you turn this book's pages, the illustrations will give you a sense of what baseball has meant to America for the past 100 years. In particular, the faces of the

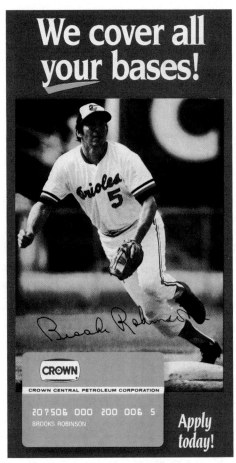

Publisher: Crown Central Petroleum Corp., Baltimore, MD • Manufacturer: Not Indicated • Type: Chrome Business Reply Card • Postmark: Not Used
Value: $5 Unsigned

players—some legends, some all but forgotten—leap out at you in a way they just don't seem to do with traditional baseball cards. Once you've looked at each picture, take time to read Ron's accompanying text. It captures many of the details that made the players, teams, and parks so memorable.

If you're a collector of baseball postcards like Ron, I think you'll find this book, with its illustrations and postcard prices, to be a handy resource. And if, like me, you're just a fan of the game, I hope this book brings you a little closer to your heroes. Either way, you should enjoy it for years to come

Brooks Robinson
July 15, 1999

INTRODUCTION

In the United States, picture postcards date to 1893, when a series was issued to celebrate the Columbian Exposition (World's Fair) in Chicago. The earliest documented card pertaining to major league baseball is a 1900 real-photo card showing Honus Wagner and two of his Pittsburgh Pirate teammates, Tommy Leach and Duff Cooley.

As postcards became more common and less expensive to produce, baseball clubs seized at them. The earliest known team postcard, showing the 1903 New York Giants, was issued by Falk of New York. Two years later, the Philadelphia Athletics released an entire series of 20 ornate cards celebrating their American League championship.* Not to be outdone, the New York Giants—who defeated the Athletics in the 1905 World Series—had their own cards produced by the Ullman Company of New York. All of the Giants pictured wore uniforms with the words "World Champions" emblazoned across the chests. The Rhotograph Co. also issued 1905 cards featuring Giants players as well as some New York Highlanders.

These early postcards differ from modern specimens in a crucial way. Prior to 1907, postcard backs were reserved exclusively for addresses; by law, messages could be written only on the card fronts. Then the government began to permit cards with divided backs that could share a message and the mailing address.

The same year saw the introduction of another postcard innovation: color. Until 1907, all baseball postcards were black-and-white. The Morgan Stationery Co. of Cincinnati broke the mold, issuing a set of 10 full-color cards using photos taken at Palace of the Fans, the Reds' ballpark. Second baseman Miller Huggins is the only identified player in the set, making him the first major leaguer depicted on a color postcard.

Expensive to produce, color postcards remained rare through the first half of the century. But some publishers found unique ways to add color without adding expense. G.F. Grignon, for example, produced in 1907 16 cards with small black-and-white portraits of Cubs players, each set against a green background, along with a posed teddy bear and a two-line verse. Across town, George W. Hull produced black-and-white cards depicting 10 members of the 1906 world champion White Sox.

Championship teams were great fodder for early baseball postcards. Various Detroit publishers issued a plethora of Tiger postcards from 1907–09, when the team won three consecutive American League pennants. A.C. Dietsche produced 16 cards with action scenes set against black backgrounds. In 1907, when the Tigers met the Cubs in the World Series, Dietsche also produced a set of 16 Cubs postcards with sepia backgrounds.

That same World Series inspired H.M. Taylor to issue a set of eight black-and-white Tiger cards. The Wolverine News Co. published cards similar to the Taylors that are also very collectible. Another news publisher, *The Detroit Free Press,* published a set of 12 green-and-cream Tiger cards that year. Topping and Co. issued the most ornate of the early Tiger sets in 1909, publishing 20 known cards each with a black-and-white head shot of a player inside a yellow star.

During this same period, the Brush Motor Car Co. issued a rare set that showed Tiger stars endorsing its products. Brush was the first in a long line of Detroit automakers that used Tiger players to promote cars. (See "Advertising Postcards," p. 9.)

Of course, the Tigers weren't the only players to command postcards as the 1910s approached. In 1908, Cleveland's American League Publishing Co. issued 15 cards featuring prominent local players as well as the game's premier stars, Ty Cobb and Honus Wagner. This marked a new era in baseball postcards. Prior to this, postcard series had featured only players of regional interest. Now "the national pastime" was producing national stars, and postcard publishers began to take this into account.

In 1909, the Rose Co. of Philadelphia crafted an ambitious postcard series featuring players from all 16 major league teams as well as Scranton of the New York State League. To date, 160 cards have been identified. These beautiful cards each have a green background with a gold embossed circle behind a black-and-white head shot of a player. Highly desired by modern collectors, Rose cards of common players sell for around $75, while top stars bring hundreds of dollars.

From 1909 through 1916, Chicago publisher Max Stein—who also operated under the name United States Publishing House—issued at least 25 different cards featuring top players and teams of the era. Nearly all Max Stein postcards command a minimum of $100, with higher sums for Hall of Famers and White Sox third baseman Buck Weaver, banned from baseball in the fallout of the 1919 Black Sox scandal. A Stein card of Olympic star Jim Thorpe, who played six years in the majors from 1913–19, is a real sleeper.

The Novelty Cutlery Co. of Canton, Ohio, became the first advertiser to employ national baseball stars for postcards. Included among its gray cards is one showing Cobb and Wagner together—in a photo obviously taken during the 1909 World Series between Pittsburgh and Detroit—that today brings close to $1,000. The same images later appeared on sepia cards with no publisher listed. Today, the sepia cards bring about $100 each, the more attractive Novelty cards about 10 percent more.

In 1915, *The Sporting News* got into the postcard

---

*A group of 19 sold for nearly $3,000 in a 1994 Leland's auction.

business, issuing a set of six color-tinted cards. The set sells today for $1,500–$2,000 in mint condition.

While postcards featuring national stars were prospering, local cards were still produced in abundance. From 1909–11, St. Louis photographer H.H. Bregstone issued a series of photo postcards featuring top Browns and Cardinals. In 1912, when the Red Sox reigned as American League and world champions, the *Boston Daily* and *Boston Sunday American* published postcards of the team. After the Cincinnati Reds defeated the Chicago White Sox in the 1919 World Series, an anonymous manufacturer published a set of 24 Reds cards on poor quality board. Unattractive and in relative abundance, these cards have never caught on with collectors.

In 1921, the Exhibit Supply Co. of Chicago began producing Arcade (also called "Exhibit") cards of baseball players for sale in vending machines at amusement parks. Even though the pure Exhibit cards had black backs, many people mailed them as postcards. Over the years, a few Exhibit cards were produced with light postcard backs, some of them marked, "Not to be used in Exhibit machines." In 1922, the Eastern Exhibit Supply Co. of Philadelphia issued a set of 20 sepia cards with pure postcard backs with the word "Correspondence" on the left side of the divided back and the word "Address" on the right.

Through the 1920s and '30s, while Exhibits remained popular, baseball postcards passed out of favor. Of course, there were exceptions, including one provided by Detroit Tigers star Hank Greenberg, who had his own postcard printed in the '30s to accommodate autograph requests. After World War II, postcards enjoyed a resurgence in popularity, thanks in part to two baseball radio announcers.

In 1948, a set of 12 Washington Senators postcards sponsored by Gunther Beer and Senators radio broadcaster Arch McDonald was made available exclusively through radio station WTOP. Extremely rare today, these cards bring in excess of $100 each in pristine condition.

That same year, Cleveland Indians owner Bill Veeck began issuing photo postcards of his players. In 1949, Tribe announcer Van Patrick began sending the cards to fans who wrote to him. Between them, McDonald and Patrick made baseball postcards fashionable again.

The St. Louis Cardinals joined the postcard parade in '49, issuing the first of many annual series. At first, player photos shared space with a team schedule; later, the calendar was replaced by a team message. Beginning in 1956, the message was dropped, and the player photos gained greater prominence.

Pennsylvanians also enjoyed new baseball postcards in 1949, though not team issues. Film Fotos Inc. of New York issued an outstanding Pittsburgh Pirates photo set, while the Olmes Studios of Philadelphia produced a beautiful series of Athletics photo postcards. Olmes continued the practice for several years. In 1950, when the Phillies won the National League pennant, Olmes even issued a photo postcard of ace pitcher Robin Roberts, the only non-Athletic in its series.

Also in 1950, a familiar name began to appear on the backs of real-photo postcards: Kodak. The photography giant became virtually the only source of paper for these types of cards. Thus almost all real-photo cards produced after 1950 have a Kodak mark on their backs.*

As the prosperous '50s wore on, baseball postcards continued to proliferate. Chicago lensman George Brace, a longtime photographer of major league players, began giving players postcards to send to fans. During this same period, Detroit photographer J.D. "Charley" McCarthy expanded his postcard range from the Tigers to include players from every major league team.

Having reintroduced single-player postcards in Cleveland, it was only natural for Bill Veeck—and his astute marketing director, Rudy Schaefer—to issue player postcards in St. Louis when they took over the Browns in 1951. Veeck's team continued to produce Browns postcards for the three years the team remained in St. Louis. When the Browns moved to Baltimore and became the Orioles in 1954, the new management kept the postcard tradition alive.

In Virginia, Don Wingfield began producing brilliant real-photo postcards of Washington Senators stars in 1955, then began to issue printed postcards featuring other teams' players. A year later, in Wisconsin, Spic and Span Dry Cleaners of Milwaukee issued 18 oversized postcards of the Braves.

In the late '50s and early '60s, photographer Norman Paulson joined the player postcard business, both under his name and as National Press. In that same period, Graphic Arts Service of Cincinnati issued 16 cards, primarily of Detroit Tigers. L.L. Cook Postcard Publishers in Milwaukee turned out more than 20 photo cards of Braves and Brewers players from the '50s through 1971.

COLOR POSTCARDS

Though they were introduced early in the 20th century, color postcards did not become common until the 1950s. In 1953, Long Island photographer Louis Dormand began producing color postcards of major league stars. The 38 players featured are primarily Yankees, with a few others who came through Yankee Stadium mixed in. These cards were issued as premiums by the Mason Candy Company and used by players to correspond with fans.

Some of the most beautiful color postcards of the 1950s came from the Bill and Bob Photographic Studio of Bradenton, Florida, where the Milwaukee Braves trained. Today, their 15 Braves cards are all highly col-

---

*One way to judge the authenticity of a postcard is to look for a Kodak mark on the back. If the card is supposed to predate 1950 but says "Kodak," it's a fake. A number of such counterfeit cards entered the market in 1994.

lectible. Two other popular color cards of that decade are Don Wingfield's only color postcard, which features Harmon Killebrew, and a card of Yankee outfielder Hank Bauer produced by the Hayes Co. of Fort Hayes, Kansas.

While the 1960s featured numerous color cards, the most popular were produced by New York photographer Louis Requina. All of Requina's color cards except one feature Yankees.

The Los Angeles Dodgers emerged as a postcard staple soon after the club moved to California. Since 1959, its second season in Los Angeles, the Dodgers have produced cards every year, with the exception of a period from 1987–1991.

Two Californians stand out among recent color postcard photographers: Doug McWilliams of Berkeley and Barry Colla of Santa Clara. McWilliams began in 1970, producing beautiful color postcards of Oakland Athletics players. His work was so outstanding that players from other teams sought him out to do cards until 1985, when he stopped publishing postcards.

Colla has been the premier publisher of color postcards for players and teams since 1983, when he produced a San Francisco Giants series. Subsequent cards have featured the Dodgers, Mets, Twins, and Blue Jays. In 1989, Colla began producing eight-card sets featuring individual stars.

In recent years, some teams have begun to issue Player Message Cards (PMCs), which feature a player on the front and a message from that player that takes up the entire back. The Mets, Twins, and Orioles have been issuing PMCs instead of postcards in recent years, some produced by Colla.

Other cards of recent vintage are postcard-sized, but have backs filled entirely with biographical information about the featured players, making them impossible to send as postcards. I designate cards like these as Player Information Cards (PICs), and they are not included in this book.

For a definitive work on color postcards, see Mark Bowers' *Color Postcards 1953-1995*, an illustrated checklist of every color postcard known to exist.

ADVERTISING POSTCARDS

As previously noted, American businesses realized early the promotional power of baseball. When the Detroit Tigers were kings of the American League (1907–09), Brush Motor Car Co. lined up Tiger stars to extol the virtues of Brush automobiles. After winning the 1910 World Series, Philadelphia A's stars were signed to endorse Monarch typewriters with a set of black-and-white postcards.

Over the years, Tiger players have frequently been used to promote various automotive products. After winning the 1935 World Series, Tiger player/manager Mickey Cochrane endorsed B.F. Goodrich tires. In 1962, Ford issued 16 cards showing Tiger players, coaches, and a trainer standing next to one of their cars. The players used the postcards to answer autograph requests. In the late '60s and early '70s, Tiger stars Bill Freehan and Mickey Lolich endorsed Chrysler cars.

Another popular and scarce postcard set, issued in 1946 by Sears stores in East St. Louis, featured players from both the Browns and Cardinals. Thirty cards of each team were produced. Several years later, Roger Maris of the Cardinals appeared on an oversized postcard promoting AAMCO products. After he hit 61 home runs in 1961, Maris appeared on a postcard with restauranteur Sam Gordon, who purchased the record-breaking ball.

In recent years, Nationwide Insurance has produced PICs of the Pittsburgh Pirates, while Coca-Cola produced cards for the Los Angeles Dodgers in 1985 and 1986. In 1994, David Sunflower Seeds issued postcards that selected Dodger players used to answer autograph requests.

COOPERSTOWN PLAQUE CARDS

Since the National Baseball Hall of Fame and Museum opened in Cooperstown, New York, postcards have been issued that reproduce the plaques made to commemorate those players named to the Hall. All the members of the shrine, from 1936 to the present, have been so depicted. The Albertype Co. of Brooklyn produced the Hall of Fame plaque postcards until 1952, when the Artvue Postcard Co. took over. Later, Curt Teich of Chicago became the publisher. The early sepia cards published by Albertype and Artvue today tend to run in the $5–$10 price range. If signed by their respective Hall of Famers, they can bring hundreds of dollars apiece. Unsigned plaques from recent years usually can be had for 25–50 cents, while signed cards bring considerably more.

–Ron Menchine

1900-09

The dawn of the 20th century brought momentous changes to major league baseball, changes that are still felt today. In 1901, the American League was formed as a rival to the National League. Following the formation of the National League in 1876, other leagues—including the Union Association, American Association, Players League, and Federal League—tried briefly to compete, but eventually disappeared. Only the American League still thrives. The success of the AL led in 1903 to the advent of the World Series, which captivates America to this day. In 1906, the first crosstown Series pitted the NL's Chicago Cubs, who had won a record 116 games, against the rival White Sox, who had won the pennant despite posting a league-low .230 team batting average. The Cubs were heavily favored, but the "Hitless Wonder" White Sox—behind the brilliant pitching of Ed Walsh, Doc White, and 20-game winner Nick Altrock—shocked Chicago and the world, winning the Series in six games. The Cubs, who fielded the legendary double-play trio of Joe Tinker, Johnny Evers, and Frank Chance, as well as pitchers Ed Reulbach, Jake Pfiester, and Three Finger Brown, went on to win the 1907 and '08 Series with virtually the same lineup.

The rise of the American League also created the need for new ballparks. By 1903, Philadelphia's Columbia

Publisher: V.O. Hammon Publishing Co., Chicago, IL • Manufacturer: V.O. Hammon • Type: Black & White • Postmark: Chicago, IL, Oct. 16, 1906
Value: $150

Park, New York's Hilltop Park, and Boston's Huntington Avenue Grounds had sprung up in the nation's greatest cities. Like the parks before them, these arenas were constructed from wood, and thus were susceptible to the fires that destroyed many early ballparks. Then in 1909, the first modern baseball stadiums built of steel and concrete opened: Shibe Park in Philadelphia and Forbes Field in Pittsburgh. They were considered the final word in architecture and fan comfort.

Within the parks, legends were in the making. Managers such as Connie Mack of the Philadelphia Athletics, John McGraw of the New York Giants, Frank Chance of the Chicago Cubs, and Hughie Jennings of the Detroit Tigers established reputations as brilliant leaders, while players such as Napoleon Lajoie, Ty Cobb, Ed Walsh, Walter Johnson, Sam Crawford, Honus Wagner, Frank Chance, Joe Tinker, and Johnny Evers, to mention only a few, earned their status as all-time superstars. Then there's the remarkable Cy Young who, despite being 33 years old at the turn of the century, still ranked as one of the game's great pitchers, winning two games in the 1903 World Series as he helped the Boston Puritans upset the Pittsburgh Pirates in the first of the modern Fall Classics. You'll meet these people and many more as we revisit the 20th century's first decade.

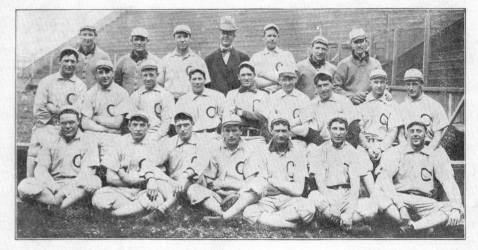

Publisher: F.P. Burke, Chicago, IL • Manufacturer: Not Indicated • Type: Black & White
Postmark: Chicago, IL, Oct. 15, 1906 • Value: $175–$200

Publisher: Not Indicated • Manufacturer: Not Indicated • Type: Real Photo • Postmark: Not Used • Value: $1,000–$1,500

1900 TOMMY LEACH, DUFF COOLEY, & HONUS WAGNER, Pittsburgh Pirates

The three nicely attired young men in this photograph hardly project the image of professional baseball players. Don't let appearances fool you, however. All three were prominent members of the 1900 Pittsburgh Pirates. From left to right, they are Tommy Leach, Duff Cooley, and Honus Wagner, one of the finest players in baseball history. This extremely rare item is the earliest known postcard to feature major league baseball players.

The Pirates of 1900 finished in second place in the eight-team National League, 4½ games behind the Brooklyn Superbas. It was the first year these players were members of the Pirates. Prior to 1900, Leach and Wagner had played with the NL's Louisville Colonels, which merged with the Pirates when the league contracted from 12 teams to eight.

First baseman Cooley, who came from the Philadelphia club, batted just .201 in Pittsburgh and was traded to Boston after the season. It was an aberration for a player who compiled a .294 average in his 13 major league years.

On the other hand, Wagner had an outstanding season, leading the NL with a .381 average, the highest in his brilliant 21-year career. "Winning my first batting title in 1900 was my greatest thrill in baseball," Wagner later recalled. Although Wagner became famous as a shortstop, he played in right field that season, making the transition to short in 1901.

Leach was a utility player in 1900, seeing time at third base, shortstop, second base, and in the outfield, and batting .213 in 51 games. He accrued a .269 average over 19 seasons, retiring in 1918.

1901 COLUMBIA PARK, Philadelphia Athletics

In 1901, Ben Shibe and Connie Mack obtained a franchise for a Philadelphia team nicknamed the Athletics in the new American League, and they hurriedly sought a location for a ballpark. In his autobiography, *My 66 Years in the Big Leagues,* Connie Mack discusses the search:

We now had our franchise but we had no team and no park. What I learned about Philadelphia, I learned from walking the entire city, inspecting every vacant lot. We were in such a hurry to get started that we thought we might have to take a city playground. Finally we decided upon a site at 29th Street and Columbia Avenue and got it on a 10-year lease. Columbia Park is the name we gave it. We had just five weeks after leasing the park to put up the stands in order to keep the franchise. It didn't take us long to construct a single-decked, wooden grandstand.

Columbia Park, in a section of Philadelphia called Brewerytown, was ready for the opening game on

COLUMBIA BALL PARK, PHILADELPHIA, PA.

Publisher: Not Indicated • Manufacturer: Not Indicated
Type: Color Pre-Linen • Postmark: Not Used • Value: $200

April 24, 1901. Two days of rain delayed the official opening until April 26, when an overflow crowd of more than 10,000 watched the Athletics lose to the Washington Senators, 5-1. However, the Athletics' second baseman, Napoleon Lajoie—whom Shibe and Mack had financially induced to jump from the National League's Phillies—shone as the team's star, with three hits in the losing cause. Lajoie's batting exploits were a portent of things to come, as he went on to lead the AL with a remarkable .426 batting average, more than 80 points better than the league's second-leading hitter. Nap played head and shoulders above everyone else that year, becoming the AL's first triple crown winner as he also led the league with 14 home runs and 125 RBI.

The Athletics finished fourth in 1901, then came back in '02 to post the AL's best record. They succeeded a bit too early to play in a postseason series, however, as the first NL/AL World Series didn't occur until 1903.

1901 EDDIE PLANK, Philadelphia Athletics

In 1901, when Connie Mack was creating his American League team in Philadelphia, he went looking for quality players. In his book, *My 66 Years in the Big Leagues,* he wrote of one of his successes: "I found a boy wonder at Gettysburg College who looked like a comer to me. His name was Eddie Plank."

Plank left Gettysburg College to become a Hall of Fame pitcher, never spending a single day in the minor leagues. During his first season with the Athletics, the 5-foot 11½-inch left-hander won 17 games and lost 13. The next season, he went 20-15 as the A's won their first pennant. It proved to be the first of eight 20-win seasons for Plank—seven with the A's and one with the St. Louis Terriers of the Federal League.

By the time his career ended in 1917, Plank had proven himself to be the best left-handed pitcher in major league history. He pitched more shutouts and complete games than any lefty before or since. To this

EDWARD S. PLANK, Pitcher

Publisher: The Monarch Typewriter Co. • Manufacturer: Not Indicated
Type: Black & White • Postmark: Not Used • Value: $200–$250

day, Plank's career victory total of 326 wins stands third-best all time for left-handers, behind only Warren Spahn and Steve Carlton. In his best season, 1904, he went 26-17. Of course, some of Plank's success must be attributed to his teams. During his stint in Philadelphia, the A's won six pennants and went to five World Series (there was no World Series when the A's won the 1902 pennant).

Plank joined Mack in the Hall of Fame in 1946.

1903 NEW YORK GIANTS

This postcard is the earliest known to show a major league team. The players were photographed on the staircase of New York's famous Waldorf Astoria Hotel. Baseball had an image problem in the early years, as many of the players were hard-drinking rowdies. Associating the Giants with the grand Waldorf Astoria, one of the world's finest hotels, was probably an attempt to bring the club more respectability.

In his first full season as manager, John McGraw took the New York Giants from a last-place finish in

1902 to second place in 1903. McGraw learned his managing craft as one of the stars of the famous Baltimore Orioles of the 1890s, and was years ahead of his contemporaries as a strategist and innovator. As was the case with many of McGraw's future Giant teams, pitching was the strength in 1903. Right-hander Joe McGinnity, second from the left in the second row, led the National League with 32 wins, while Christy Mathewson, seated to the right of McGinnity, was the league's second-best pitcher with 29 victories. McGinnity and Mathewson were eventually elected to Baseball's Hall of Fame. Another future Hall of Famer, Roger Bresnahan, who led the 1903 Giants in batting with a .350 average, sits at the bottom left.

Publisher: Thaddeus Wilkerson, New York, NY • Manufacturer: Thaddeus Wilkerson • Type: Real Photo • Postmark: Not Used
Value: $1,500–$2,000

1903 HILLTOP PARK, New York Highlanders

American League president Ban Johnson was anxious to put a franchise in New York because he knew a team in the nation's largest city would bring the league instant credibility—and perhaps more money. When the American League was founded in 1901, it had franchises in Baltimore, Boston, Chicago, Cleveland, Detroit, Milwaukee, Philadelphia, and Washington, D.C. In 1902, the members remained the same with the exception of Milwaukee, whose franchise moved to St. Louis. The Baltimore Orioles finished the 1902 season in last place and in financial straits. Johnson was able to switch the franchise to New York, finding two New Yorkers, Frank Farrell and Bill Devery, to purchase the Baltimore franchise for $18,000.

The transported club found a playing site on Broadway between 165th and 168th Streets, and hastily constructed a wooden ballpark that became known as Hilltop Park because of its high elevation. When John W. Gordon was hired to operate the team as president, his last name reminded someone of the famous British military unit known as Gordon's Highlanders. Based on this association and Hilltop Park's location, the team was dubbed the New York Highlanders.

Hilltop Park opened on May 1, 1903, with the Highlanders beating the Washington Senators 8-1 before an overflow crowd of 16,293. This photograph by Thaddeus Wilkerson shows the wooden grandstand as it looked from center field. The water visible in the background is the Hudson River.

Publisher: Photo by Falk • Manufacturer: Photo by Falk
Type: Real Photo • Postmark: Not Used • Value: $1,000–$1,500

Publisher: Not Indicated • Manufacturer: Not Indicated • Type: Real Photo • Postmark: Not Used • Value: $1,000–$1,500

1903 HUNTINGTON AVENUE GROUNDS, Boston Puritans

Although the American League was founded in 1901, 1903 was the first year that the champions of the American League and National League met in a World Series. Pittsburgh owner Barney Dreyfuss contacted Boston owner Henry Killilea in August, when it became apparent that his Pirates and the Puritans (later called the Red Sox) would win their respective League championships. He suggested a best-of-nine format for the first inter-league championship series since the 1890s. In the 1880s and 1890s, the champions from the National League and rival American Association had faced off in a lengthy World Series. When the American Association was absorbed into the National League in 1892, the top two teams met in what was called the Temple Cup Series. The last such series had taken place in 1897, when the Baltimore Orioles defeated the Boston Beaneaters four games to one.

The wooden structure shown above is Boston's Huntington Avenue Grounds, site of the first game of the modern World Series. The Pirates, led by player/manager Fred Clarke and incomparable shortstop Honus Wagner, had won their third straight National League pennant and were heavy favorites over the upstart Puritans. The park was built to hold about 8,500 spectators, but 16,242 crammed inside that day. Most went away disappointed,

as Boston's 28-game winner Cy Young gave up four first-inning runs and was clearly outpitched by Deacon Phillippe. The Pirates won the game, 7-3. The Puritans fell behind three games to one, then won four in a row, as Young had two victories and Bill Dinneen recorded three wins. Phillippe was magnificent throughout the Series, gaining all three Pirates victories, but the Puritans emerged as champions of the world.

1905 PHILADELPHIA ATHLETICS

The 1905 Philadelphia Athletics, adroitly managed by Connie Mack, won 92 games and lost 56. Heavy in pitching talent, the A's had three 20-game winners in 1905, but no batter posted a better batting average than team captain Harry Davis' .284. Eccentric Rube Waddell, one of baseball's most famous characters (pictured third from the right with arms folded in the top row of the photograph atop the facing page), earned pitching's triple crown with the league's best record (27-10), lowest ERA (1.48), and most strikeouts (287). Left-hander Eddie Plank (third from the left in the middle row) posted a 24-12 record, while right-hander Andy Coakley enjoyed his finest major league season with 18 wins and 8 defeats.

In order to save money during baseball's early days, teams frequently made two players share a single bed during road trips. Catcher Ossee Schreckengost ("Schreck"),

PHILADELPHIA AMERICAN LEAGUE BASE BALL TEAM ("ATHLETICS")
Reading from left to right are: Top row—Murphy, Davis, Hanley, Waddell, Knight, Bender. Middle row—Seybold, Coakley, Plank, L. Cross, Schreck, Lord. Lower row—M. Cross, Hoffman, Barton, Hartsel, Dygert, Powers.

Publisher: Not Indicated • Manufacturer: Not Indicated
Type: Black & White • Postmark: Not Used • Value: $150–$200

seated second from the right in the middle row, had a clause written into his contract that forbade his roommate, Waddell, from eating animal crackers in bed.

As great as the A's pitchers were, the New York Giants pitchers proved to be even better in the 1905 World Series, winning four games to one without allowing a single earned run. Christy Mathewson pitched three shutouts for New York, while Joe McGinnity pitched one. Philadelphia's only win came on Chief Bender's four-hit shutout in the second game, with Philadelphia scoring three unearned runs off two Giant errors.

1905 NEW YORK GIANTS

If the New York Giants were afraid to play the American League champion Boston Puritans in the 1904 World Series, they more than made up for it in 1905. In his autobiography, *My Thirty Years in Baseball*, John McGraw candidly admitted that Giants owner John Brush "did not see why we should jeopardize the fruits of our victory by recognizing and playing against the champions of an organization that had been formed to put us out of business." Perhaps the Boston Puritans' stunning upset of the National League's Pittsburgh Pirates in the 1903 World Series sparked this reaction.

In any case, the issue was resolved in 1905, and the Giants made amends for their previous reticence. The club's 105 wins nearly matched its 1904 total of 108. Christy Mathewson was again a 30-game winner, leading the NL with 31 victories against only 8 losses. Mathewson also compiled the league's best ERA, 1.27. Mike Donlin, in his first year as a Giants outfielder, led the team with a .356 batting average, third-best in the National League. The Giants beat the Philadelphia Athletics in that year's World Series, the only one in history in which every game was a shutout.

The Giants were the toast of New York in 1905, and this photograph—one of the first baseball postcards produced in color—shows a few of the team's stars. Of

Publisher: Souvenir Postcard Co., New York, NY • Manufacturer: J.T. Dye, New York, NY • Type: Color Pre-Linen • Postmark: Not Used • Value: $150–$200

the six players shown, four are pitchers, and all of those are right-handers. After Mathewson, Red Ames recorded 22 wins, Joe McGinnity had 21 victories, and Dummy Taylor won 16 games. Left fielder Sam Mertes, to the left of Mathewson, led the Giants with 108 RBI. Sam Bowerman, pictured on the extreme left, batted .269 with 41 RBI as he shared catching duties with future Hall of Famer Roger Bresnahan.

1905 JOHN McGRAW, New York Giants

John McGraw posted Hall of Fame numbers during his 16 years as a player, primarily as a third baseman with the famous Baltimore Orioles, who won three consecutive National League championships (1894–96). A fiery competitor, he personified the rough-and-tumble days of 1890s baseball, frequently letting his fists do the talking. His lifetime batting average of .333 ranks among the game's best. But McGraw is best remembered for his managerial skills. In 33 seasons with the original Orioles

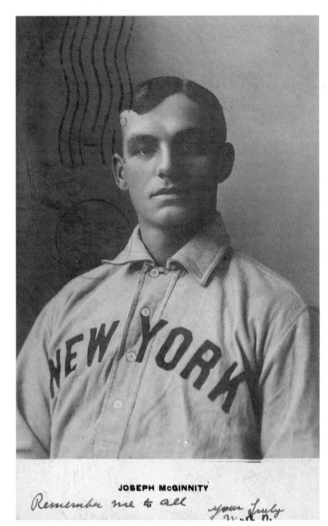

JOSEPH McGINNITY

Remember me to all   your truly
m... D..

Publisher: The Rhotograph Co., New York, NY • Manufacturer: The Rhotograph Co. • Type: Real Photo • Postmark: Brooklyn, NY, Aug. 13, 1907 • Value: $200–$250

ROTOGRAPH SERIES   MANAGER - J. J. Mc. GRAW. N.Y. NATIONAL BASEBALL TEAM

Publisher: The Rhotograph Co., New York, NY • Manufacturer: The Rhotograph Co. • Type: Real Photo • Postmark: Not Used • Value: $250–$300

and the New York Giants, McGraw managed his teams to a career 2,763 wins and 1,948 losses, for a percentage of .586. During his 30 years in charge, the Giants won 10 pennants and three world championships, finishing out of the first division only four times.

McGraw was one of baseball's great innovators, credited with developing the hit-and-run. He also had an uncanny ability to assess talent, frequently turning other teams' busts into stars. Because of McGraw's long tenure in baseball, his memorabilia is plentiful. Nearly every postcard of the Polo Grounds produced from 1909–1930 has a cameo insert of McGraw in the upper right-hand corner.

This 1905 Rhotograph postcard at left is the earliest image of McGraw as Giants manager. He was still slim enough to play in three games for the Giants and steal a base. In later years, good living at some of New York's finest restaurants greatly increased his girth.

1905 JOE McGINNITY, New York Giants

New York Giants manager John McGraw said that Christy Mathewson was the best pitcher he had ever seen, but he rated right-hander Joe McGinnity in the top echelon of all-time greats. In his autobiography, *My Thirty Years in Baseball,* McGraw said of McGinnity, "He was pretty nearly as good as Matty. Joe had pretty nearly everything a pitcher needs, including a puzzling underhand ball and a baffling change of pace."

On three occasions, McGinnity pitched and won both games of a double-header—but that's not how he earned the nickname "Iron Man." The moniker was given to him because he worked in an iron foundry during the off-season. In only 10 seasons in the major leagues, McGinnity won 242 games against 142 losses, an average of more than 24 victories a year. Breaking in with the Baltimore Orioles in 1899, Joe won 28 games during his first year, leading all National League pitchers. To prove his success was not beginner's luck, he won 29 games for Brooklyn in 1900, again leading the NL. When the American League was organized in 1901, McGinnity left the NL to join John McGraw's AL club in Baltimore. He won 24 games with the Orioles, finishing second to Boston's Cy Young, who led the American League with 33 victories.

In 1902, when McGraw left the Orioles to become manager of the New York Giants, McGinnity followed him back to the National League. With the Giants in 1903, he led the NL with 31 wins, then garnered a career-high 35 victories in 1904. Unquestionably one of the finest pitchers of all time, "Iron Man" McGinnity was elected to the Hall of Fame in 1946.

1905 CLEVELAND NAPS

Napoleon Lajoie performed brilliantly in the major leagues for 21 years, mainly as a second baseman. He had a unique distinction, becoming the only player in major league history to have a team named after him.

When Cleveland was a member of the National League in the 1890s, the team was called the Spiders. In 1901, when the franchise became a charter member of the rival American League, the first team was called the Blues. In 1902, the club was referred to as the Broncos, but like Blues, the nickname never caught on with the fans. A Cleveland newspaper conducted a poll among fans to select a new name, and respondents voted overwhelmingly to call the team the Naps in honor of Lajoie, who had joined the club during the 1902 season, establishing himself among fans with a .366 batting average. Lajoie remained Cleveland's star player for 12 seasons and managed the club for five seasons, coaching it to 397 wins and 330 losses from 1905–1909. The team's best season under Lajoie was 1908, when it finished in

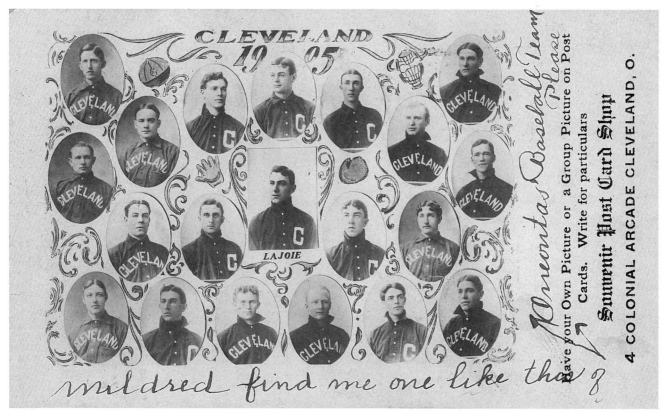

Publisher: The Souvenir Postcard Shop, Cleveland, OH • Manufacturer: The Souvenir Postcard Shop • Type: Real Photo
Postmark: Cleveland, OH, June 3, 1907 • Value: $750–$1,000

second place, half a game behind the Detroit Tigers.

The 1905 photograph on p. 17 shows Napoleon Lajoie in his first season as Naps manager, surrounded by his team, which finished fifth in the AL with 76 wins and 78 losses. The picture appears on the first known advertising postcard—it promotes the Souvenir Post Card Shop in Cleveland—to feature a baseball theme.

Nap had previously played with the National League Philadelphia Phillies, but jumped to Connie Mack's Athletics when offered more money to play in the new league. The Phillies brought an injunction against Lajoie, preventing him from playing anywhere in Pennsylvania. In order to keep his premier star in the American League, Mack sent him to Cleveland, where the injunction was invalid.

1905 NAPOLEON LAJOIE, Cleveland Naps

Napoleon Lajoie was not only the American League's first triple crown winner, but also was one of the greatest second basemen in baseball history. In 1901, with the Philadelphia Athletics, Lajoie batted a robust .422 and led the league with 14 home runs and 125 RBI, tremendous figures in the dead-ball era. Nap also topped the league in doubles (48), hits (229), runs (145), and putouts (395, according to *Total Baseball*). Seldom has a player so completely dominated a league. However, after only one game with the A's in 1902, he was sent to Cleveland.

1906 MATTY FITZGERALD, New York Giants

Matty Fitzgerald was a New York Giants catcher who played in only 11 major league games—four in 1906 and seven in 1907. Yet he appears in one of the rarest postcard sets ever issued: the Ullman series of 1906, which shows the defending world champion Giants. In 1906, Matty went 4 for 6 with 2 runs and 2 RBI in his four games. In 1907, he was only 2 for 15, and his major league career ended almost as quickly as it began. But he will be forever remembered as one of the Giants captured in the Ullman Postcard set of 1906.

Publisher: Raymond Kahn Co., Cleveland, OH
Manufacturer: Not Indicated • Type: Black & White • Postmark: Not Used
Value: $750–$1,000

Publisher: The Ullman Manufacturing Co., New York, NY • Manufacturer: The Ullman Manufacturing Co. • Type: Black & White
Postmark: Not Used • Value: $150–$200

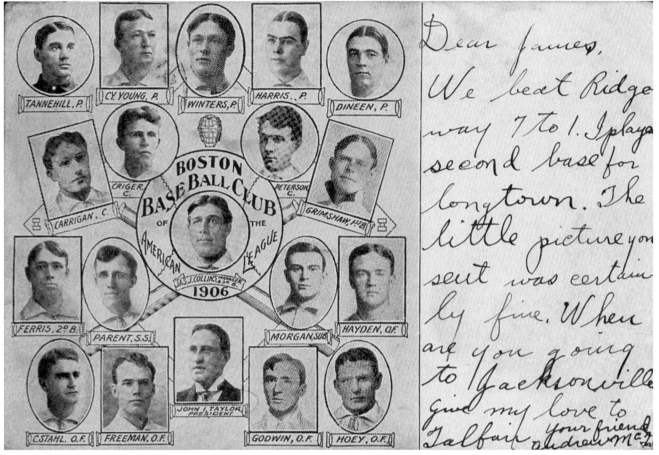

Publisher: Sporting Life Publishing Co., Philadelphia, PA • Manufacturer: Sporting Life Publishing Co. • Type: Sepia
Postmark: Ridgely, SC, Sept. 9, 1907 • Value: $300

1906 BOSTON RED SOX

It's hard to believe any team with immortal right-hander Cy Young in its lineup could finish last, but that's exactly what happened to the 1906 Red Sox. In fact, Young's record of 13 wins and 21 losses was the worst of his career, which began in 1890 with the Cleveland Spiders and ended in 1911 with the Boston Braves. (His 511 wins over those 22 seasons is the all-time highest total.) Hall of Famer Jimmy Collins, the club's manager/third baseman, played in only 37 games and was replaced as skipper late in the season by center fielder Jake Stahl. Boston's 35-79 record no doubt triggered Collins' departure.

During this period, *The Sporting Life* rivaled *The Sporting News* as the baseball bible. In 1906, the paper published an extremely rare set of 16 sepia postcards featuring all major league teams. Any postcards from this early period showing Hall of Fame players tend to command top dollar, and even though Young and Collins were both well past their peaks, this card of the 1906 Red Sox is no exception.

Incidentally, "Old Cy" bounced back the next season with 21 wins and captured 21 more in 1908, proving he was far from washed up after his dismal 1906 season.

Publisher: Simplicity Co., Chicago, IL • Manufacturer: Not Indicated
Type: Black & White • Postmark: Not Used • Value: $200

1907 WORLD SERIES

When the Simplicity Co. of Chicago published this post-card prior to the 1907 World Series between the Cubs and Tigers, the company made sure it had all the bases covered. Even though the Cubs, with their 116 wins, had been heavily favored to beat the crosstown rival White Sox in the 1906 World Series, the American League champs stunned the baseball world, beating the Cubs in

Publisher: Simplicity Co., Chicago, IL • Manufacturer: Not Indicated • Type: Black & White • Postmark: Not Used • Value: $150

six games. In 1907, the Cubs won 107 and lost 45, while the Tigers won the AL pennant with a more modest mark of 92-58 under manager Hughie Jennings. Detroit was led by the incomparable Ty Cobb, who topped the league in batting (.350) and RBI (116). Another Hall of Famer, center fielder Sam Crawford, was second to Cobb with a .323 batting average. Tiger pitching was outstanding, too, as Wild Bill Donovan and Ed Killian each won 25, while George Mullin won 20 but lost the same number. The Cubs had the Hall of Fame infield of Tinker, Evers, and Chance, plus superb pitching led by Orval Overall (23-8) and Hall of Famer Three Finger Brown (20-6). The World Series with the Tigers was no contest. The Cubs won four games to none, with the first game pitching duel between Donovan and Overall and Ed Ruelbach ending in a 3-3, 12-inning tie. The Cubs won the next four games, with Jake Pfiester, Ruelbach, Overall, and Brown registering complete-game triumphs.

Both of these cards (p. 19 and above) are valuable, but the card with the Cub in the coffin is much more so.

1907 WORLD SERIES

Frank Chance's Cubs won four National League pennants and two world championships during his eight seasons as player/manager. Highly respected by opponents and teammates alike, Chance exuded confidence, as is apparent in the photograph below, taken during the

1907 World Series between the Cubs and Detroit Tigers. The Cubs easily disposed of the Tigers, winning four games to none after the first game ended in a 3-3 tie. Opposing player/manager Hughie Jennings and Tigers ace pitcher Wild Bill Donovan seem to be looking at Chance in awe. Perhaps they're eyeing the matching diamond starburst ring and tie pin Chance is wearing as he kibitzes on the Tigers bench before a game.

A native of Fresno, California, Chance signed with the Cubs in 1898 as a catcher. Although he was a good catcher, Chance became a star after he converted to first base in 1902. Chance's playing career ended with the New York Yankees in 1914 after he appeared in just one

Publisher: H.M. Taylor, Detroit, MI • Manufacturer: Not Indicated • Type: Black & White • Postmark: Detroit, MI, Oct. 16, 1907 • Value: $150–$200

game. Over 17 seasons, his clutch hitting and inspirational leadership made him one of the most respected players in baseball history.

Because he crowded the plate when he batted, Chance was frequently hit by pitched balls—to such a degree that he developed severe headaches and ultimately required surgery. The "Peerless Leader" was only 47 years old when he died in 1924. He was posthumously elected to the Baseball Hall of Fame in 1946.

1907 JOE TINKER, Chicago Cubs
1907 JOHNNY EVERS, Chicago Cubs
1907 FRANK CHANCE, Chicago Cubs

Franklin P. Adams, a noted newspaper columnist for the *New York Evening Mail*, never played an inning of professional baseball. But his contribution to the game's history will forever be a part of baseball lore. An ardent New York Giants fan, Adams became increasingly frustrated watching his beloved team suffer heartbreaking defeats to the Chicago Cubs. The Cubs' double-play combination of second baseman Johnny Evers and shortstop Joe Tinker continually distressed him with superb fielding that frequently snuffed the Giants' offense. Cubs manager Frank Chance played first base and was on the receiving end of many a rally-ending double-play ball. Adams poured out his disappointment on his typewriter, composing "Baseball's Sad Lexicon," one of the most famous poems ever written about America's pastime.

> *These are the saddest of possible words—*
> *"Tinker to Evers to Chance"*
> *Trio of Bear Cubs and fleeter than birds—*
> *"Tinker to Evers to Chance"*
> *Thoughtlessly pricking our gonfalon bubble*
> *Making a Giant hit into a double*
> *Words that are weighty with nothing but trouble—*
> *"Tinker to Evers to Chance"*

Frank Chance would have made the Hall of Fame playing in any era. In 17 seasons, he had a lifetime .296 batting average and twice led the National League in stolen bases, with 67 in 1903 and 57 in 1906, despite his husky 6-foot, 190-pound size. The rest of the trio's induction is more disputable. Although Johnny Evers and Joe Tinker were outstanding players in their own right, many baseball historians say that Adams' poem immortalized them and was instrumental in their election to the Hall of Fame. For the record, Evers had a career .270 batting average over 18 seasons, while Tinker batted .263 in 15 seasons.

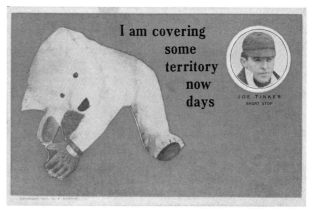

Publisher: G.F. Grignon, Chicago, IL • Manufacturer: Not Indicated
Type: Color Pre-Linen • Postmark: Not Used • Value: $200–$250

Publisher: G.F. Grignon, Chicago, IL • Manufacturer: Not Indicated
Type: Color Pre-Linen • Postmark: Lansing, MI, Jan. 27, 1908
Value: $200–$250

Publisher: G.F. Grignon, Chicago, IL • Manufacturer: Not Indicated
Type: Color Pre-Linen • Postmark: Not Used • Value: $200–$250

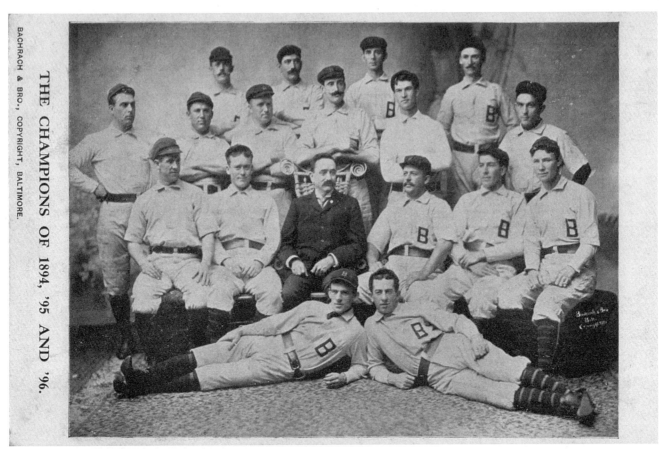

THE CHAMPIONS OF 1894, '95 AND '96.

Publisher: Bachrach Bros., Baltimore, MD • Manufacturer: Not Indicated • Type: Black & White • Postmark: Not Used • Value: $400–$500

1907 BALTIMORE ORIOLES REMEMBERED

In 1907, the city of Baltimore celebrated its 100th anniversary with a Homecoming Week. The festivities included honoring one of the great baseball teams of all time, the 1894, '95, and '96 Orioles, who won three consecutive National League pennants. No less than seven future Hall of Famers played on those teams: manager Ned Hanlon, catcher Wilbert Robinson, first baseman Dan Brouthers, third baseman John McGraw, shortstop Hughie Jennings, right fielder Wee Willie Keeler, and left fielder Joe Kelley. After their playing days ended, John McGraw, Hughie Jennings, and Will Robinson became highly successful major league managers with the New York Giants, Detroit Tigers, and Brooklyn Dodgers, respectively.

Right-hander Bill "Wizard" Hoffer appeared headed for a Hall of Fame career when he won 31 games in his rookie year of 1895, followed by 25 wins in '96 and 22 in '97. But the bane of all pitchers—arm trouble—forced him out of the game. Traded to Pittsburgh in mid-season '98, he went 3-4 with the two teams and 8-10 for the Pirates the following year. He stayed out of baseball in 1900, then tried a comeback with the Cleveland Blues in the AL's first season of 1901, winning 3 and losing 8 before he retired for good.

The NL Orioles were the most hated team in baseball during their pennant-winning seasons, as they played with a ferocity never equaled. The club invented such things as the hit-and-run and squeeze bunt. A more colorful team never existed. Although this postcard was produced more than 10 years after the club's glory days, the original photograph was taken during those championship seasons.

1907 PALACE OF THE FANS, Cincinnati Reds

"Palace of the Fans." Just the name conjures up an image of the ultimate in ballparks, and this Cincinnati

Publisher: The Morgan Stationery Co., Cincinnati, OH • Manufacturer: Not Indicated • Type: Color Pre-Linen • Postmark: Not Used • Value: $500–$750

ballpark was considered just that when it opened in 1902. For fans' convenience, there were two bars below the stands that sold whiskey and beer. After having a few drinks, imbibers could retire to seats below the main grandstand along both foul lines. The area was called "Rooter Row," and you can imagine what choice comments could come from this section during the course of the game.

The ballpark derived its name from its wooden columns and pillars, copied from buildings—called palaces—shown at the 1893 Columbian Exposition. The design was a popular architectural style of the day; however, being wood, it was susceptible to fire. In the fall of 1911, fire destroyed a large section of the grandstand. It was rebuilt on the same location, using steel and concrete, before the next season. But since columns and pillars were no longer the architectural vogue, they were omitted from the new Redland Field.

This photograph, revealing all the splendors of the Palace, was shot at the opening game of the 1907 season. It was not a good year for the Reds, who finished sixth in the National League with a record of 66 wins and 87 losses.

1907 MILLER HUGGINS, Cincinnati Reds

While Miller Huggins is best remembered as manager of the outstanding New York Yankees teams of the 1920s, he also spent 13 seasons as a scrappy second baseman for the Cincinnati Reds and St. Louis Cardinals. Only 5 feet 6 inches tall, Huggins was an excellent fielder with good range and an astute student of the game. He was also a graduate of the University of Cincinnati Law School, though he never practiced law.

Huggins compiled a .265 lifetime batting average, with a .304 average at St. Louis in 1912 his best mark. In 1913, he launched his second career as player/manager of the Cardinals. Jumping to the Yankees in 1918, Huggins led the club to three straight pennants beginning in 1921, and to the first of three world championships under his tutelage in 1923. Huggins' 1927 Yankees are considered the best team in history. Featuring such Hall of Fame sluggers as Babe Ruth, Lou Gehrig, Tony Lazzeri, and Earle Combs, this lineup earned the nickname Murderers' Row. Add Hall of Fame pitchers Waite Hoyt and Herb Pennock to the mix, and the Yankees were virtually invincible. Huggins was still managing the Yankees in September 1929 when he became ill and entered a New York hospital. He died there September 25.

When the Morgan Stationery Co. issued a set of postcards in 1907 featuring various baseball scenes involving the Reds and their opponents, Miller Huggins was the only Cincinnati player featured. He was probably

Publisher: The Morgan Stationery Co., Cincinnati, OH • Manufacturer: Not Indicated • Type: Color Pre-Linen • Postmark: Not Used • Value: $350–$500

selected because of his status as Cincinnati's leading hitter among starting players in 1906, with a .292 batting average. Today, this color postcard is one of the most desirable Huggins collectibles. (See p. 200 for a full-color look at this postcard.)

1907 TY COBB, Detroit Tigers

The Detroit Tigers won their first American League pennant in 1907, the year that Ty Cobb won the first of his 12 AL batting championships. "Tyrus Cobb at Bat" (p. 24) shows Cobb at 20 years of age, already considered a star. Cobb batted .350 and drove in 119 runs in 1907, his first full season in the majors. It was an outstanding record, but Cobb managed to improve on it in later years, retiring in 1928 with a lifetime .367 average, the highest in baseball history. In his final season, at age 42, Cobb batted .323. Three times during his brilliant career, he hit better than .400, including a career-high .420 in 1911. If Cobb had a major disappointment during his fabulous career, it was that he never played on

"Tyrus Cobb" at Bat.

Publisher: H.M. Taylor, Detroit, MI • Manufacturer: Not Indicated • Type: Black & White • Postmark: Detroit, MI, Oct. 9, 1907 • Value: $400–$500

Publisher: A.C. Dietsche Co., Detroit, MI • Manufacturer: A.C. Dietsche Co.
Type: Black & White • Postmark: Not Used • Value: $400–$500

a team that won a World Series. Cobb played in three World Series with the Tigers in 1907, 1908, and 1909, and Detroit lost them all.

Ty Cobb is rated as the fiercest competitor in the history of the game and the greatest base stealer of his day. Rube Bressler of the Philadelphia Athletics pitched against Cobb beginning in 1914, and said of his adversary, "Cobb had that terrible fire, that unbelievable drive. His determination was fantastic. I never saw anybody like him. It was his base. It was his game. Everything was his."

During the 1936 balloting for induction to the Baseball Hall of Fame, Ty Cobb had more votes than anyone, including Babe Ruth. The "Georgia Peach" was truly a baseball immortal.

1907 TY COBB, Detroit Tigers

Ty Cobb is recognized as the greatest hitter of all time, but he was also a respectable fielder. Postcards like this one (at left), which shows Cobb in pursuit of a fly ball, are much more scarce than cards of Ty in a batting pose. The dark background tends to diminish the beauty of the card.

This card was produced by A.C. Dietsche of Detroit in 1907. For such early issues, Dietsche cards are surprisingly plentiful and thus aren't nearly as valuable as

Tiger postcards produced by Wolverine, Topping, and H.M. Taylor. Of all the Tiger cards Dietsche produced over a three-year period, this and the team postcard of 1909, which shows wooden Bennett Park in the background, command the most money.

1907 SAM CRAWFORD, Detroit Tigers

SAM CRAWFORD, Bunting

Publisher: Wolverine News Co., Detroit, MI • Manufacturer: Not Indicated
Type: Black & White • Postmark: Not Used • Value: $250–$300

Called "Wahoo Sam" because he was born in Wahoo, Nebraska, Sam Crawford always played in the shadow of Ty Cobb. For the 12 seasons that Crawford and Cobb played together in the Detroit Tigers' outfield, Cobb attracted most of the attention. Nevertheless, Crawford was one of the hardest hitters of the dead-ball era. His record of 311 career triples stands as the all-time best. Sam retired in 1917, before the lively ball of the 1920s came into use. Had he played during that era, there's no telling how many home runs he might have hit. As it was, he twice led his league in homers, hitting a career-high 16 the first time, in 1901 when he played with Cincinnati. He also had 108 RBI that year, third

best in the league. The feat was especially impressive given that the Reds offered few opportunities for anyone to drive in runs that season.

Crawford thrice topped the American League in RBI, with 120 in 1910, 104 in 1914, and 112 in 1915. His 18-year totals show 1,525 RBI to go with his .309 career average. Crawford was elected to Baseball's Hall of Fame in 1956.

1907 HUGHIE JENNINGS, Detroit Tigers

"Wee-A-Ah" was the rallying cry of Detroit manager Hughie Jennings as he encouraged his team from the third-base coaching box. Jennings would pull up fistfuls of grass from around the box, raise his left foot, and with clenched fists shout as loud as he could. His antics made him a crowd attraction. What's more, the call seemed to work, as the Tigers won three consecutive American League pennants in 1907, '08, and '09.

Jennings was born in the coal-mining town of Pittston, Pennsylvania, on April 2, 1870. He began his

Publisher: Brush Automobile Co., Detroit, MI • Manufacturer: Not Indicated
Type: Blue & White • Postmark: Not Used • Value: $400–$500

ST. LOUIS BROWNS. 1908

Bailey Schweitzer Hoffman Ferris Yeager C. Jones Criss Spencer Stephens McAleer T. Jones Williams Dinneen Hartzell Stone Pelty Howell O'Connor Wallace Powell Blue Waddell

Publisher: Star Photo Co., St. Louis, MO • Manufacturer: Not Indicated • Type: Triple Fold • Postmark: Not Used • Value: $750–$1,000

professional career as a catcher with Allentown, then joined the American Association's Louisville team in 1891 after impressing manager Jack Chapman in an exhibition game. At Louisville, he switched to first base and later to shortstop, where he gained his greatest fame. He was Louisville's full-time shortstop when the club joined the National League in 1892, but played only 23 games with the team in 1893 before being traded to Baltimore. There he became one of the most important members of the Orioles, batting .335 in 1894, .386 in 1895, and .401 in 1896 as the team won three consecutive National League pennants.

While the Orioles earned a reputation as the rowdiest and toughest players in baseball during the 1890s, Jennings was a warm, friendly person with laughing blue eyes and a marvelous sense of humor that endeared him to everyone.

1908 ST. LOUIS BROWNS

St. Louis Browns memorabilia and triple-fold postcards are both extremely rare, making the 1908 Browns item above a unique collectible. The Browns were often a second-division ballclub, but they finished a respectable fourth in 1908, their 83-69 record leaving them just 6 1/2 games behind pennant-winning Detroit. The Browns' roster included two future Hall of Famers that season: left-hander Rube Waddell and shortstop Bobby Wallace. Waddell, pictured on the right of the card, won 19 games, while Wallace batted .253 and dazzled defensively. Wallace is shown fourth from the right, wearing an opened Browns jacket. With white buttons, white trim, and a fleur-de-lis logo on both sleeves, these jackets established the Browns as the best dressed baseball team of the period.

Note the size of the glove being held by second baseman Hobe Ferris, fourth from the left. It's about half the size of gloves worn by infielders today.

WADDELL, p
St. Louis "BROWNS" American B. B. League.
BY N. N. BREGSTONE 1318 CASS AV. ST. LOUIS

Publisher: Bregstone, St. Louis, MO • Manufacturer: Bregstone
Type: Real Photo • Postmark: Not Used • Value: $1,000

1908 RUBE WADDELL, St. Louis Browns

Philadelphia Athletics manager Connie Mack once called Rube Waddell "the greatest left-hander I ever saw." One of the zaniest characters in baseball history, Waddell was also too much for Mack to handle due to his unpredictability and propensity for drinking to excess. Thus, despite his 129 victories in six seasons with the A's, Waddell was dealt to the St. Louis Browns after the 1907 season. The first time he faced the A's on

May 19, 1908, Waddell beat them. On July 29, again opposing his ex-teammates, he promised a record strikeout performance—and gave it, fanning 16.

Rube had a blazing fastball and screaming curve. With the Pittsburgh Pirates in 1900, he led the league with 130 strikeouts and an ERA of 2.37, but had only an 8-13 record to show for his efforts. Pirates manager Fred Clarke found Rube impossible to control and let him go to the Cubs. Mack induced Waddell to join the Athletics in 1902, but eventually Mack, too, gave up on him.

Waddell's 13-year career began with the Louisville Colonels in 1897 and ended with the Browns in 1910, when the pitcher went 3-1. His final big-league totals showed 191 victories and 141 defeats. Rube's eccentricity only enhanced the Waddell legend. The kid who never grew up was inducted into the Hall of Fame in 1946.

1908 THREE FINGER BROWN, Chicago Cubs

If you're ever looking for an inspiring story of an individual overcoming a handicap and even turning it to his advantage, you need look no further than Mordecai "Three Finger" Brown, one of baseball's all-time best pitchers.

Spending the summer on his Uncle David Beasley's farm, the seven-year-old Brown injured his right hand in a grinding machine accident that required the amputation of his index finger and badly mangled his middle finger. "It was a terrible thing at the time," Beasley said years later, "but when he grew up, the maimed hand enabled him to get unusual breaks on his pitches."

Brown went on to become the Chicago Cubs' star pitcher. He beat New York Giants great Christy Mathewson nine straight times when they opposed each other on the mound. Brown won 20 or more games during six consecutive years from 1906 to 1912 and was instrumental in the Cubs' National League–pennant wins in 1906, 1907, 1908, and 1910.

Perhaps his most memorable game occurred at New York's Polo Grounds on October 8, 1908, when the Cubs faced the Giants in a playoff for the pennant. The competition was so intense, Brown received death threats. "I had a half dozen 'Black Hand' letters in my coat pocket. 'We'll kill you if you pitch and beat the Giants,'" he said later. Brown didn't start the game, but Jack Pfiester ran into difficulty in the first inning, as the Giants scored one run and had two runners on base with two out. Brown was summoned from the bullpen by manager Frank Chance. He struck out the Giants' Art Devlin, ending the inning, and Chicago went on to beat Mathewson and the Giants, 4-2. "I was about as good that day as I ever was in my life," he said. "That year, I had won 29 games, and what with relief work, had been in 43 winning ballgames."

Brown concluded his 14-year major league career in 1916 with a total of 239 wins and 129 losses.

Publisher: Novelty Cutlery Co., Canton, OH • Manufacturer: Not Indicated
Type: Gray & White • Postmark: Not Used • Value: $350–$500

1908 CHICAGO CUBS

Although postcards of the 1906 and 1907 National League champion Chicago Cubs surface frequently, those showing the world champion Cubs of 1908 are relatively scarce. Perhaps it's because '08 was the third consecutive year the Cubs won the pennant, and the players were basically the same. Thankfully, the Suhling Co. of Chicago deemed the club worthy of further documentation, producing not only a 1908 postcard of the team (p. 28), but several featuring individual players. We know it was Suhling because the cards bear the Suhling logo: a dollar sign inside a shield. If you come across a card on gray paper stock with this logo on the back, it's a Suhling.

The 1908 Cubs defeated the Giants by one game for the pennant. They won the replay of the famous game in which Fred Merkle failed to touch second base, rescinding a Giants victory. Three Finger Brown won

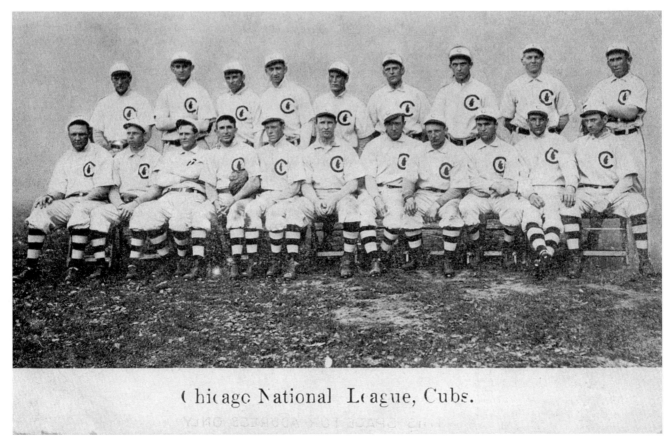

Chicago National League, Cubs.

Publisher: Suhling Co., Chicago, IL • Manufacturer: Suhling Co. • Type: Black & White • Postmark: Viola, IL, Aug. 26, 1908 • Value: $400–$500

his 29th victory of the season in the playoff, then took two more in the World Series as the Cubs beat the Tigers in five games. Orvie Overall won the other two, while Chicago's Hall of Fame infield led the offense. Second baseman Johnny Evers batted .350, first baseman/manager Frank Chance hit .421, and shortstop Joe Tinker drove in five runs. During the regular season, Evers' .300 average led the team. Pitcher Ed Reulbach was second to Brown with 24 wins.

1908 CHRISTY MATHEWSON, New York Giants

On any list of the greatest pitchers in baseball history, Christy Mathewson is almost always near the top. In his autobiography, *My Thirty Years in Baseball*, New York Giants manager John McGraw called Matty "the greatest pitcher I ever saw." That's high praise coming from a Hall of Famer who played or managed in the major leagues from 1891 through 1932.

For 17 big-league seasons, Mathewson was McGraw's meal ticket, winning 373 games—all but one for the Giants. The total puts Mathewson in third place behind Cy Young and Walter Johnson in career victories. The similarity between Mathewson and Johnson is striking. Both were about the same size—Christy 6 feet 1¹/₂

inches and 195 pounds, Walter 6 feet 1 and 200 pounds—and both had fastballs second to none. In addition, both were beloved figures who inspired fans and teammates alike.

A graduate of Bucknell University, where he starred on the Bisons' baseball and football teams, Mathewson came to the majors in 1900, posting an unimpressive 0-3 record. But the next year, Matty went 20-17 and was on his way to superstardom. In 1903, '04, and '05, Christy won 30, 33, and 31 games, respectively. In the 1905 World Series against Philadelphia, Matty almost single-handedly beat the Athletics, winning three times without allowing a run. In 1908, he won a career-high 37 games as the Giants lost the pennant in a playoff to the Chicago Cubs.

While serving in the U.S. Army in France during World War I, Mathewson was gassed and never fully recovered. Just seven years later, at a sanatorium in Saranac Lake, New York, he died of tuberculosis. His loss was felt by the millions who held him in high esteem. He was truly an American legend.

Publisher: The Rose Co., Philadelphia, PA • Manufacturer: The Rose Co.
Type: Color Pre-Linen • Postmark: Not Used • Value: $1,000–$1,500

1908 CY YOUNG, Boston Red Sox

When Denton True Young joined the Cleveland Spiders of the National League in 1890, the 6-foot 2-inch right-hander had already earned his nickname "Cy"—short for cyclone, in tribute to his fastball. Young was given the name by Ohio sportswriters in 1888, when he pitched for Canton in the Tri-State League.

In 1901, when the American League was formed, Young joined the junior circuit's Boston franchise. That put him in position to participate in the first modern World Series in 1903, where he won two games and led the Puritans, as the Boston franchise was then known, to a stunning upset over the Pittsburgh Pirates of the established National League.

When Cy Young's 22-year major league career ended, he had compiled 511 career victories, a record that probably will never be broken. He won 20 or more games in one season 16 times, including 14 years in a row. The last of those 14 years was 1908, when a 41-year-old Young won 21 games for the Red Sox. He pitched three no-hitters and led his league in shutouts

seven times. Young accomplished all of this under less-than-perfect conditions. As he said years after his career was over, "There were disadvantages playing back then, including poor fields, poorer equipment, bad food, lousy traveling conditions, no showers, sooty trains, and noisy rooming houses so full of bedbugs they'd keep you up all night."

Young was inducted into the Hall of Fame in its inaugural year, 1937. He is immortalized by the Cy Young Award, given annually to the top pitcher in both the American and National Leagues.

Publisher: A.C. Williams, Boston, MA • Manufacturer: Not Indicated
Type: Black & White • Postmark: Unionville, MD, March 12, 1912
Value: $400–$500

"Cy" Young as a Fox Hunter.

Publisher: Hugh C. Leighton, #8824, Portland, ME • Manufacturer: Not Indicated • Type: Color Pre-Linen • Postmark: Not Used • Value: $300–$400

1908 CY YOUNG, fox hunter

This rare postcard of Cy Young as a fox hunter shows how players used to stay in shape during the off-seasons. Long before the fancy weight rooms and exercise machines so prevalent today, players stayed in condition by pursuing such outdoor activities as game hunting, frequently in groups. Babe Ruth frequently enjoyed hunting trips with some of his Yankee teammates between the World Series and spring training. Cy Young obviously benefited from his outdoor hunting trips. Not only did he set the all-time record for career wins (511), he lived to be 88 years old.

1908 ED WALSH, Chicago White Sox

When John McGraw ranked the top pitchers of all time in his autobiography, the Giants manager included Ed Walsh. According to McGraw, "Walsh was easily the most famous and effective of all the spitball pitchers. A big factor in his value to a team was his marvelous endurance. Aside from his spitball, Walsh had tremendous speed and splendid control."

Walsh was certainly one of the game's most durable hurlers. His 464 innings pitched in 1908 still stands as the modern record. During that remarkable season, Walsh started 49 games, completed 42, won 40, lost

Publisher: George W. Hull, Chicago, IL • Manufacturer: Not Indicated
Type: Black & White • Postmark: Chicago, IL, Sept. 27, 1907
Value: $250–$300

only 15, and threw 11 shutouts while compiling a 1.42 ERA. The White Sox's workhorse pitched $41^{2}/_{3}$ innings over the final eight days of the season in a futile effort to give Chicago the pennant. The team finished $1^{1}/_{2}$ games behind the Tigers. Still, it was an improvement over the club's third-place finish in 1907, when Walsh won 25 games and led the AL with an ERA of 1.60.

Following his virtuoso performance in 1908, Walsh didn't win 20 games until 1911, when he won 26. He notched 27 wins in 1912, the last year he pitched more than 100 innings. In 1913, his arm began to hurt, and he never fully recovered. Perhaps leading the league in innings pitched four times finally took its toll.

Walsh went 8-3 before his injury set in, then won only five more games the remainder of his career. He retired in 1917 with 195 wins against only 126 losses and an all-time best 1.82 ERA. Big Ed certainly earned his election to the Hall of Fame in 1946.

1909 SHIBE PARK, Philadelphia Athletics

Publisher: Frank H. Taylor, Philadelphia, PA • Manufacturer: Not Indicated
Type: Color Pre-Linen • Postmark: Pittsburgh, PA, Oct. 8, 1909
Value: $1,000–$1,500

When Connie Mack and Ben Shibe built Columbia Park in 1901, they realized it was a temporary structure. As the Philadelphia Athletics had greater success, they required a more modern facility. In 1908, when word of a new facility began to circulate, publisher Frank H. Taylor created postcards showing the park approximately one year before its opening. Different postcards were published in 1908 and 1909, distinguishable by the information on them. The postcards published in 1908 read: "The greatest ball park in the world, 21st Street and Lehigh Avenue, Philadelphia. Seating Capacity 23,000. Steel and Concrete construction. Will open for season of 1909." For the postcards published in 1909: "Shibe Park Athletic Baseball Club, American League. 21st Street and Lehigh Avenue, Philadelphia. The largest and best appointed baseball park in the world." Shibe Park proved worthy of these lofty accolades.

The '09 card shown above depicts Shibe Park upon its completion. Taylor's postcards are considered very rare and desirable among collectors. This card brought more than $1,100 in a 1998 auction.

1909 POLO GROUNDS, New York Giants

Albert Goodwill Spalding was one of baseball's pioneers. A star pitcher and outstanding manager in the first professional league, the National Association, Spalding won 207 games and lost 56 with the NA's Boston Red Stock-

POLO GROUNDS, 157th STREET AND EIGHTH AVENUE
Can be reached by Sixth and Ninth Avenue Elevated direct to the grounds, and Broadway Subway, stopping at 155th St., and a short walk to the grounds. Seating capacity estimated at 40,000.
Reserved Seats as well as Box Seats on sale by A. G. Spalding & Bros., No. 126 Nassau St. and No. 29 W. 42nd St.

Publisher: A.G. Spalding & Bros., New York, NY • Manufacturer: Not Indicated • Type: Color Pre-Linen • Postmark: Not Used • Value: $1,000–$1,500

COPYRIGHTED 1909, PITTSBURGH ATHLETIC CLUB

PITTSBURGH BASE B

ings during that organization's five-year existence. Gambling and rowdyism were rampant in the National Association, and Spalding led a group that formed a new league to be free of those problems. Called the National League, it launched in 1876, with Spalding as pitcher and manager of the Chicago White Stockings. He had a 46-12 pitching record that year in leading the White Stockings to the new league's first pennant.

Spalding was also a shrewd businessman who saw the potential of baseball. He opened a chain of sporting-goods stores throughout the country called A.G. Spalding & Bros. He also sold tickets to games in the major cities. The rare postcard on p. 31, showing the Polo Grounds, indicates that tickets for games could be purchased at Spalding's New York stores: "Polo Grounds, 157th Street and Eighth Avenue. Can be reached by Sixth and Ninth Avenue Elevated direct to the grounds. Seating capacity estimated at 40,000. Reserve seats as well as Box Seats on sale by A.G. Spalding and Bros., No. 126 Nassau St. and No. 29 W. 42nd St." This postcard was issued in 1908 or 1909, when the stadium at the Polo Grounds was basically a wooden structure.

1909 PITTSBURGH PIRATES

The Pittsburgh Pirates enjoyed a glorious season in 1909. First the club moved into a new, ultramodern ballpark—Forbes Field—in mid-season. Then the team went on to win the world championship, beating the Detroit Tigers in the World Series, four games to three. It was superstar Honus Wagner's last Fall Classic, and he made the most of it, batting .333 and driving in six runs. Another Hall of Famer, player/manager Fred

Clarke, drove in seven runs and scored seven.

This extremely rare triple-fold postcard pictures Clarke (on the right), Wagner (third from the right), and a host of other greats. Right-hander Babe Adams (seventh from the right) was the Pirates' pitching star in the '09 Series, winning three games, including a six-hit shutout in the deciding game. Right-handers Howie Camnitz and Vic Willis each went 0-1 in the Series, but helped the Pirates get there, winning 25 and 22 games, respectively, during the regular season. Adams was 12-3 in the '09 season with a team-low 1.11 ERA. Wagner led the Pirates offensively during the regular campaign, leading the National League with a .339 batting average and 100 RBI.

1909 WORLD SERIES

Unquestionably the most famous players of the century's first decade were the Detroit Tigers' Ty Cobb and the Pittsburgh Pirates' Honus Wagner. When Detroit and Pittsburgh met in the 1909 World Series, baseball fans argued as to who was the better player. The publisher of this postcard (facing page) gave them equal billing— almost. Wagner's picture is slightly larger than Cobb's. Perhaps clairvoyance was at work. The Pirates won the World Series in seven games as Wagner batted .333, compared to .231 for Cobb. Cobb was 22 years old that season, while Wagner was 35 and far more experienced.

Lifetime, Cobb had the edge at the plate, posting a .367 average in 22 seasons versus Wagner's .327 in 21 seasons. Both men were exceptionally fast, outstanding base runners who led their leagues numerous times in stolen bases. Baseball historians continue to debate over the merits of each player. In the final analysis, the title on this postcard may sum it up best: They were indeed "Two of a Kind."

Publisher: R.W. Johnston Studios, Pittsburgh, PA • Manufacturer: R.W. Johnston Studios • Type: Sepia Triple Fold
Postmark: Pittsburgh, PA, Oct. 8, 1909 • Value: $1,000–$1,500

Publisher: W.W. Smith, Pittsburgh, PA • Manufacturer: Davis & Mason, Pittsburgh • Type: Black & White • Postmark: Pittsburgh, PA, Oct. 8, 1909 • Value: $1,000

Publisher: The Rose Co., Philadelphia, PA • Manufacturer: The Rose Co.
Type: Color Pre-Linen • Postmark: Not Used • Value: $1,000–$1,500

1909 WALTER JOHNSON, Washington Senators (above)

1909 WALTER JOHNSON & GERMANY SCHAEFER, Washington Senators (right)

Right-hander Walter Johnson, who pitched brilliantly for 21 seasons with the Washington Senators, is ranked by many as the fastest pitcher ever. Nicknamed "The Big Train" because his fastball roared to home plate like a speeding locomotive, the 6-foot-1, 200-pound Johnson was discovered pitching semi-pro baseball in Weiser, Idaho during the summer of 1907. He joined the Senators that August, at the age of 19, without any minor league experience. The photograph used on this extremely rare Rose postcard (above) shows young Walter Johnson in his second season of major league baseball.

Johnson had a very unusual pitching motion. He didn't use a windup. When he was ready to pitch, he twisted his body around to the right until he was facing second base. Then, with a sweeping delivery from just

below the waist, Johnson sent his exploding fastball toward home plate. Johnson's unique style baffled opposing batters for most of his career. His lifetime record of 413 wins and 277 losses is truly remarkable considering that for most of his years, the Washington Senators were a second-division club. It wasn't until 1924, late in his career, that he had his first chance to pitch in a World Series. He won the seventh and deciding game against the New York Giants at the age of 37, giving the Senators their only world championship.

Germany Schaefer was baseball's first clown, running the bases backward on at least one occasion. Schaefer played every position except catcher during his 15 years in the majors, starting in 1901 with the Cubs. Later stops included Detroit, Washington, and Cleveland, where he played one game with the Indians in 1918. He had his finest season with the Senators in 1911, batting .334 in 125 games. He also batted .320 for the Senators in 1913, appearing in 52 games.

Schaefer left the majors with a .257 career batting average. His two-game, three-out pitching stint left him

Publisher: Walter Johnson • Manufacturer: Not Indicated • Type: Real Photo
Postmark: Not Used • Value: $500–$750

with an astronomical 18.00 ERA. But his clowning on
and off the field made him extremely popular. This
postcard shows Germany and his wife sitting next to his
good friend and battery-mate, Walter Johnson, and
Johnson's wife Hazel.

Author's Note: This postcard has particular meaning
for me since it was given to me by Walter's grandson
Henry Thomas, a close friend and award-winning
author.

1909 TOM JONES, Detroit Tigers

First baseman Tom Jones was a member of the 1909
American League champion Detroit Tigers and is part
of a 20-card set published by Topping & Co. that year.
Because of the beauty and scarcity of the set, even lesser
known players like Jones command $150. Hall of Famers
like Cobb, Crawford, and Jennings bring $350 to $500.

Jones broke into the bigs with the Baltimore Orioles
in 1902, compiling a career-high .283 batting average in
37 games. He began the '09 season with the St. Louis
Browns, but was traded late in the summer to Detroit,
where he managed to bat .281 in 44 games. He
remained with the Tigers for the last of his eight big-
league seasons in 1910. Never a prolific batter, Jones
retired with just a .251 career average, but he was one
of the better glove men of his era, finishing with a lifetime .984 fielding average.

Publisher: Topping & Co., Detroit, MI • Manufacturer: Not Indicated
Type: Color Pre-Linen • Postmark: Not Used • Value: $150–$200

1910-19

The construction of ultramodern stadiums made of steel and concrete continued from 1910 through 1919. Cleveland's new League Park replaced the original wooden structure on the same site in 1910. That same year, spacious Comiskey Park—named for owner Charles Comiskey and billed as "The Baseball Palace of the World"—opened in Chicago.

Some construction came as a result of destructive fires. After flames claimed the wooden Polo Grounds in New York, a new steel and concrete facility took its place. In 1911, American League Park in Washington, D.C., burned to the ground while the Senators were at spring training. Remarkably, a new park was ready for the season opener less than five weeks later. Cincinnati's Palace of the Fans became another fire casualty in 1911 and was replaced by Redland Field, which opened on the same location in 1912. That same year, Boston's Fenway Park and Detroit's Navin Field opened. Navin Field was built on the site of Bennet Park, which it replaced. In 1913, Ebbets Field—named, like Navin Field, after its owner—opened in Brooklyn to rave reviews.

A slew of ballparks opened in 1914, as a third Major League—the Federal League—arose to challenge the powers that were. The most notable of those stadiums was Weeghman Park in Chicago, named after the owner of the Federal League's Whales. Today, that park is known as Wrigley Field and is home to the Cubs. Also in 1914, a park that stood the test of time less successfully, Braves Field, opened on Boston's Commonwealth Avenue, only a few blocks north of Fenway Park.

Inside the new "modern" ballparks, players performed feats that filled the seats. Detroit's Ty Cobb enhanced his reputation as the greatest hitter in history, batting .420 and .410 in back-to-back seasons in 1911 and 1912. The Red Sox's Babe Ruth, a young left-hander from Baltimore, went about establishing himself as one of the finest pitchers in the game—as well as a phenomenal long-ball hitter.

As baseball's premier team, the Red Sox won world championships in 1912, before Ruth's arrival, and in 1915,

OPENING DAY FEDERAL LEAGUE BALL PARK, CHICAGO.

NOW NATIONAL LEAGUE PARK, CUBS

Publisher: Gerson Bros., Chicago, IL • Manufacturer: Not Indicated • Type: Color Pre-Linen • Postmark: Not Used • Value: $40–$50

'16, and '18 after he joined them. The Philadelphia Athletics, under Connie Mack's guidance, won the world championship in 1910 and '11, but when they lost to the Braves in a stunning upset in 1914, Mack broke up the team. The Chicago White Sox were world champs in 1917 and were heavy favorites to win again in 1919, but lost to the Cincinnati Reds. The loss prompted an investigation that resulted in eight White Sox stars being banned from baseball.

Not even America's pastime could ignore the war that began raging across Europe in 1914, particularly after the U.S. joined the fray in 1917. To drum up support, military units began performing at ballparks nationwide—often joined by players in baseball uniforms who marched with bats instead of rifles over their shoulders.

HOW THE NEW CLEVELAND GRAND STAND WILL LOOK

DETAILS :—Length of grand stand, 503 feet; length of pavillion, 423 feet; distance from home plate to grand stand, 76 feet; distance from first base to grand stand, 78 feet; distance from third base to grand stand, 70 feet; home plate to right field fence on foul line, 290 feet; home plate to left field fence on foul line, 385 feet. Seating capacity: 260 front box seats, $1.25; 340 rear box seats, $1.00; 2,400 reserved seats, $1.00; 7,700 grand stand seats, 75 cents; 6,500 pavilion seats, 50 cents, 2,000 bleacher seats, 25 cents; total seats, 19,200. Made of steel and concrete.

A. G. SPALDING & BROS., 741 EUCLID AVE.

Publisher: A.G. Spalding & Bros., #613, Cleveland, OH
Manufacturer: Not Indicated • Type: Pre-Linen • Postmark: Cleveland, OH,
May 11, 1910 • Value: $1,000

1910 PHILADELPHIA ATHLETICS

Publisher: Not Indicated • Manufacturer: Not Indicated • Type: Black & White
Postmark: Philadelphia, PA, Sept. 9, 1910 • Value: $300–$400

The 1910 Philadelphia Athletics employed a fine blend of pitching, defense, and hitting to win the American League pennant by 14½ games over the second-place New York Highlanders. Jack Coombs won 31 games and lost 9 to lead a pitching staff that featured two other future Hall of Famers: Chief Bender, who won 23 and lost 5, and Eddie Plank, who won 16 and lost 10. The infield included Captain Harry Davis at first base,

Eddie Collins at second base, Jack Barry at shortstop, and Frank "Home Run" Baker at third base. Collins and Baker also made the Hall of Fame.

When the Athletics entered the American League in 1901, someone commented, "There is not enough room for two teams in Philadelphia. The Athletics will be a white elephant." Co-owner and manager Connie Mack adapted the white elephant as his team symbol, and it remains so today, although the A's have since relocated.

1910 MIKE POWERS, Philadelphia Athletics

In baseball's illustrious history, hundreds of special days and nights have been held for various players. None were sadder than when Michael "Doc" Powers, catcher for the Philadelphia Athletics, was honored posthumously by the fans of Philadelphia. The event was held at Shibe Park on June 30, 1910, to raise money for Powers' family. Powers had died from intestinal gangrene in 1909.

This rare promotional postcard was issued to draw attention to "Doc" Powers' Day. The back of the card has a poignant message from A's owner Connie Mack, which says in part:

The sad death of Dr. Powers, a little over a year ago, took from our midst one who was esteemed by all. He was loveable, kindly, and faithful in all of his duties, and of a

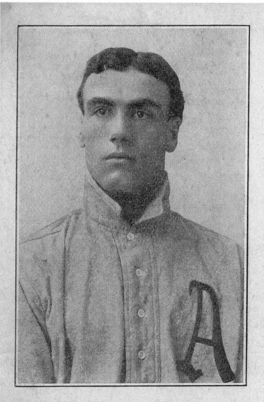

Publisher: Philadelphia Athletics, Philadelphia, PA • Manufacturer: Not Indicated • Type: Black & White • Postmark: Not Used • Value: $200–$300

disposition that only saw the bright side of things and the good in life. Almost his last words were, 'I am not thinking of myself, I am thinking of my wife and three little ones.' The Athletic Club wishes that this one great desire shall be accomplished—that his widow shall not want and his children will be given the education he had planned for them. All receipts of this day will be turned over to his widow. We want this fund to be a grand one and trust we may have your help in this cause by the presence of yourself and your friends, Connie Mack.

Powers, a graduate of Holy Cross, became a doctor while pursuing his 11-year major league career, which began in 1898 with the Louisville Colonels. "Doc" was behind the plate for the first game in Philadelphia Athletics history, in 1901 at Columbia Park, and played his last game for the A's in 1909, just prior to his untimely death at age 29. Although his career batting average was only .216, Powers was an extremely intelligent catcher, obviously loved by all who knew him.

1910 JIM MORONEY, Philadelphia Phillies

Publisher: Jimmy Moroney, Phiadelphia, PA • Manufacturer: Not Indicated
Type: Black & White • Postmark: Not Used • Value: $350–$400

Jimmy Moroney was an obscure left-handed pitcher who won 2 and lost 6 over three seasons with three different National League teams. He broke in with his hometown Boston Braves in 1906, starting, completing, and losing three games. He returned to the majors in 1910 with the Phillies as a relief pitcher, winning one and losing two with an ERA of 2.14 in 12 games. His final season was 1912, when he appeared in 10 games for the Cubs, all but three in relief, and finished 1-1.

With limited pitching success, Moroney decided the bar business would prove more lucrative. This advertising postcard pictures Jim in his major league uniform and a bottle of his own brand of whiskey, which he sold at his bar in Philadelphia. It also serves as a scorecard.

Moroney died in his adopted city of Philadelphia in 1929, but left behind as a legacy one of the more unusual postcards ever published.

1911 FRANK BAKER, Philadelphia Athletics

Frank "Home Run" Baker earned his nickname by walloping two game-winning round-trippers for the Philadelphia Athletics in the 1911 World Series. Those homers enabled the A's to defeat the New York Giants, four games to two. In the dead-ball era, Baker led the American League in homers for four straight years (1911–1914). When Connie Mack refused to pay Baker what the player felt he was worth, Baker sat out the entire 1915 season, playing with a semi-pro team in Pennsylvania. Mack traded Baker to the New York Yankees in 1916, where he played on two pennant winners—the Yanks' first—in 1921 and 1922. Home Run's finest all-around season was 1912, when he topped the league with 10 home runs, drove in a league- and career-high 133 RBI, and had his finest ever batting average, .347. While his lifetime average was a solid .307, he thrived in World Series competition, batting a robust .363 in 25 games over six Series.

Baker, who grew up on a farm in Trappe, Maryland, was extremely strong, using a 52-ounce bat—20 ounces more than today's average. He was also an astute judge

Publisher: Not Indicated • Manufacturer: Not Indicated • Type: Real Photo
Postmark: Not Used • Value: $200

of talent, recommending fellow Maryland eastern shore native Jimmy Foxx to his old adversary Connie Mack. Foxx went on to star with the A's, Red Sox, Cubs, and Phillies, hitting 534 career home runs.

In addition to his power-hitting prowess, Baker was a solid fielder with speed enough to steal 38, 40, and 34 bases from 1911–1913. But it was those game-winning homers in the 1911 World Series that established his reputation as a baseball immortal. He was elected to the Hall of Fame in 1955.

1911 CHIEF BENDER, Philadelphia Athletics

When Philadelphia A's manager Connie Mack needed a clutch victory, he would often call upon Chief Bender, who seldom let him down. A Chippewa Indian graduate of Carlisle Indian School, Chief won 212 games against only 127 losses during his 16 seasons in the majors. Bender joined the A's in 1903 and was the bellwether of Mack's staff along with left-hander Eddie Plank. Three times, Chief led the American League in

Compliments of **THE MONARCH TYPEWRITER COMPANY**

CHARLES A. BENDER, Pitcher

Publisher: The Monarch Typewriter Co., Philadelphia, PA • Manufacturer: Not Indicated • Type: Black & White • Postmark: Not Used • Value: $200–$250

winning percentage. His best all-around season came in 1910, when his 23 wins and .821 percentage were the league's best. He picked up another victory in the World Series that year, as the A's defeated the Cubs. He also threw a no-hitter against Cleveland in 1910.

After leading the AL with an .850 winning percentage in 1914 thanks to a 17-3 season, Chief jumped to the Baltimore Terrapins of the Federal League, where he had a disastrous 4-16 season in 1915. He finished his career with the Phillies, winning 15 and losing 9 over two seasons. Chief made 10 World Series appearances with the Athletics, winning 6 and losing 4.

1911 EDDIE COLLINS, Philadelphia Athletics

Edward Collins
Philadelphia Athletics.
Published by
The Sporting News

Publisher: The Sporting News, St. Louis, MO • Manufacturer: The Sporting News • Type: Color Pre-Linen • Postmark: Not Used • Value: $250–$300

Eddie Collins was a superb all-around ballplayer who compiled a .333 batting average over 25 major league seasons and earned a well-deserved spot in the Hall of Fame in 1939. Yet even though the second baseman hit .303 or better in 19 of his 25 seasons, he never led the league in batting.

Collins joined Connie Mack's Philadelphia Athletics in 1906, remaining with them through 1914, when he was traded to the White Sox. He remained in Chicago through the 1926 season—including 1919, the year of the Black Sox scandal. Known to be a man of complete integrity, Collins reportedly never was approached by gamblers to fix the 1919 World Series.

Starting with Philadelphia in 1909, Collins didn't bat below .308 for eight consecutive seasons. After subpar seasons in 1917 and '18, he batted .319 in '19, igniting a 10-year run of seasons in which he hit .303 or better. Extremely fast, Eddie led the AL in stolen bases four times, swiping a career-high 81 in 1910. From 1912–14, he led the league in runs with 137, 125, and 122. When his career was winding down in 1927, Collins returned to the Athletics at the ripe old age of 40 and led the league in pinch-hitting with 12 hits in 34 at bats.

1911 FRANK SCHULTE, Chicago Cubs

Publisher: Max Stein, Chicago, IL • Manufacturer: Not Indicated
Type: Sepia • Postmark: Not Used • Value: $150–$200

Before the advent of Most Valuable Player awards, the Chalmers Motor Car Co. selected the year's finest player and presented him with a Chalmers automobile. In 1911, the first recipient of the Chalmers Award for the National League was Frank "Wildfire" Schulte, an outfielder with the Chicago Cubs who led the league with 21 home runs and 107 RBI. His slugging percentage of .534 was also the league's best. His .300 batting average was a career second-best.

In his 15 years in the major leagues, Schulte never came close to matching those figures again. Nevertheless, he retired with a respectable .270 lifetime batting average. Though he was never accorded HOF honors, Frank Schulte was the National League's finest player in 1911.

1911 CLEVELAND NAPS VS. ALL-STARS

Publisher: Not Indicated • Manufacturer: Not Indicated • Type: Real Photo
Postmark: Not Used • Value: $3,000–$5,000

Right-hander Addie Joss of the Cleveland Naps had a fabulous, if relatively short, nine-year pitching career. He won 160 games and lost 97 from his first big-league season until illness forced him out of the game in 1910 and soon after took his life.

Tall, handsome, and well educated, Joss became an immediate fan favorite when he joined Cleveland's American League club in 1902, winning 17 games that season. Two years later, Joss won his first ERA title with a league-low 1.59. In 1907, he led the AL with 27 wins. On October 2, 1908, he achieved that rarest of pitching highs, throwing a perfect game against the Chicago White Sox in a 1-0 win over Big Ed Walsh. The effort capped a 24-win season in which Joss led the AL with a 1.16 ERA.

Everything seemed to be going well for Joss when he was struck by tubercular meningitis. His record slipped to 14-13 in 1909 and to 5-5 in 1910—although one of those five wins was a no-hitter. He left the game after only 13 appearances that season. On April 14, 1911, Joss died.

To raise money for Joss' wife and son, an All-Star

Publisher: Elite Postcard Shop, Washington, DC • Manufacturer: Elite Postcard Shop • Type: Real Photo • Postmark: Not Used • Value: $1,500–$2,000

team faced the Naps on July 11 at League Park. A Cleveland newspaper described it as "the greatest array of players ever seen on one field." The illustrious rosters included Ty Cobb, Eddie Collins, Sam Crawford, Frank "Home Run" Baker, Tris Speaker, Walter Johnson, and Napoleon Lajoie, all destined for the Hall of Fame. Note that Cobb, the Tigers star, second from the right, is wearing a Cleveland uniform. Perhaps he forgot to bring his own outfit to the game. The All-Stars defeated the Naps, 5-3, raising more than $13,000 for the Joss family.

1911 AMERICAN LEAGUE PARK,
Washington Senators

On March 17, 1911, while conducting spring training in Atlanta, the Washington Senators received terrible news. A plumber working with an acetylene torch at the team's ballpark, located at 7th Street and Florida Avenue in the District of Columbia, had accidentally set fire to the wooden structure. President Tom Noyes, though badly shaken by the news, said he would have a new park ready for opening day on April 12. The Elite Postcard Shop of Washington documented the con-

Publisher: Elite Postcard Shop, Washington, DC • Manufacturer: Elite Postcard Shop • Type: Real Photo • Postmark: Not Used • Value: $1,500–$2,000

struction of the new park, shooting a series of postcard photos starting on April 1—only 11 days before the park was scheduled for completion. Two of the cards are illustrated here.

Postcard #1 shows construction workers on April 1, placing the wooden beams that will support the rows of seats. A second card, not pictured, reproduces a photo taken later in the day that shows the construction workers preparing the wooden support beams for the grandstand.

A third photo, taken five days later on April 6, shows

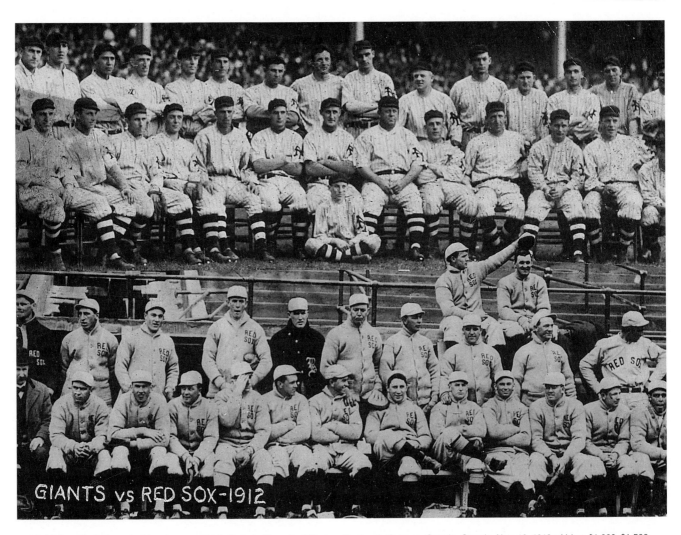

GIANTS vs RED SOX-1912

Publisher: Not Indicated • Manufacturer: Not Indicated • Type: Real Photo • Postmark: Oshawa, Ontario, Canada, Nov. 16, 1912 • Value: $1,000–$1,500

concrete poured in specific areas of the ballpark, while workers continue to build support beams in other sections. Photo-card #18 from April 10 shows seats being installed.

These extremely rare postcards are part of a larger set that show the creation of the new ballpark through opening day, when the park was opened as planned. *Washington Post* sports editor Joe Jackson provided commentary describing this memorable event: "As 16,000 exuberant 33rd degree fans rose with the incoherent babble of sound that is the cry of the rooter, President William Howard Taft posed for a moment, swung his arm, and hurled the ball straight and true to Dolly Gray, the Washington pitcher." President Taft, an avid baseball fan, had begun the tradition of throwing out the ceremonial first ball the previous year. This Washington tradition continued until the city lost its major league franchise in 1971, with each president through Richard Nixon participating in at least one season-opening game.

1912 WORLD SERIES

The 1912 World Series between the Boston Red Sox and New York Giants was one of the most hotly contested in history. The Red Sox beat the Giants four games to three, with an eighth game ending in a 6-6 tie. Both teams were loaded with superstars, and the drama throughout was incredible.

In the eighth and final game, played in Boston, the Red Sox scored two runs in the bottom of the 10th inning, as Giants outfielder Fred Snodgrass dropped a fly ball and first baseman Fred Merkle let Tris Speaker's foul pop get away. Christy Mathewson was the hard-luck loser by a score of 3-2, while Smoky Joe Wood picked up his third World Series win in relief of Hugh Bedient. Outfielders Tris Speaker and Harry Hooper of the Red Sox are enshrined in the Hall of Fame, as are Giants manager John McGraw and pitchers Mathewson and Rube Marquard. The Red Sox were the dominant team in baseball during this decade, winning the World Series in 1912, '15, '16, and '18.

RICHARD (RUBE) MARQUARD, NEW YORK (Giants)

Publisher: United States Publishing House, Chicago, IL • Manufacturer: United States Publishing House • Type: Sepia • Postmark: Not Used • Value: $200–$250

1912 RUBE MARQUARD, New York Giants

When left-handed pitcher Rube Marquard joined the New York Giants in 1908, he was named "The $11,000 Beauty." The title was based on the fact that he had been purchased from the Indianapolis club of the American Association for that amount, an unheard of sum for a player. Marquard did not become an instant star with the Giants. In fact, he lost his only game his first season. The New York press began referring to him as "The $11,000 Lemon." In 1909, he won six games and lost 13. Manager John McGraw recognized Marquard's problem, later describing it in his book, *My Thirty Years in Baseball:* "It was his nervousness over living up to a great reputation that seemed to upset him. As a result, he developed problems in controlling his pitches. So fearful was he of not being able to get the ball over when it came down to two [strikes] and three [balls] that he would simply toss it over straight as a string. In other words, he had so

much stuff that he was afraid to use it."

After Marquard mastered control of his pitching—which required two full seasons—he became one of the best pitchers in baseball. He went 24-7 in 1911 and won 26 games in 1912. He was almost perfect in the 1912 World Series against the Boston Red Sox, allowing only one run in 18 innings and winning two games. In 1913, he had 24 wins and 10 losses.

Marquard completed his 18-year career in 1925 with a lifetime total of 205 victories. "The $11,000 Beauty" was elected to the Hall of Fame in 1971.

1912 HARRY HOOPER, Boston Red Sox

Harry Hooper played 17 seasons with the Red Sox and White Sox, batting .281 in his career, but he is best remembered as one of the finest outfielders in baseball history. His barehanded grab of a potential Larry Doyle home run in the eighth game of the 1912 World Series

Publisher: Harry Hooper • Manufacturer: Not Indicated • Type: Black & White • Postmark: Capitola, CA, Feb. 17, 1949 • Value: $50

assured Boston victory over the Giants. Still, Hooper was also a fine clutch hitter who led the Red Sox past the Phillies in the 1915 World Series, batting .350 with 2 HR and 3 RBI. Hooper batted .304 or better five times, including a career-best .328 with the White Sox in 1924. Indirectly, Hooper was responsible for Babe Ruth's success. He suggested to manager Ed Barrow that Ruth be converted to a full-time outfielder, even though he was the Red Sox's star pitcher, reasoning he was more valuable to the team playing every game than pitching every fourth.

Hooper played with four World Series winners in four tries with the Red Sox, batting .293 in championship games. He was elected to the Hall of Fame in 1971, and was the oldest living member of the Hall when he died in 1974 at age 87.

1912 JOE WOOD, Boston Red Sox

Right-hander Smoky Joe Wood earned his nickname from a blazing fastball that ranks among baseball's all-

Publisher: Max Stein, Chicago, IL • Manufacturer: Max Stein • Type: Sepia
Postmark: Not Used • Value: $50

time best. In 1912, he was baseball's finest pitcher, leading the American League with 34 wins (against 5 losses) and a brilliant .872 winning percentage while compiling a 1.91 ERA. He capped that season with three victories in the 1912 World Series, helping his Red Sox defeat the New York Giants four games to three. However, the 344 innings he pitched during the regular season, along with 22 more in the World Series, took a tremendous toll on his arm. Although Wood went 35-14 in his remaining years, he never again recaptured his remarkable form of 1912. His last hurrah as a pitcher came in 1915, when he paired the league's best ERA (1.49) with the top winning percentage (.750), going 15-5.

Traded to Cleveland in 1917, Smoky Joe became an outfielder and played through the 1922 season. He hit .296 in 1918 and .366 in 66 games with the Indians in 1921. He was a member of the Indians' 1920 world championship team, giving him a second World Series ring.

Smoky Joe may never make the Hall of Fame because of his relatively brief tenure as a pitcher. Still, his 11-year record of 116 wins, 57 losses, and a 2.03 ERA warrants a closer look.

Publisher: Not Indicated • Manufacturer: Not Indicated • Type: Real Photo
Postmark: Not Used • Value: $150–$200

1912 CLYDE MILAN, Washington Senators

Clyde Milan was one of the fastest outfielders of his day, twice leading the American League in stolen bases, with 88 in 1912 and 75 in 1913. He spent his entire 16-year career with the Washington Senators, from 1907, when he made the roster, until 1922, his one season as player/manager. That year, the Senators finished 69-89, sixth in the AL. Milan stayed with the team as a coach for many years after.

Milan compiled a lifetime .285 batting average, hitting .301 or better four times, including a career-high .322 in 1920. His 79 RBI in 1912 was another career topper. His lifetime total of 495 stolen bases ranks among the best in baseball history.

The postcard above, labeled "The Climbers," was

Publisher: R.S. McConnell, Southern Pines, NC • Manufacturer: R.S. McConnell • Type: Real Photo • Postmark: Not Used • Value: $1,500–$2,000

produced by an unknown Washington photographer around 1912, after the Senators climbed from a seventh-place finish in 1911 to second in 1912 (and 1913), thanks mainly to the pitching of right-hander Walter Johnson, who won 32 games in '12 and 28 in '13.

1914 BALTIMORE TERRAPINS

Originally organized in 1913 as an independent league in the Midwest, the Federal League consisted of six teams: Chicago, Cleveland, Covington (Kentucky), Indianapolis, Pittsburgh, and St. Louis. John T. Powers of Chicago was elected as the league's president. In June of the first year, the Covington franchise moved to Kansas City. But the rest of the league was successful enough that owners decided to expand to eight teams for 1914, electing a new president, Chicagoan James A. Gilmore.

Gilmore had grandiose plans to compete with the National and American leagues. At that time, baseball's Reserve Clause enabled teams to control and reserve players even after their contracts had expired. On August 2, 1913, the Federal League owners held a secret meeting. They decided to invade the East Coast, adding teams in Baltimore and Brooklyn. Furthermore, they would ignore the Reserve Clause and sign major league players not under contract.

Player/manager George Stovall of the St. Louis Browns became the first player to ignore the Reserve Clause and jump to the Federal League, signing to take the same position with Kansas City. Others soon followed, including many big-name players. Philadelphia Phillies second baseman Otto Knabe became the Baltimore Terrapins' player/manager with a three-year contract worth $30,000, three times the sum he was making with the Phillies. This photograph of the Terrapins, providing the earliest known postcard of a Federal League club, shows the team beginning spring training on March 11, 1914, at Southern Pines, N.C. Note the many different major league uniforms worn by the players, as their Terrapin outfits had not arrived. Player/manager Knabe is kneeling on the left, holding a bat. One month after the photo was taken, the team began its season at Baltimore's new Terrapin Park.

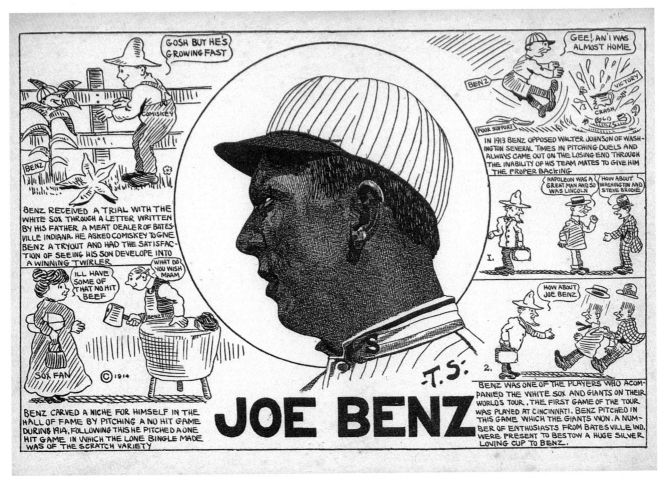

Publisher: E & S Publishing Co., Chicago, IL • Manufacturer: Not Indicated
Type: Blue & White • Postmark: Not Used • Value: $200–$250

1914 JOE BENZ, Chicago White Sox

Right-hander Joe Benz pitched nine seasons with the Chicago White Sox from 1911 through 1919, winning 76 games and losing 75. Although he won 14 games in 1914, he led the league with 19 defeats despite an excellent ERA of 2.26. In 1915, he won 15, this time losing 11. His 2.42 lifetime ERA attests to his skill as a pitcher. With better batting support, he undoubtedly would have won many more games. He has the distinction of appearing in one of the rarest postcard sets. Published by E & S Publishing Co. of Chicago in 1914, it shows caricatures of prominent players of the day.

1915 BRAVES FIELD, Boston Braves

When it opened on August 18, 1915, Braves Field was proudly proclaimed the largest ballpark in the world, with a capacity of approximately 45,000. That opening day, 56,000 fans crammed the yard to watch the game, with another 6,000 turned away. At the end of the season, the World Series came to Braves Field, although the Braves failed to win the National League pennant.

Publisher: Ruge & Badger, Boston, MA • Manufacturer: Not Indicated
Type: Color Pre-Linen • Postmark: Not Used • Value: $100–$125

The club generously allowed the AL-champion Red Sox to use their new field, which seated 10,000 more fans than Fenway Park, as thanks for the Braves' use of Fenway Park in 1914.

In their first years in the new park, the Braves remained fairly competitive, finishing in second place in 1915, and third place in 1916. They fell to sixth place in 1917, seventh in 1918, and last in 1922 and 1924. The Braves didn't win a pennant until 1948. In the interim, the Red Sox won pennants in 1915, 1916, and 1918, capturing the hearts of Boston fans. The Braves maintained the claim of having the finest and largest stadium until Yankee Stadium was built in 1923. Still, many people seemed to feel that Braves Field never had the homey environment of Fenway Park.

1915 WALTER JOHNSON & GABBY STREET, Washington Senators

Publisher: The Sporting News, St. Louis, MO • Manufacturer: The Sporting News • Type: Color Pre-Linen • Postmark: Not Used • Value: $300–$400

This postcard of Walter Johnson and catcher Gabby Street was issued by *The Sporting News* in 1915. The hard-throwing, right-handed Johnson was considered the fastest and best pitcher in baseball. He led the American League in wins for four consecutive seasons, with 36 victories in 1913, 28 in 1914, 27 in 1915, and 25 in 1916. Before Johnson ended his pitching career in 1927, he took the wins title one more time, winning 23 games in 1924.

Gabby Street left the Washington Senators in 1911, long before the postcard above was issued. The photo-

graph must have been taken during his last season with Washington. Street caught 28 games with the New York Highlanders in 1912. He retired as an active player in 1931 after making one appearance as a catcher with the St. Louis Cardinals, where he was a manager. Considered a brilliant handler of pitchers, Street helped to develop Johnson. He achieved some notoriety as the first man to catch a baseball thrown out of the Washington Monument, 550 feet above the ground. The feat had been attempted by others, including Pop Schriver, a catcher with the Chicago Colts, in 1894. Twelve balls were thrown out to Street, and every one hit a wall of the monument on the way down. He caught the 13th ball over his head, staggering as the impact almost drove his glove into the ground, but holding on to the ball.

1916 GROVER ALEXANDER, Philadelphia Phillies

Grover Cleveland Alexander had many highlights during his 20-year major league pitching career, but none more

Publisher: The Girard Bank, Philadelphia, PA • Manufacturer: Not Indicated
Type: Chrome • Postmark: Not Used • Value: $1–$3

memorable than his performance in the seventh game of the 1926 World Series. The Cardinals were hanging precariously to a 3-2 lead in the seventh inning of Game 7 when the 39-year-old right-hander was summoned from the bullpen. The bases were loaded, but Alexander struck out Tony Lazzeri and shut out the heavily favored Yankees in the final two innings to give the Cardinals their first world championship.

Alexander made his major league debut with the Phillies in 1911 and promptly led the NL in victories with 28, a rookie record that still stands. After winning 20 in 1912 and 22 in 1913, Alexander topped all pitchers in victories for four consecutive seasons, winning 27 in 1914, 31 in 1915 (when the Phillies won their first pennant), 33 in 1916 (his career high), and 30 in 1917. He did it again with the Cubs in 1920, winning 27. Alexander was also a five-time ERA champ, leading the NL in 1915–17, 1919, and 1920. His four one-hitters in 1915 and 16 shutouts in 1916 remain major league records.

Alexander missed nearly all of the 1918 season serving in France as an artillery sergeant during World War I. He returned suffering from epilepsy and became a heavy drinker, but continued to excel despite these obstacles. Traded to the Cubs prior to the 1918 season, he went 2-1 before joining the army. He was dealt to St. Louis in 1926, and after his brilliant work in the World Series, the 40-year-old won 21 and lost only 10 for the Cardinals in 1927.

During his three-decade career, Alexander picked up 373 victories, tying him with Christy Mathewson as the National League's all-time winningest pitcher. During World Series appearances in 1915, 1926, and 1928, he won three and lost two. Grover Cleveland Alexander was elected to the Hall of Fame in 1938.

1919 CINCINNATI REDS

The 1919 Cincinnati Reds are arguably the most under-appreciated team in baseball history. When it was learned in 1920 that eight Chicago White Sox players had conspired with gamblers to fix the 1919 World Series, many jumped on that to demean the Reds' victory. However, looking objectively at the '19 Reds, the accomplishment was no fluke. Center fielder Edd Roush led the National League with a .321 batting average. The team's pitching was superb, as Dutch Ruether, Slim Salee, and Hod Eller had three of the top four winning percentages in the league. Right-hander Eller was 20-9 with a 2.39 ERA. Left-hander Ruether went 19-6, leading the NL with his .760 winning percentage, while the 6-foot-3 left-hander Sallee was 21-7 with a 2.06 ERA. Defensively, the Reds were exceptional. Second baseman Morris Rath led the league in putouts (345), assists (452), and double plays (59), while Heinie Groh topped third basemen in putouts (171)

CINCINNATI REDS, WORLD'S CHAMPIONS 1919

Publisher: Not Indicated • Manufacturer: Not Indicated • Type: Black & White • Postmark: Not Used • Value: $750–$1,000

and double plays (22). In addition, the Reds' overall record of 96 wins and 44 losses was considerably better than the White Sox's 88-52 mark. Make no mistake, the 1919 Reds were an outstanding all-around team and deserve a lot more appreciation than they have received.

1919 EDD ROUSH, Cincinnati Reds

Edd Roush was not only a superb center fielder and hitter, he was also a man of strong convictions. He sat out the entire 1930 season because the Giants tried to cut his salary. Roush came up with the White Sox in 1913 for nine games, but after getting only one hit in 10 trips to the plate, he was sent back to the minors for more seasoning. He resurfaced with the Indianapolis Hoosiers in the Federal League in 1914, helping them to the championship with a .325 batting average in 74 games.

EDDIE ROUSH, *Center Field*
Cincinnati "Reds" World's Champions 1919

Publisher: Not Indicated • Manufacturer: Not Indicated • Type: Black & White • Postmark: Not Used • Value: $100

Publisher: Max Stein, Chicago, IL • Manufacturer: Max Stein • Type: Sepia • Postmark: Not Used • Value: $200

When the club moved to Newark in 1915, Roush became a full-time player, batting .298.

Following that season, the Federal League folded, leading Roush to join the New York Giants in 1916. After several run-ins with manager John McGraw, Edd was traded to Cincinnati, where he became one of baseball's premier stars. Realizing his mistake, McGraw tried frequently to get Roush back to the Giants, finally succeeding in 1927.

With the Reds, Roush led the National League in batting in 1917 with a .341 average and again in 1919, when he batted .321. That year, he was instrumental to the Reds' first National League championship. And while he batted only .214 in the 1919 World Series against the infamous Black Sox of Chicago, he had 7 RBI and was a big factor in the Reds' victory.

Roush used a 48-ounce bat—the heaviest made by Louisville Slugger—compiling a lifetime batting average of .325. Back-to-back .352 batting averages in 1921 and 1922 were his highest. Elected to the Hall of Fame in 1962, Roush died in 1988 at the age of 94. The postcard at right, part of a 25-card set issued after the 1920 Series, is among the most prized Roush collectibles.

1919 BUCK WEAVER, Chicago White Sox

Buck Weaver was a better-than-average third baseman who spent his entire nine-year career with the Chicago White Sox—and wound up being among the eight White Sox who were banned from baseball for life. Max Stein was a famous Chicago photographer, skilled at capturing all aspects of American life but particularly adept at chronicling baseball. Their paths crossed when Weaver became the subject of the Stein postcard pictured above.

All Stein postcards are very desirable, but this particular one, although not the most valuable, is my favorite. It's a montage of Weaver's life as a baseball player. Stein captures Buck enjoying a conversation with attractive women before the game as well as performing his duties as a third baseman.

In the 1919 World Series against the Reds, Weaver was outstanding, batting .324 and playing flawlessly in the field. Yet he was kicked out of baseball following the 1920 season, the year the Black Sox scandal broke. Ironically, it was his finest season in the majors, as he batted .333, scored a career-high 104 runs, and drove in a career-best 75 runs.

1920-29

Baseball entered the Roaring '20s with a whimper. In 1920, America learned that eight members of the Chicago White Sox took gamblers' money to fix the 1919 World Series with Cincinnati. Disillusioned fans stayed away from the stadiums in droves, questioning the integrity of the game. It took the immortal Babe Ruth to bring them back time and time again with his remarkable home run hitting. Traded from Boston to the New York Yankees in 1920, Ruth and his bat made Yankees tickets the hottest in the Big Apple. Even though the New York Giants beat the Yankees in the 1921 and '22 World Series, the Yankees outdrew the Giants by huge margins at the Polo Grounds, which the teams shared. Frustrated, Giants manager and part-owner John McGraw told the Yankees to vacate the Polo Grounds and build a ballpark of their own. Consequently, Yankee Stadium—dubbed "The House that Ruth Built"—

opened in 1923 across the Harlem River in the Bronx, within sight of the Giants' park. In their own stadium, the Yankees finally won their first World Series, defeating the Giants, to whom they had lost in 1921 and '22.

Ruth couldn't have picked a better time to introduce himself to the world. As he arrived in New York, radio was coming of age. The 1921 Giants/Yankees World Series was the first to be broadcast, as stations WJZ in Newark, N.J., and WBZ in Springfield, Mass., joined to re-create the games. By telephone from the press box at the Polo Grounds, *Newark Call* reporter Sandy Hunt relayed each play to WJZ program supervisor Thomas Cowan, who described Hunt's comments over the two-station network. The next year, as the number of radio receivers in America climbed to three million, the World Series was broadcast live from the ballpark.

New York's World Series monopoly concluded in 1924, when the Washington Senators won their only world championship. The Senators were American League champs again in 1925 but lost the Fall Classic in seven games to the Pittsburgh Pirates. The St. Louis Cardinals surprised the baseball world in 1926, winning the National League pennant and subsequently crushing the Yankees in the World Series.

HARLEM RIVER YANKEE STADIUM AND POLO GROUNDS NEW YORK CITY

Publisher: Gravotone Co., New York, NY • Manufacturer: Not Indicated • Type: Black & White • Postmark: Not Used • Value: $250–$300

Publisher: RCA Victrola • Manufacturer: Not Indicated • Type: Government Postal • Postmark: Not Used • Value: $50–$75

Yankee dominance asserted itself in 1927 and '28 as the team demolished the Pirates and Cardinals four straight in each World Series. Ruth, first baseman Lou Gehrig, and the rest of Murderers' Row supplied most of the punch.

Meanwhile, another dynasty was being established by Connie Mack in Philadelphia. Starting in 1929, the A's won three consecutive American League pennants and two world championships. The offense, centered around Hall of Famers Jimmie Foxx, Al Simmons, and Mickey Cochrane, was supplemented by superb pitching, led by Hall of Famer Lefty Grove, who won 20, and George Earnshaw, who led the league with 24 victories. Unfortunately, 1929 was the start of a worldwide depression, and baseball attendance suffered accordingly—particularly in Philadelphia, where Connie Mack eventually was forced to sell most of his stars just to survive.

1920 WORLD SERIES

Where Brooklyn Watched the World's Series, Fulton St. at DeKalb Ave., Brooklyn, N. Y.

Publisher: E.C. Kropp Co., #29519N, Milwaukee, WI • Manufacturer: E.C. Kropp • Type: Color Pre-Linen • Postmark: Brooklyn, NY, July 20, 1922 Value: $20–$30

This illustration shows how baseball fans followed the fortunes of their favorite teams before the advent of radio and television. Large, electric scoreboards were set up in downtown locations for huge crowds to watch. In Brooklyn, during the 1920 World Series between the Dodgers and Cleveland, a scoreboard was placed on the corner of Fulton Street and DeKalb Avenue. After this postcard was published, the proprietor of the store in the picture imprinted the cards to promote a sale on men's clothes. Most of the Brooklyn fans were disappointed with the results of the World Series, which the Dodgers lost, five games to two. Hopefully, the proprietor of the store had better results with his sale.

1920 WILBERT ROBINSON, Brooklyn Dodgers

Wilbert Robinson and John McGraw played for the famous Baltimore Orioles team that dominated baseball throughout most of the 1890s. Although Robinson, the veteran catcher, was 10 years older than third baseman McGraw, they became the best of friends—and partners in a combination gym, restaurant, and bowling alley in Baltimore, called The Diamond. There, the pair originated duckpin bowling. To save money, when the larger pins became damaged, the alley shaved them down to a smaller size and continued to use them. Some customers preferred them, and the idea spread to other parts of the country.

John McGraw became manager of the New York Giants in 1902, and a year later, Robinson joined him as his principal coach and confidant. Known as "Uncle Robbie," Robinson was as kindhearted as he was large—his weight grew to almost 300 pounds from his playing weight of 215 pounds. Robinson spent most of his time developing pitchers, including Christy Mathewson, Rube Marquard, and Joe McGinnity.

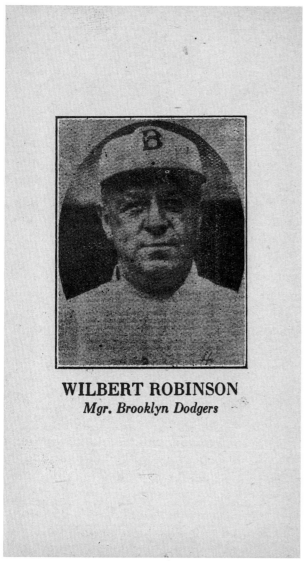

WILBERT ROBINSON
Mgr. Brooklyn Dodgers

Publisher: Not Indicated • Manufacturer: Not Indicated • Type: Black & White • Postmark: Not Used • Value: $200–$250

By 1913, the relationship between Robinson and McGraw deteriorated to the point that the two no longer spoke to one another. Robinson resigned as the Giants' coach and became manager of the Brooklyn Dodgers. His career as Dodger manager lasted for 19 years, ending in 1931 with 1,399 wins and 1,398 losses, plus a 3-9 record in two World Series losses, one in 1916, the other in 1920. The photograph above was taken in 1924. Robinson died on August 8, 1934, only six months after McGraw. They're buried only a few yards apart, achieving a closeness that eluded them in their later years of life.

1920 TRIS SPEAKER, Cleveland Indians

Tris Speaker's 22 years as a major league outfielder began in 1907 with the Boston Red Sox; he batted .304 or better in 18 of those seasons. In 1916, he went to Cleveland, where he launched his Indians career with a .386 batting average, winning his only batting title. In 1919, Speaker was named player/manager of the Indians, and he led them to the world championship in 1920.

Whether at bat or in the field, Speaker's performance was consistently splendid. Though he wasn't a prolific home run hitter, Speaker had power enough to lead the American League in doubles eight times and finish his career with the record for most doubles in baseball history (792). His throwing arm was equally strong. Speaker holds the records for double plays (139) and unassisted double plays (4) by an outfielder. He held the record for most career putouts by an outfielder until it was broken by Willie Mays.

In 1927, Speaker played for the Washington Senators, then finished his career in 1928 with the Philadelphia Athletics. He had a career total of 3,515 hits and a .344 batting average. Tris Speaker was inducted into the Baseball Hall of Fame in 1937.

TRIS SPEAKER
CLEVELAND AMERICANS

Publisher: Eastern Exhibit Supply Co., Philadelphia, PA
Manufacturer: Eastern Exhibit Supply Co. • Type: Browntone
Postmark: Not Used • Value: $100–$125

URBAN CLARENCE FABER
CHICAGO A.L. 1914-1933
DURABLE RIGHTHANDER WHO WON 253,
LOST 211, E.R.A. 3.13 GAMES IN TWO DECADES
WITH WHITE SOX. VICTOR IN 3 GAMES
OF 1917 WORLD'S SERIES AGAINST GIANTS.
WON 20 OR MORE GAMES IN SEASON
FOUR TIMES, THREE IN SUCCESSION.

NATIONAL BASEBALL HALL OF FAME & MUSEUM
Cooperstown, New York

Publisher: Not Indicated • Manufacturer: Not Indicated • Type: Greentone
Postmark: Not Used • Value: $60–$75

1920 RED FABER, Chicago White Sox

Urban "Red" Faber toiled 20 years with the Chicago White Sox, 15 of which saw the team finish in the second division. Yet Faber still won 254 games, earning a spot in the Hall of Fame for his remarkable perseverance. With better clubs, Faber undoubtedly would have won many more games. After posting a 10-10 record in his initial season of 1914, Red showed a portent of things to come with a 24-10 record in 1915. Faber was a 20-game winner for three consecutive years in 1920, '21, and '22, finishing 23-13, 25-15, and 21-17, respectively. Red also was ERA champ in '21 with a 2.48 mark and again in '22 with a 2.80. In Faber's only World Series appearance in 1917, he won three games, helping the White Sox to the championship. Faber was the last legal spitball pitcher in the American League when he retired in 1933, using it and a fine fastball to account for his success. He was elected to the Hall in 1964.

H. W. ARLIN   C. C. WYLAM

CONCERT ANNOUNCERS

Station KDKA
"THE PIONEER BROADCASTING STATION OF THE WORLD"

Westinghouse Electric & Manufacturing Co.
East Pittsburgh, Pa.

POST STUDIO ANNOUNCERS

G. S. RYAN   T. F. HARNACK

Publisher: Westinghouse Electric Co., #O.C. 1543, Pittsburgh, PA • Manufacturer: Not Indicated • Type: Sepia • Postmark: Not Used • Value: $100–$150

1921 HAROLD ARLIN, broadcaster

Every baseball broadcaster of the past 70 years owes a debt of gratitude to Harold W. Arlin, shown in the upper left corner of this postcard. Arlin was a foreman for Westinghouse who moonlighted as a concert announcer for the company's radio station, KDKA in Pittsburgh. He became the first radio announcer for a baseball game on August 5, 1921.

Speaking into a telephone that had been converted into a microphone by Westinghouse engineers, Arlin described the game between the Pittsburgh Pirates and Philadelphia Phillies at Forbes Field as it happened. He broadcast from a box seat located at ground level, as the elevated radio and TV booths of today did not exist.

Arlin was also the first person to broadcast Davis Cup tennis matches and a football game between Pittsburgh and West Virginia played that fall at Pittsburgh Stadium. His work in sports and other duties was so good that KDKA gave him the title "First Full-Time Radio Announcer in the World." In later years, reflecting on the initial broadcast years, Arlin modestly said, "No one had the foggiest idea, the slightest hint of an inkling, that what we started would take off like it did."

1921 HARRY HEILMANN, Detroit Tigers

Outfielder Harry Heilmann was one of the greatest right-handed batters in history, compiling a .342 average over 17 seasons. He had the misfortune of playing the outfield with Ty Cobb, and never received the acclaim Cobb did. But aside from fellow Hall of Famer Rogers Hornsby, Heilmann has no peers as a right-handed batter. He won four batting titles, hitting .394 in 1921, .403 in 1923, .393 in 1925, and .398 in 1927. Primarily a line-drive hitter, Heilmann blasted a career-best 21 homers in 1922. He drove in at least 103 runs eight times, including a career-high 139 RBI in 1921—the same season he led the American League with 237 hits.

Publisher: Eastern Exhibit Supply Co., Philadelphia, PA • Manufacturer: Eastern Exhibit Supply Co. • Type: Browntone • Postmark: Not Used
Value: $100–$125

Heilmann was not an instant star. When he broke in with the Tigers in 1914, he batted only .225. During his first four seasons with Detroit, his best average was .282. But once he began to hit .300 (with a .320 average in 1919), he continued for 12 straight seasons.

When his playing days ended, Heilmann stepped into the Tigers' broadcasting booth and served as an outstanding play-by-play announcer for many years. He was elected to the Hall of Fame in 1952.

1922 ROGERS HORNSBY, St. Louis Cardinals

Publisher: Block Bros., St. Louis, MO • Manufacturer: Block Bros.
Type: Real Photo • Postmark: Not Used • Value: $500–$750

This extremely rare real-photo postcard proclaims Rogers Hornsby as the world's greatest hitter—and during the mid-'20s, when this card was produced, Hornsby was just that. From 1920–1925, he won six consecutive NL batting titles. During this period, when he was at his zenith, Rajah batted .370, .379, .401, .384, .424, and .403, averaging better than .400 over the last five of those seasons. Even Ty Cobb, the all-time major league batting leader, never had such a five-year stretch. Hornsby is second to Cobb with a .358 lifetime batting average.

After leading the Cardinals to the world championship in 1926 as player/manager, Hornsby was traded to the New York Giants, where he promptly hit .361. Dealt to the Boston Braves for the 1928 season, he again held a player/manager position while hitting .387 and earning his seventh and last batting title.

Hornsby was a complete player who hit for power along with his remarkable average. He led the NL in home runs in 1922 with 42 and in 1925 with 39. He was RBI champ four times, with 152—a career best–in 1922. The Rajah had great eyesight and did everything possible to protect it, including not attending movies during his career. The last of Hornsby's 23 seasons came in 1937 when, as manager of the St. Louis Browns, he appeared in 20 games and managed to bat .321. He was elected to the Hall of Fame when he first became eligible in 1942.

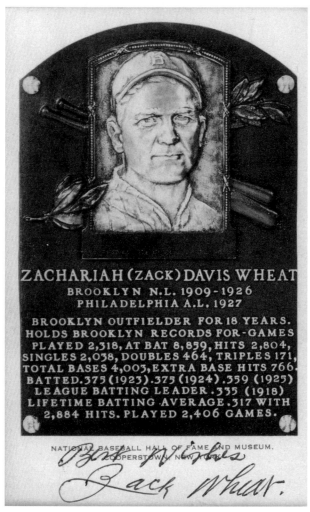

Publisher: National Baseball Hall of Fame and Museum, Cooperstown, NY
Manufacturer: Artvue • Type: Black & White • Postmark: Not Used
Value: Signed $200, Unsigned $10

1922 ZACH WHEAT, Brooklyn Dodgers

Zach Wheat was the complete package for the Brooklyn Dodgers. The right-handed hitting outfielder was a career .317 batter as well as a superb defensive specialist. His arm was particularly strong and accurate. Wheat batted .300 14 times, leading the league in 1918 with a .335 batting average. Twice, in 1923 and '24, he batted .375 but failed to win the batting title. Wheat drove in a career-high 112 runs in 1922 and drove in 103 in 1925. After 18 seasons with the Dodgers, he joined the Philadelphia Athletics in 1927, hitting .324 in 88 games. Wheat was elected to the Hall of Fame in 1959. Evidence of his popularity came when he edged Frankie Frisch of the Giants and Babe Ruth of the Yankees as the most popular player in New York. This early Hall of Fame plaque, signed by Wheat, has a value of $200.

1922 EPPA RIXEY, Cincinnati Reds

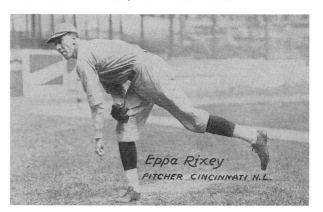

Publisher: Not Indicated • Manufacturer: Not Indicated • Type: Yellowtone
Postmark: Not Used • Value: $60–$75

Eppa Rixey pitched 21 years in the major leagues, nearly all with second-division ballclubs. Until Warren Spahn broke his record, Eppa was the winningest left-hander in big league history with 266 victories. Fresh from the University of Virginia campus, Rixey joined the Phillies in 1912—without spending a day in the minors—and won 10 and lost 10. His finest season with Philadelphia was 1916, when he led the National League with 22 wins. After being traded to the Cincinnati Reds in 1921, he was the NL's top winner again in 1922 with 25 triumphs. Rixey also recorded 20 victories in 1923 and 21 in 1925. The 6-foot 5-inch, 210 pounder had superb control throughout his career, averaging just over 1.5 walks per game. He was elected to the Hall of Fame in 1963, just prior to his death several months later.

Publisher: Not Indicated • Manufacturer: Not Indicated • Type: Greentone
Postmark: Not Used • Value: $100–$150

1923 FRANKIE FRISCH, New York Giants

Hall of Fame second baseman Frankie "Fordham Flash" Frisch acquired his nickname by going directly from Fordham University to the New York Giants in 1919. A hard-nosed competitor famous for coming through in clutch situations, Frisch played 19 seasons, compiling a .316 batting average. In his eight seasons with the Giants, the team won eight pennants and two World Series championships. Prior to the 1927 season, Frisch was dealt to the Cardinals, where he stayed through 11 seasons, four pennants, and two World Series titles. A switch-hitter, Frisch ran off 11 straight .300 seasons, including a career-high .348 in 1923. In 1921, 1927, and 1931, he led the league in steals with 49, 48, and 28, respectively. Though not a power hitter, Frankie drove in 100 or more runs three times, with 114 in 1930 his career high.

Frisch became player/manager of the Gashouse Gang Cardinals in 1933 and led them to the championship in '34. His managerial career continued for 16 years with the Cardinals, Pirates, and Cubs. In the end, his teams won 1,137 and lost 1,078, finishing second three times but never again winning a pennant. Frisch then became one of the first network baseball telecasters. He was elected to the Hall of Fame in 1947.

1923 RAY SCHALK, Chicago White Sox

Publisher: Exhibit Supply Co., Chicago, IL • Manufacturer: Exhibit Supply Co.
Type: Browntone • Postmark: Not Used • Value: $75–$100

In his 1932 autobiography, New York Giants manager John McGraw named Ray Schalk the finest catcher in the American League. He wrote, "Schalk is a hard and accurate thrower and because of a wonderful pair of hands he is seldom disabled. He is also very fast on the bases and is a good hitter. I regard him as the best backstop the American League has ever produced." McGraw liked Schalk so much, he signed the catcher as a part-time player in 1929, after Schalk's career with the White Sox had ended.

Born in Harvel, Illinois, on August 12, 1892, Schalk was signed by the Chicago White Sox in 1912. Though

YANKEE STADIUM
NEW YORK

©PICTORIAL PRESS N.Y.

Publisher: Pictorial News Co., #NY440, New York, NY • Manufacturer: Not Indicated • Type: Color Pre-Linen • Postmark: Not Used • Value: $40–$50

many considered him too small for baseball at 5 feet 9 inches and 165 pounds, he proved them wrong, catching more than 100 games per season in 11 consecutive years, leading all catchers in putouts for seven of them. An innovator, Schalk was the first catcher to back up plays at first base and third base, and on several occasions made putouts at second base. He was also an excellent handler of pitchers, catching four no-hitters during his 18-year career. Schalk wasn't a great threat offensively; he never hit .300, and retired with a .253 batting average and 12 career home runs. But his defense earned him election to the Hall of Fame in 1955.

1923 YANKEE STADIUM, New York Yankees

Yankee Stadium has been called "The House That Ruth Built." George Herman "Babe" Ruth of the New York Yankees was larger than life and baseball's dominant star for nearly two decades. More than 40 years after his death in 1948, he remains the best known personality in baseball history. His popularity and home run exploits made him the game's greatest attraction in the 1920s, when the Yankees shared the Polo Grounds with the New York Giants. Both teams were winning pennants at that time, and the Giants beat the Yankees in the 1921 and 1922 World Series—yet, thanks to Ruth, the Yankees had more fans, a fact that infuriated Giants manager John McGraw.

McGraw wanted Ruth and the Yankees out of the Polo Grounds. Yankees owner Jake Ruppert responded by building the largest, finest facility in baseball—directly across the Harlem River from the Polo Grounds.

The artist's rendition of a proposed design, pictured in the bottom right corner of this postcard, shows a fully enclosed structure. During construction, the design was changed to allow open center field bleachers. The primary photograph shows the stadium on opening day, April 18, 1923, with an inset illustration of the original enclosed design. The Osborne Engineering Co. of Cleveland, Ohio, designed the stadium, and the White Engineering Co. of New York built it in 284 days. The park covers 10 acres in the Bronx between 157th and 161st Streets and from River Avenue to the Major Deegan Expressway.

Officially, 74,200 fans were inside the stadium for the grand opening, while 20,000 more clamored to get in but went away disappointed when the gates were locked. The people inside were entertained by the music of the Seventh Regiment Band, directed by John Phillip Sousa. For many fans, the best music was the sound of Ruth's bat hitting a three-run homer as the Yankees beat Boston, 4-1. As *The New York Times* reported the next day, "The biggest crowd in baseball history rose to its feet and let loose the biggest shout in baseball history after Ruth's dramatic home run."

Publisher: Not Indicated • Manufacturer: Not Indicated • Type: Purpletone
Postmark: Not Used • Value: $60–$75

1924 DAZZY VANCE, Brooklyn Dodgers

Right-hander Dazzy Vance first reached the major leagues in 1915, pitching in nine games with the Pittsburgh Pirates and New York Highlanders. He posted an 0-4 record and was sent back to the minors. Recalled by New York in 1918, Dazzy was far from dazzling, as his 15.43 ERA in two innings will attest. He bounced from one minor league team to another, winding up with New Orleans in 1922. The Brooklyn Dodgers wanted catcher Hank DeBerry from the Pelicans, who insisted they take Vance as well. The Dodgers reluctantly agreed, stumbling upon one of the best deals in team history. Vance returned to the majors at age 31 and proceeded to lead the National League in strikeouts from 1922–28. He led the league in victories with 28 in 1924 and 22 in 1925. He won 22 again in 1928, losing 10 as he compiled a league-best 2.09 ERA. He was also the ERA champ in 1930 (2.61) despite a 17-15 record.

Vance had blinding speed, as his strikeout record indicates, and he threw his curve with almost as much zip as his fastball. A colorful character both on and off the field, Vance became one of the biggest gate attractions in baseball. Traded to St. Louis in 1933, he pitched $1\frac{1}{3}$ innings in the 1934 World Series, striking out 3. His career ended back in Brooklyn in 1935. Dazzy's career totals show 197 wins and 140 losses—remarkable figures when you consider he notched his first win at age 31.

1924 WASHINGTON SENATORS

The 1924 Senators gave Washington, D.C., its first American League pennant and its only world championship. Skillfully led by 27-year-old "Boy Manager" Bucky Harris and league-leading pitcher Walter Johnson, the Senators finished the '24 season with 92 wins, 62 losses, and a two-game advantage over the second-place New York Yankees. The '24 World Series was arguably the most exciting in baseball history, as the Senators won the seventh and deciding game against John McGraw's Giants in 12 thrill-packed innings. It was poetic justice that Johnson was the winner in relief after suffering two earlier losses, including a 12-inning, 4-3 loss in the Series opener.

Four Hall of Famers graced the Senators' lineup that season. In addition to Harris and Johnson, outfielders Sam Rice and Goose Goslin were subsequently inducted into baseball's shrine. The real-photo postcard of the '24 champions (p. 59) shows three of the four Hall of Famers—Johnson, Harris, and Rice—sitting together in the front row, with Goslin at the right end of the row. Two of the most colorful clowns in baseball history, Nick Altrock and Al Schacht—who served as Senator coaches as well as crowd pleasers—are at the opposite ends of the second row. Note the crazy angle of Altrock's cap at the right end. Schacht played in only 53 major league games over three seasons, winning 14 and losing 10 for the Senators in 1919, '20, and '21, while gaining notoriety as the "Clown Prince of Baseball." Left-hander Altrock won 22 games for the 1905 Chicago White Sox and 20 more in 1906, when the Hitless Wonders became world champs. Nick was 1-1 in the World Series against the Cubs, winning the first game, 2-1, and losing the fourth, 1-0.

Publisher: Not Indicated • Manufacturer: Not Indicated • Type: Real Photo • Postmark: Not Used • Value: $750–$1,000

1925 MAX CAREY, Pittsburgh Pirates

Max "Scoops" Carey, born Maximilian Carnarius, was a late bloomer whose greatest season came in 1925, when he was 35 years old. Max not only had a career-high .343 batting average, he almost single-handedly led the Pirates to the world championship over Washington, batting .458 in seven games. Max was a speed merchant who led the National League in stolen bases 10 times, still a major league record. In 1921, he pilfered 51 bases in 53 attempts.

Carey was studying to become a Lutheran minister at Concordia College in 1908 when he convinced the manager of the Central League's South Bend club that he was better than the team's current shortstop. The manager agreed, but to protect his amateur status, Max changed his name to Carey. A year later, he was up with the Pirates as an outfielder. He remained at that post, becoming one of the finest fielders of all time.

Although 1925 was his finest season, Max batted .302 or better a total of seven times, concluding his 20-year career with a .285 batting average. Elected to the Hall of Fame in 1961, Max died in 1976 at the age of 86. His autographed Hall of Fame plaque postcard is valued at $95.

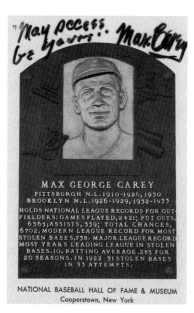

Publisher: National Baseball Hall of Fame and Museum, #5DK690, Cooperstown, NY • Manufacturer: Curt Teich, Chicago, IL • Type: Chrome Postmark: Not Used • Value: $95 Signed, $1 Unsigned

Publisher: Denby Cigar Co., Chicago, IL • Manufacturer: Not Indicated
Type: Black & White • Postmark: Not Used • Value: $200–$250

1925 KIKI CUYLER, Pittsburgh Pirates

Kiki Cuyler was a versatile outfielder who did everything well. In 15 major league seasons, he batted .300 or better 10 times, retiring in 1938 with a .321 lifetime average. In addition to hitting solidly, Cuyler was an adept base stealer, leading the league four times. Some called him a right-handed Ty Cobb.

Cuyler played one game with the Pittsburgh Pirates in each of the 1921 and 1922 seasons, then came up for 11 in 1923 before making the club for good in 1924, batting .354. The next year, he batted .357 and scored a then-record 144 runs, finishing second to Rogers Hornsby in the MVP balloting as he led the Pirates to a World Series victory—literally. It was Cuyler's bases-loaded double off Walter Johnson in the eighth inning of the seventh game that gave Pittsburgh the championship.

The Pirates returned to the World Series in 1927, but Cuyler never took the field, thanks to a dispute with Pittsburgh manager Donnie Bush. The outfielder was dealt to the Cubs before the next season. In Chicago,

he went on to bat better than .350 two more times, including a career-high .360 in 1929. His 18 home runs with Pittsburgh in 1925 marked another career high, as did his 134 RBI with Chicago in 1930. He was named to the Hall of Fame in 1968, some 18 years after his death.

1925 PIE TRAYNOR, Pittsburgh Pirates

Harold "Pie" Traynor spent his entire 17-year major league career with the Pittsburgh Pirates, establishing himself as one of the finest third baseman in baseball history. His .320 career batting average attests to his hitting skills, but he rivals fellow Hall of Famer Brooks Robinson as the best fielding third baseman of all time. Using a glove with a felt interior instead of leather, Traynor gobbled up everything hit toward third—particularly bunts and slow rollers.

Starting in 1925, Traynor batted .317 or better for six consecutive seasons, with his best mark coming in 1930,

Publisher: Not Indicated • Manufacturer: Not Indicated • Type: Purpletone
Postmark: Not Used • Value: $75–$100

when he batted a career-high .366. He drove in 100 runs or more seven times, with 124 RBI in 1928 his career best. Traynor helped the 1925 Pirates win the world championship, hitting .346 in a seven-game thriller against the Washington Senators. His only other World Series appearance came in 1927 against the New York Yankees; he batted .200 as the Pirates were overwhelmed by Ruth, Gehrig, and company in four straight.

The soft-spoken Traynor became player/manager of the Pirates during the 1934 season. Finishing second in 1938, the Pirates lost the pennant on the final day of the season to the Cubs on Gabby Hartnett's dramatic home run in the dark. Despite a losing record in 1939, his final year as manager, Pie won 457 games against only 406 losses during his six-year managerial career. Pie was elected to the Hall of Fame in 1948, regarded by many as the greatest ever to play the hot corner.

1925 SAM RICE & GOOSE GOSLIN,
Washington Senators

Publisher: Not Indicated • Manufacturer: Not Indicated • Type: Real Photo
Postmark: Not Used • Value: $300–$500

Postcards of Hall of Famers always command more money than cards of ordinary players, but when two appear on one card, it's even more special. This 1925 photo postcard of Hall of Fame outfielders Sam Rice and Goose Goslin, produced by an unidentified Washington photographer, is particularly rare. Rice played in right field and Goose covered left for the two-time American League and 1924 world champion Senators, and both had distinguished careers.

Goslin batted .316 over 18 seasons in the majors, playing with the Senators from 1921 until 1930, when he was traded to the St. Louis Browns. Goose returned to the Senators in 1933 for another AL championship, then was traded to Detroit in 1934, where he helped the Tigers win the AL pennant and, the next year, a world championship. He again returned to the Senators in 1938 to finish his major league career.

Sam Rice had almost identical statistics to Goslin, batting .322 over 20 big league seasons from 1915 through 1934, all but the last with Washington. Rice led the American League in hits twice, with 216 in both 1924 and 1926. Sam also led the AL with 63 stolen bases in 1920. In 15 games over three World Series with the Senators, he batted .302. His real name was Edgar Charles Rice, but Senators owner Clark Griffith mistakenly called him Sam early in his career, and the name stuck.

1925 BUCKY HARRIS & JOE JUDGE,
Washington Senators

Bucky Harris was dubbed the "Boy Manager" when he led the Washington Senators to the world championship in 1924 at the age of 27. Leading by example, he batted

Publisher: Not Indicated • Manufacturer: Not Indicated
Type: Real Photo • Postmark: Not Used • Value: $300–$500

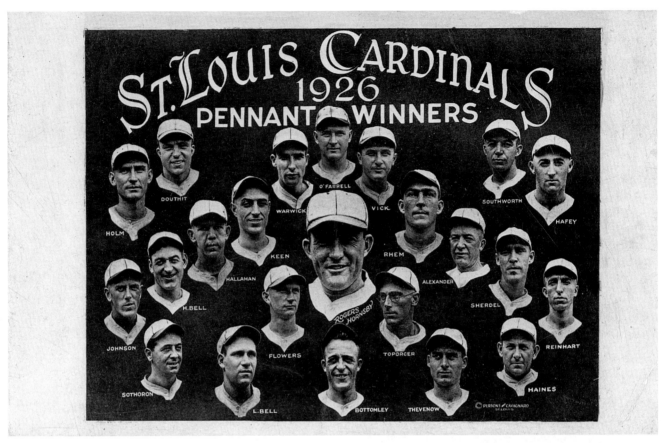

Publisher: Process Photo Studios, Chicago, IL • Manufacturer: Process Photo Studios • Type: Real Photo • Postmark: Not Used • Value: $400–$500

.333 in the World Series, scoring five runs with seven RBI as the Senators outlasted the New York Giants in seven. Overall, Harris was an outstanding second baseman, batting .274 over 12 big league seasons. In 1925, when the photo postcard on p. 61 was produced by an unknown Washington photographer, Harris enjoyed one of his finest seasons, batting .287 while driving in 66 runs in guiding the Senators to their second consecutive pennant. He went on to manage six different teams over 29 seasons, winning his third AL pennant and second world championship with the New York Yankees in 1947. He was elected to the Hall of Fame in 1975.

Pictured with Harris on this postcard is first baseman Joe Judge, who had a .314 batting average in '25 and also drove in 66 runs. The Senators knew they had a future star when Joe came up to the majors in 1915 and batted .415 in 12 games. He accrued his highest batting average in 1920, when he batted .333. Judge hit better than .300 on nine other occasions. His top RBI total was 93 in 1928. He played 20 years in all, 18 of those with the Senators, retiring with 2,352 hits and a .298 batting average—not quite enough to put him in the Hall of Fame to date.

1926 ST. LOUIS CARDINALS

The 1926 St. Louis Cardinals surprised the baseball world, winning the franchise's first National League pennant and defeating the heavily favored New York Yankees in the World Series. The title gave St. Louis its first championship since Chris Von der Ahe's St. Louis Browns won the American Association pennant in 1889. Hall of Famer Sunny Jim Bottomley led the NL with 120 RBI in '26, while his 19 home runs were second to the 21 hit by Chicago's Hack Wilson. Another Cardinal star, third baseman Les Bell, led the team with a .325 batting average and drove in 100 runs. Player/manager Rogers Hornsby batted .317 and drove in 93 runs during the regular season.

But the real story of the Cardinals' World Series triumph was the magnificent pitching of Hall of Famer Grover Cleveland Alexander, who at age 37 won two games while saving the seventh and final, pitching $2\frac{1}{3}$ scoreless innings in relief of another Hall of Famer, Jesse Haines. A fifth Cardinal Hall of Famer, outfielder Chick Hafey, had 21 putouts in the Series. The Cardinals outscored the Yankees 31-21 over seven games.

Publisher: Not Indicated • Manufacturer: Not Indicated • Type: Purpletone
Postmark: Not Used • Value: $100–$125

Publisher: National Baseball Hall of Fame and Museum, Cooperstown, NY
Manufacturer: Curt Teich, Chicago, IL • Type: Chrome
Postmark: Not Used • Value: $30 Signed, $1 Unsigned

1927 LEFTY GROVE, Philadelphia Athletics

Lefty Grove is generally regarded as the finest left-hander in American League history. Already 25 when he reached the majors in 1925 with the Athletics, Grove won 300 games before he retired following the 1941 season. Lefty won 20 games for the first time in 1927 and did it again seven more times during his career, including a lifetime-best 31-4 record in 1931. During a fabulous 1930 season, he won 16 in a row. He led the league in wins four times. Grove was equally adept at winning postseason games, as his 4-2 World Series record attests.

Grove was particularly effective against the New York Yankees and Murderers' Row, stopping their streak of 308 games without a shutout in August 1938. In 10 seasons against Grove, Babe Ruth hit only nine home runs off him.

Lefty was traded from the A's to the Red Sox in 1934, and in 1935 won 20 games for the final time. With his fastball gone, Grove relied on guile to reach the 300-win plateau, notching seven victories in 1941, his final season. Grove was inducted into the Hall of Fame in 1947.

1927 LLOYD WANER, Pittsburgh Pirates

Joining his older brother Paul in the Pittsburgh Pirates outfield in 1927, rookie Lloyd "Little Poison" Waner promptly batted .355 and led the league by scoring 133 runs. He and Paul, who was the National League MVP that year, were mainly responsible for the Pirates' pennant, along with fellow Hall of Famer Pie Traynor. In the World Series against the Yankees, Lloyd performed brilliantly, batting .400, but it was not enough to prevent a Yankee sweep.

Lloyd weighed only 132 pounds in 1927, but he got from home to first quicker than anyone of his era. Because of his great speed, he was superb defensively, getting a tremendous jump on balls. Obviously no slouch as a hitter, he batted .300 or better 10 times in his first 12 seasons, finishing his 18-year career in 1945 with a lifetime .316 batting average. Lloyd was honored with election to the Hall of Fame in 1967, 15 years after Paul, with whom he roamed the Pirates outfield for 14 seasons. Little Poison's autographed Hall of Fame plaque postcard commands $30 in today's market.

1927 PAUL WANER, Pittsburgh Pirates

Publisher: Not Indicated • Manufacturer: Not Indicated • Type: Purpletone
Postmark: Not Used • Value: $75–$100

Many fine brother combinations have shared the field in baseball history. But the only such pair in the Hall of Fame are Paul "Big Poison" Waner and his younger brother Lloyd. Paul, older by three years, won three National League batting titles, hitting .380 in 1927, .362 in 1934, and .373 in 1936. He won the MVP in 1927, leading the Pirates to the pennant with a league-topping 131 RBI. Big Poison batted above .300 14 times during his 20 seasons, finishing in 1945 with the Yankees as a career .333 career hitter.

Paul reached the majors in 1926, a year before his brother. The two were mainstays in the Pittsburgh outfield from 1927–1940. In their first year together, they went to the World Series. Even though the Pirates lost four straight to the Yankees, Paul had a respectable 5 for 15 showing with 3 RBI. Primarily a line drive hitter, Paul connected for 3,152 hits in his lifetime. He was inducted to the Hall of Fame in 1952.

1927 BENGOUGH, COMBS, HOYT, & LAZZERI, New York Yankees

Player and team postcards were sparse in the 1920s and '30s, and nearly all produced during that era are of the real-photo variety. The Exhibit Supply Co. of Chicago picked up the slack, producing Exhibit cards of the more prominent players starting in 1921. Some of these had postcard backs, but most were blank-back cards. Both varieties were frequently sent through the mail.

In 1929, the company began issuing Exhibits that showed four players per card. The "four-on-one" sample here is particularly desirable because three of the four are Hall of Famers. Earle Combs, Waite Hoyt, and Tony Lazzeri starred for the Yankees when that club dominated baseball. The other man pictured here, Benny Bengough, who backed up Hall of Fame catcher Bill Dickey in the early part of the latter man's career, played 10 seasons, eight with the Yankees.

Combs, a graduate of Western Kentucky University who was known affectionately as "The Kentucky

Publisher: Exhibit Supply Co., Chicago IL • Manufacturer: Exhibit Supply Co.
Type: Red Tone • Postmark: Not Used • Value: $100–$125

Colonel," was a superb outfielder. He batted .325 over 12 seasons and .350 in four World Series. Right-hander Waite Hoyt won 237 games over 21 seasons, including a league-leading 22 in 1927, when the Yankees were considered the greatest team of all time. His .759 winning percentage that season also led the league. Tony "Poosh 'Em Up" Lazzeri was a superb second baseman for 14 seasons, all but two with the Yankees. He left the game in 1939 with a .292 lifetime batting average. During his second season with the Yankees in 1927, he batted .309 with 18 home runs and 102 RBI.

1930-39

The Great Depression began with the Wall Street crash of 1929 and continued with a vengeance through the 1930s. One of the many casualties of America's economic desperation was baseball attendance. People barely had the money to buy food, let alone admission tickets. Philadelphia was particularly hard hit by the Depression. Connie Mack's Athletics were world champions in 1930 and American League champs in '31, but one of the greatest teams of all time drew Shibe Park crowds considerably smaller than one would expect. Finally, Mack was forced to sell off future Hall of Famers Jimmie Foxx, Al Simmons, Mickey Cochrane, and Lefty Grove—the cornerstones of the champion A's—to save the franchise. Among the four, only Foxx remained with the team by 1934; he was sold off after the '35 season, when the A's finished last.

Philadelphia's loss proved to be the gain of sister cities. Cochrane went to the Detroit Tigers as player/manager and led the team to the '34 AL pennant and the '35 world championship. The St. Louis Cardinals, who lost to the A's in the 1930 World Series, kept their abundance of Hall of Famers intact. Jim Bottomley, Chick Hafey, Johnny Mize, Frankie Frisch, Dizzy Dean, Pepper Martin, and Leo Durocher contributed to the team's success as the Cards dethroned the world champs in '31 and gained the crown again in '34.

The Washington Senators, with player/manager Joe Cronin at the helm, won their last AL pennant in 1933. In the World Series, the Senators lost to the New York Giants, who were led by HOF player/manager Bill Terry. Terry also led the Giants to pennants in 1936 and '37, but the club lost to the Yankees in the World Series both years.

New York teams were not as dominant in the '30s as they had been in the previous decade, but the Big Apple remained the center of the baseball universe. The Yankees won five pennants between 1930 and 1939, while the Giants won three.

Babe Ruth remained a Yankee mainstay in the early years of the decade. In 1932, the Babe batted .341, but for the first time in seven years he failed to win the home run crown. His impressive total of 41 was second to Jimmie Foxx's 58. As the decade wore on, Lou Gehrig took over for Ruth in many offensive departments while playing in every game. The Iron Horse's consecutive-game streak finally ended in 1939 when he was benched by a terminal illness, amyotrophic lateral sclerosis, now known as Lou Gehrig's disease.

Baseball celebrated its centennial year in 1939, and it's fitting that the Cincinnati Reds, America's first professional team, won the National League pennant that season. But in the World Series, the Reds fell to the Ruth-less, Gehrig-less Yankees of new superstar Joe DiMaggio, who won the AL batting title with a .381 average. By the end of the decade, baseball seemed to be in good health again. But dark clouds appeared on the horizon as a new war in Europe and Asia threatened to leave its mark upon the world.

Publisher: National Baseball Hall of Fame and Museum • Manufacturer: Curt Teich, Chicago, IL • Type: Linen • Postmark: Not Used • Value: $25

The humble son of an immigrant German mother, Henry Louis Gehrig went on to become one of the most revered baseball players of all time. A product of Columbia University, the Iron Horse briefly joined the Yankees in 1923, batting .423 in 13 games. He returned to the minors in 1924, but got called up again for 10 games in which he batted .500. Lou came up for good in 1925 and became the Yankee's mainstay at first base, playing in almost every game for 14 seasons. His record of 2,130 consecutive games played remained the Iron Man standard until it was broken by Baltimore Orioles shortstop Cal Ripken Jr. in September 1995.

Gehrig and Babe Ruth formed the greatest one-two punch in baseball history. Columbia Lou, as he was also known, drove in 100 runs or more in 13 consecutive seasons and topped 150 RBI on seven occasions. His 184 RBI in 1931 remains the American League single-season record. From 1926 through 1937, Lou never batted below .300. Even when his skills began to diminish in 1938, he still batted .295 with 29 home runs and 114 RBI.

In 1939, Gehrig was diagnosed with a terminal illness, amyotrophic lateral sclerosis, now commonly known as Lou Gehrig's Disease. He stayed in the Yankees lineup for eight more games, but his degenerative condition finally forced his retirement. On July 4, 1939, Lou was honored before an overflow crowd at Yankee Stadium and, despite his adversity, called himself "the luckiest man on the face of the earth." Elected to the Hall of Fame the very year he retired, Lou Gehrig remains a baseball idol nearly 60 years after his 1941 death.

1932 JIMMIE FOXX, Philadelphia Athletics

Discovered by fellow Hall of Famer Frank "Home Run" Baker while playing amateur ball in Sudlersville, Maryland, Jimmie Foxx was only 17 when he reached the majors as a catcher with the Philadelphia Athletics in 1925. Primarily a first baseman throughout his 20-year big-league career, Foxx was remarkably versatile, filling in at pitcher, third base, the outfield, and even shortstop for one game. In 1945, his final season, he appeared in nine games as a pitcher, compiling a 1.59 ERA and a perfect 1-0 record. There's no telling what he might have accomplished as a pitcher if he had begun earlier in his career, like fellow Marylander Babe Ruth. But like Ruth, "Double X" was far too valuable as a slugger to be out of the lineup. In fact, had it not been for revisions to Sportsman's Park in St. Louis and League Park in Cleveland, Foxx might have earned the all-time single-season home run record. Screens were added to the fences at both parks in 1932, which obviously weren't there when Ruth hit 60 in 1927. In '32, Foxx hit five drives that would have been homers against the screen at Sportsman's Park and three more in Cleveland. Had

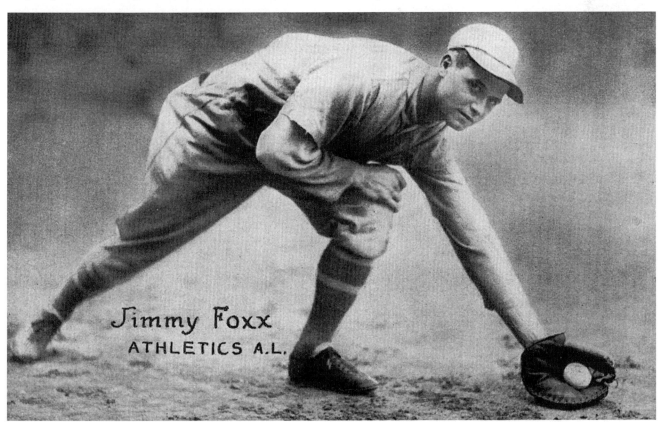

Jimmy Foxx
ATHLETICS A.L.

Publisher: Not Indicated • Manufacturer: Not Indicated • Type: Purpletone • Postmark: Not Used • Value: $100–$125

WILLIAM M. WERBER—1932 Bisons

Age, 23 years; bats and throws right; height, 5.11; weight, 164 pounds. Home, Berwyn, Md. Played with Newark, season 1931.

Publisher: Buffalo Bisons • Manufacturer: Not Indicated • Type: Browntone • Postmark: Not Used • Value: $100–$150

the screens not been there, Foxx would have walloped 66 homers, a record that would have withstood Roger Maris' 61 homers in 1961.

Still, Foxx's remarkable 1932 season (58 home runs, 169 RBI—both league highs—and a .364 batting average) earned him the league's MVP award. He followed in 1933 with his second straight MVP season, winning the triple crown with a .358 average, 48 home runs, and 163 RBI. The muscular Foxx blasted 534 career home runs, drove in 1,922 runs, and finished with a career .325 batting average. He joined the Hall of Fame roster in 1951.

1932 BILL WERBER, Buffalo Bisons

Bill Werber was an outstanding major league third baseman for 11 seasons, compiling a .271 lifetime batting average. Extremely fast, he led the American League in stolen bases three times, twice with the Boston Red Sox (40 in 1934, 29 in 1935) and once with the Philadelphia Athletics (35 in 1937).

An all-American at Duke University, Werber signed with the New York Yankees in 1930 and briefly cracked the lineup, batting .286 in four games that season. He spent the next two years in the International League with the Newark Bears and Buffalo Bisons. The

extremely rare postcard pictured above was part of a Boys Day promotion by the Bisons on July 30, 1932. It was included with three other Bison cards in an envelope given to all youngsters attending the game. Such promotions were almost unheard of during the Great Depression—particularly at the minor league level—but the Bisons somehow managed it.

Bill made it back to the Yankees in 1933 and was promptly traded to the Red Sox, where he enjoyed his best season in '34, adding a .321 batting average to his league-leading steals total. He was dealt to the A's in 1937, then to the Reds in March 1939. In Cincinnati, Werber played for consecutive National League champions in '39 and '40. He played a big role in the Reds' 1940 World Series championship over the Detroit Tigers, batting .370 in seven games.

1932 LEFTY O'DOUL, Brooklyn Dodgers

Lefty O'Doul may be the finest hitter left out of the Hall of Fame. O'Doul began his major league career as a pitcher, but had little success in that regard. In four seasons with the Yankees and Red Sox, he compiled a 1-1 record and 4.87 ERA in 34 appearances. After the 1923 season, the Red Sox released him to the San Francisco Seals in the Pacific Coast League, where he concentrated

Meet "LEFTY" O'DOUL!
AT HIS BEAUTIFUL COCKTAIL ROOM
209 POWELL ST. - SAN FRANCISCO, CALIF.
A Favorite Meeting Place for Celebrities of the Sports World

ENTRANCE

Publisher: Lefty O'Doul's, #9A–H2081, San Francisco, CA • Manufacturer: Curt Teich Co., Chicago, IL • Type: Linen • Postmark: Not Used • Value: $100–$150

on hitting and resurrected his career.

Five years later, he joined the New York Giants as a left fielder and averaged .319 at the plate. Traded to the Phillies in 1929, he led the National League with a .398 batting average while swatting 32 home runs and driving in 122 runs. In 1932, playing with Brooklyn, O'Doul won his second batting championship, averaging .368. He was traded to the Giants in the middle of the 1933 season and helped the club win the NL pennant and then the World Series against the Washington Senators. O'Doul retired in 1934 with a .349 lifetime average. His seven years as an outfielder weren't enough to get him into the Hall.

1932 CHUCK KLEIN, Philadelphia Phillies

Chuck Klein played 17 years in the major leagues, primarily with the second-division Phillies, where he was generally the main show. His efforts did not go unrewarded. He was named National League MVP in 1932 with a league-leading 38 home runs, 137 RBI, and a .348 batting average; without Klein's performance, the Phils undoubtedly would have finished lower than the fourth place they managed. In 1933, Klein gave a triple-crown performance with a .368 average, 28 home runs, and 120 RBI, yet the Phillies finished seventh.

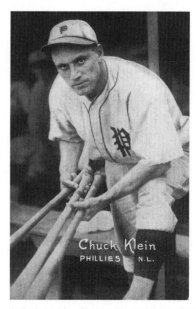

Publisher: Not Indicated • Manufacturer: Not Indicated • Type: Purpletone
Postmark: Not Used • Value: $75–$100

With the Chicago Cubs in 1934, Klein batted .301. He got to play in his first World Series the next year and hit .333 in a losing effort against Detroit. Klein's most memorable season was 1930, when he batted .386, walloped 40 homers, and had 170 RBI—all career highs—yet failed to finish first in any category. Even so, he did lead the league defensively that year, posting 44 assists as an outfielder—a modern record that still stands. Klein and his lifetime .320 average were finally elected to the Hall of Fame in 1980.

1932 BABE RUTH, New York Yankees

Babe Ruth is the most famous player in baseball history. Today, more than 50 years after his death, the Babe is still an icon. Born George Herman Ruth on February 8, 1895, in Baltimore, Md., he acquired his nickname when Jack Dunn, owner of the International League Orioles, signed him right out of St. Mary's Industrial School at the age of 17. The other Oriole players

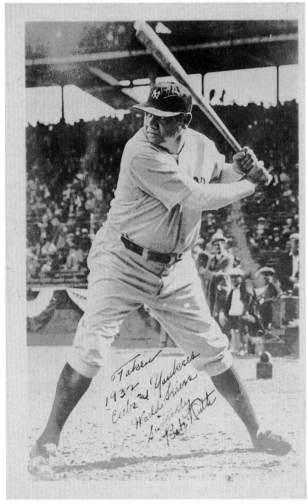

Publisher: Not Indicated • Manufacturer: Not Indicated • Type: Real Photo
Postmark: Not Used • Value: $250

referred to Ruth as Dunn's Babe, and the name stuck. A larger-than-life figure, Ruth's exploits as an eater, drinker, and womanizer rival his fame as a ballplayer. Nevertheless, many credit him with saving baseball from the Black Sox scandal. When eight members of the Chicago White Sox were banned from the game for conspiring with gamblers to throw the 1919 World Series, many fans lost their faith in the national pastime. The Bambino brought them back.

Ruth reached the major leagues with the Boston Red Sox in 1914, immediately establishing himself as one of the game's greatest pitchers. He won 23 games for the Red Sox in 1916 and 24 a year later. In his six seasons with Boston, he won 89 games while losing just 41 and compiling a brilliant 2.19 ERA. He started three World Series games for the Red Sox in 1916 and '18, winning all three while posting a 0.87 ERA. The Sox won the Series both years. At the same time, Babe's slugging skills finally led Boston manager Ed Barrow to play him in the outfield. He soon proved the wisdom of that move, leading the AL in home runs with 29 in 1919.

Following the 1919 season, Red Sox owner and Broadway producer Harry Frasee did the unthinkable. He sold Ruth and several teammates to the New York Yankees for $125,000 in cash and a $300,000 loan. The fire sale rescued Frasee financially but ruined the Red Sox for years to come. Ruth's departure has become known as the Curse of the Bambino, because the Red Sox have not won a World Series since, while the rival Yankees became the most dominant team in history. In 1920, his first year with New York, Ruth established a new single-season major league record for home runs with 54. The next year, he hit 59. In 1927, he belted 60, a mark that lasted until it was broken by Roger Maris in 1961.

Perhaps the most famous moment in Babe's remarkable career came in the 1932 World Series against the Chicago Cubs, when he appeared to call his home run shot against pitcher Charley Root in the third game. This real-photo premium postcard was taken at Wrigley Field during that dramatic series, which the Yankees won in four straight.

1933 JOE HAUSER, Minneapolis Millers

You're looking at Joe Hauser, the only man in baseball history to hit 60 or more home runs in a season in two different leagues. Joe first accomplished the feat with the Baltimore Orioles of the International League in 1930, slamming 63. The second time, in 1933, he belted 69 for the Minneapolis Millers of the American Association. That year, Wheaties produced this extremely rare postcard of Joe.

While he performed his greatest exploits in the minor leagues, Hauser had a very respectable six-year

Joe Hauser, first base
MINNEAPOLIS BASEBALL CLUB, 1933

Publisher: General Mills, Minneapolis, MN • Manufacturer: Not Indicated
Type: Black and White • Postmark: Not Used • Value: $200–$250

1933 JOE CRONIN, Washington Senators

One of the finest shortstops of his day, Joe Cronin was also a great communicator who utilized his skills to succeed as a manager, general manager, and president of the American League. Yet the seven-time All-Star was not an instant success. He came up with the Pittsburgh Pirates in 1926 and '27, but each year found him back in the minors with Kansas City. The Washington Senators purchased his contract midway through the 1928 season, and he returned to the majors, batting only .242 over the remainder of the year. But manager Bucky Harris admired Cronin's hard work and tenacity. By 1930, Joe was considered the best shortstop in the league; that year, he posted career highs in batting average (.346) and RBI (126) and earned the AL MVP award.

In 1933, Cronin replaced Walter Johnson as Senators manager, leading the team to the pennant his first year. In 1935, the Red Sox offered Washington owner Clark Griffith $250,000 plus shortstop Lyn Lary for Cronin,

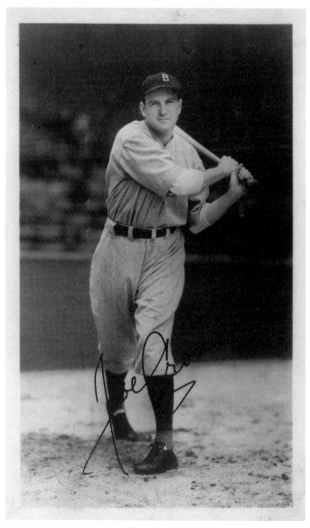

Publisher: RDM Studios, Chicago, IL • Manufacturer: RDM Studios
Type: Real Photo • Postmark: Not Used • Value: $250 signed

career in the majors. He came up with the Philadelphia Athletics in 1922, batting a career-best .323 with nine home runs and 43 RBI as a part-time first baseman. He stayed with the A's through the 1924 season, which proved to be his best overall. Joe had a .288 batting average, walloped 27 home runs, and drove in 115 runs. His RBI production was fourth in the American League that year, while his home run total was second only to that of Babe Ruth. Of course, it was considerably tougher to hit homers in Shibe Park than in Yankee Stadium. In addition, Joe led all first basemen in putouts with 1,513 and in double plays with 131.

A broken knee caused Hauser to miss the entire 1925 season. He returned to the Athletics in 1926 a shell of his former self. Hauser concluded his major league career with Cleveland in 1929, appearing in only 37 games while batting .250 with three homers and nine RBI. Altogether, his major league totals show a career .284 average, 79 home runs, and 356 RBI. Had he remained free of injuries, there's no telling what he might have accomplished. As it is, "Unser Choe" became a cult hero in his native Milwaukee, where he died in 1998 at the age of 99.

who then took over as Boston's player/manager.

Over 20 seasons, Cronin batted .300 or better eight times and drove in 100 or more runs eight times as well. His playing career ended in 1945, but he kept managing, helping the Red Sox to a pennant in 1946. In 1948, Cronin became Boston's general manager. Eleven years later, he left that job to become AL president, a post he held until 1974. He was elected to the Hall of Fame in 1956.

1934 CARL HUBBELL, New York Giants

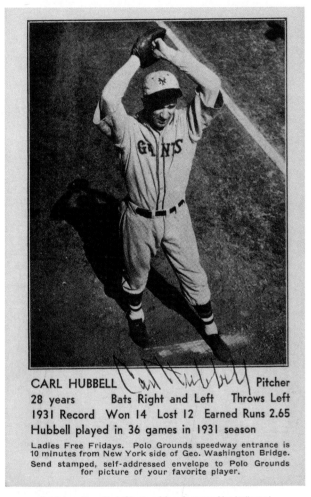

Publisher: New York Giants • Manufacturer: Not Indicated
Type: Black & White • Postmark: Not Used • Value: $150–$200

Left-hander Carl Hubbell spent his entire 16-year career with the New York Giants. At his peak from 1933 through 1937, "King Carl" was considered the best pitcher in baseball, leading the National League in 1933 with 23 wins, 26 wins in 1936, and 22 victories in 1937. The Giants won the pennant in these years, earning Hubbell a new moniker, "The Meal Ticket." Unfortunately, he couldn't always bring the team postseason success. In the 1933 World Series, the Giants defeated the Washing-

ton Senators, four games to one, as Hubbell won two. But the Giants lost the 1936 and 1937 World Series to the Yankees, with Hubbell going 1-1 each time.

Hubbell had pinpoint control and used a screwball with remarkable success. One of the most difficult pitches to throw, the screwball defies nature and places extraordinary stress on the elbow. Hubbell twisted his left wrist to the right in his release to make the ball break down and away from right-handed hitters.

In 1934, Hubbell had the chance to demonstrate his dominance. In the All-Star Game at the Polo Grounds, he faced the three most feared sluggers in baseball, Babe Ruth, Lou Gehrig, and Jimmy Foxx of the American League squad. He struck out each of them in 1-2-3 order. Hubbell continued the performance in the second inning, striking out Al Simmons and Joe Cronin before the spell was broken by Bill Dickey's single. He left the pitching mound after three scoreless innings.

Hubbell ended his career in 1943 with 253 wins and 154 losses. He joined the Hall of Fame in 1947.

1934 BABE RUTH, New York Yankees

Babe Ruth's fame spread beyond the borders of the U.S. He was also considered a hero in Japan. After his final season with the Yankees in 1934, Ruth led a team of major league All-Stars to Japan to play four exhibition games against a Japanese All-Star team. The U.S. team was greeted by a crowd of more than half a million in a huge parade. The first game was played in Tokyo on November 4, 1934, before an overflow crowd of 64,000 fans. The legend on the front of this extremely rare postcard tells the story. Translated, it reads: "This is the moment when Babe Ruth, who is called Home Run King of the World, swung hard and hit the ball. It seems the ball flew over the outfield fence and became a home run. The catcher and umpire stood still with surprise in their eyes and the smiling Babe Ruth has a look of pride and satisfaction on his face. The crowd in the stands watched in silent disbelief."

Publisher: Not Indicated • Manufacturer: Not Indicated • Type: Linen
Postmark: Not Used • Value: $750–$1,000

Connie Mack, who went along with the team as manager and goodwill ambassador for baseball, told a story relating to this home run. "A Japanese General walked 30 miles to present his sword to the first man who made a home run. He didn't seem to think it was possible to hit a ball so far that a batter could make a home run. When Babe Ruth stepped to the plate and hit the ball out of the park, the General presented his sword to the King of Swat."

1935 BILLY HERMAN, Chicago Cubs

Publisher: National Baseball Hall of Fame and Museum, Cooperstown, NY
Manufacturer: Curt Teich Co., Chicago, IL • Type: Chrome
Postmark: Not Used • Value: $15 Signed, $1 Unsigned

Hall of Fame second baseman Billy Herman was one of the best fielders in history. If you want proof, just check the record books. Even though he has been retired since 1947, Herman still holds numerous National League records, including five seasons with 900 or more chances and seven seasons leading second basemen in putouts. The All-Star game became a particular showcase for Billy; he played in 10 and compiled a .433

batting average, going 13 for 30.

Considered a master at stealing other teams' signs, Herman compiled a .304 lifetime average over 15 years, including a career-best .341 average with the Cubs in 1935. After being traded to the Dodgers late in the 1941 season, he became a spark plug in the club's successful pennant race. He had another banner year with Brooklyn in 1943, batting .330 with 100 RBI.

Herman had two unsuccessful managerial stints, with the Pirates in 1947 and the Red Sox from 1964–66, but he was highly respected as a coach with numerous teams. A master of the hit-and-run, Billy Herman is considered one of the smartest and best second basemen who ever played. He was elected to the Hall of Fame in 1975. Today, an autographed Billy Herman Hall of Fame plaque postcard is worth $15.

1935 BILL TERRY, New York Giants

New York Giants first baseman Bill Terry, the last National League player to hit .400, finished his 14-year

Publisher: Not Indicated • Manufacturer: Not Indicated • Type: Black & White
Postmark: Not Used • Value: $5 (recent vintage)

career in 1936 with a lifetime .341 batting average, the highest compiled by a left-handed hitter in modern NL history. Terry broke in with the Giants at the end of the 1923 season. Used sporadically during the 1924 season, he really came into his own in the 1924 World Series, batting .429 against Washington in a losing cause. Taking over first base permanently from fellow Hall of Famer George "Highpockets" Kelly in 1925, Terry batted .319. Beginning in 1927, he went on to bat .310 or better for 11 consecutive seasons. Terry also drove in 101 or more runs in six of those seasons, including a career-best 129 in 1930, when he led the league with 254 hits and a .401 batting average, earning the NL MVP award.

Terry frequently feuded with manager John McGraw, but he earned the skipper's respect—so much so that when illness forced McGraw to abandon his post in June 1932, he named Terry to succeed him. Terry led the Giants to the 1933 pennant and a World Series championship over his old nemesis, Washington. He also led the Giants to pennants as player/manager in 1936 and as manager in '37, but the team lost both World Series to the Yankees.

The postcard on p. 75 shows Giants manager Terry talking with the Boston Braves' Babe Ruth in 1935, the Bambino's final major league season. Terry continued managing the Giants through 1941, when he passed the reins to Mel Ott. He was elected to the Hall of Fame in 1954.

1935 MICKEY COCHRANE, Detroit Tigers

Baseball and its players have been used for advertising purposes since the game began. In 1935, as he led the Tigers to the world championship in his last year on the full-time roster, player/manager Mickey Cochrane was in demand as a spokesman for various products, including B.F. Goodrich tires. Perhaps Detroit's status as the automobile capital of the world, as well as the Tigers' success, led the manufacturer to associate itself with Cochrane. Whatever Goodrich's rationale, the company produced a lot of these cards. Copies of this postcard—identical except for the dealer's name—were mailed by Goodrich stores around the country.

A 13-year major league veteran who earned three World Series rings with the A's and Tigers, Cochrane was named to the Hall of Fame in 1947.

1935 HANK GREENBERG, Detroit Tigers

First baseman/outfielder Hank Greenberg was one of the most feared sluggers of his day, walloping 331 home runs—including a career-high 58 in 1938. There's no telling how many more he would have hit had he not missed most of the 1941 season with a broken wrist or left baseball from 1942–44 to serve in World War II.

In 1935, just two years after joining Detroit, Hank led the Tigers to the pennant, belting 36 home runs with

"I'd rather face a thousand spikes than have another blow-out."

Mickey Cochrane

Manager, Detroit Tigers

Take a tip from one who knows. Put Life-Saver Golden Ply Tires on your car today!

GOODRICH SAFETY SILVERTOWNS
with the Life-Saver Golden Ply
3 TIMES SAFER FROM HIGH SPEED BLOW-OUTS

ACADEMY SERVICE STATION
Shinglehouse, Pa.

Publisher: B.F. Goodrich Tires, Akron, OH • Manufacturer: Not Indicated • Type: Government Postal • Postmark: Not Used • Value: $75–$100

Publisher: Not Indicated • Manufacturer: Not Indicated • Type: Black & White • Postmark: Atlantic City, NJ, Sept. 22, 1936 • Value: $150–$200

170 RBI and a .328 average as he won his first of two American League MVP awards. He then led Detroit to the franchise's first World Series championship. The Tigers had also been pennant winners the year before, when Hank batted .339 with 26 homers and 139 RBI. But the team lost the World Series to St. Louis in seven games, despite Hank's .321 average and seven RBI.

Greenberg notched a career-high 183 RBI in 1937 and a personal-best 58 home runs in '39. Moved from first base to the outfield in 1940, Hammerin' Hank won his second MVP award, leading the Tigers to another pennant with a .340 batting average, 41 homers, and 150 RBI. But his .357 average and 6 RBI in the World Series weren't enough to keep Detroit from losing to Cincinnati.

After his military stint, Greenberg returned to the Tigers midway through the 1945 season, pacing the club to another pennant with a .311 average, 13 home runs, and 60 RBI. His grand slam on the final day of the season, against St. Louis, enabled the Tigers to nip the Washington Senators by a game for a return to the post-season. The club went on to defeat the Cubs in the

World Series, as Hank had two home runs and seven RBI. Sold by Detroit to Pittsburgh in January 1947, Hank considered retirement, but was enticed by the Pirates' $100,000 offer to play one more season. He went out with 25 homers and 74 RBI.

In his career, Greenberg won or shared the home run title five times, led the AL in RBI on four occasions, and compiled a .313 average over 13 seasons. He was elected to the Hall of Fame in 1956.

1936 ST. LOUIS CARDINALS

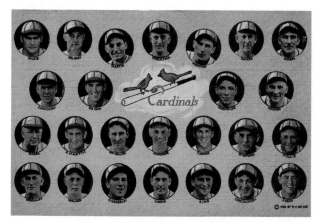

Publisher: H.A. Meade, #6A-H1554, St. Louis, MO • Manufacturer: Curt Teich Co., Chicago, IL • Type: Linen • Postmark: Not Used • Value: $200–$250

With a lineup bearing such nicknames as Dizzy, Daffy, Ducky, Pepper, Rip, the Lip, Big Cat, Pop, and Fordham Flash, one would expect the St. Louis Gashouse Gang of the 1930s to be a wild and distinctive bunch—and so they were. But they were also an awfully good team. Together, they won the National League pennant and World Series in 1931 and 1934. In 1936, when this postcard was issued, the Gashouse Gang was intact but finished the season in second place, five games behind the Giants.

They may not have won a pennant every year, but the Gashouse Gang was always a colorful group, and they thrilled crowds wherever they went. They gave outrageous quotations to media reporters, had their own band, and lived a full life. Of the group, Pepper Martin, Dizzy Dean, Frankie "Fordham Flash" Frisch, Jesse "Pop" Haines, Joe "Ducky" Medwick, Leo "The Lip" Durocher, and Johnny "Big Cat" Mize were inducted into the Hall of Fame.

1937 PAUL WANER, LLOYD WANER, & JIM WEAVER, Pittsburgh Pirates

"Big Jim" Weaver had a better-than-average major league pitching career, compiling a record of 57 wins and 36 losses in eight seasons with the Senators, Yankees, Browns, Cubs, Pirates, and Reds. At 6 feet 6 inches and

average and again in 1942 with a .330 average. The good-natured giant was a shy man who found the adoration of crowds to be embarrassing. Yet during his stint in Cincinnati, from 1932 through 1941, he became the most popular Reds player since Edd Roush. His prominent nose left him with the nickname "Schnozz," which stayed with him throughout his career. When he retired at the end of the 1947 season, he had compiled a .306 batting average with the Dodgers, Reds, Braves, and Giants. Lombardi joined the Hall of Fame roster posthumously in 1986.

1938 JOHNNY VANDER MEER, Cincinnati Reds

Left-handed fastball pitcher Johnny Vander Meer never won 20 games in a season in the major leagues, concluding his 13-year career with 119 wins and 121 losses. However, he will always be remembered in baseball history for an important accomplishment. While pitching for the Cincinnati Reds, with whom he spent the bulk of his career, Vander Meer threw no-hitters in

Publisher: Not Indicated • Manufacturer: Not Indicated • Type: Black & White • Postmark: Baltimore, MD, Sept. 26, 1939 • Value: $100

230 pounds, Weaver was one of pitching's early giants. Along with his size came remarkable strength, as this postcard illustrates. On his sturdy shoulders, Weaver bears the weight of two Hall of Fame outfielders, Paul and Lloyd Waner. Lloyd weighed 150 pounds, while Paul scaled 153. Remember, these were the days before bodybuilding and weightlifting became part of a ballplayer's daily regimen. This has become one of my favorite cards because of its uniqueness.

1938 ERNIE LOMBARDI, Cincinnati Reds

In 17 years with National League teams, Ernie Lombardi forged a reputation as one of the finest catchers—and one of the slowest men—ever to play baseball. An outstanding handler of pitchers and possessor of an excellent throwing arm, Lombardi was 6 feet 3 inches tall and weighed 230 pounds. Despite his lack of running speed, he led the National League in 1938 with a .342 batting

Publisher: Metropolitan Clothing Co., Dayton, OH • Manufacturer: Orcajo Photo Art, Dayton, OH • Type: Real Photo • Postmark: Not Used • Value: $175

Publisher: Orcajo Photo Art, Dayton, OH • Manufacturer: Orcajo Photo Art
Type: Real Photo • Postmark: Not Used • Value: $250–$300

Publisher: Val Decker Packing Co., Cincinnati, OH • Manufacturer: Orcajo
Photo Art, Dayton, OH • Type: Real Photo • Postmark: Not Used • Value:$150

back-to-back appearances, becoming the only major league pitcher to perform this feat.

On June 11, 1938, Vander Meer beat the Boston Braves at Crosley Field, 3-0, without allowing any hits. In so doing, he became the Reds' first pitcher to throw a no-hitter since Hod Eller did it in 1919. That was reason enough for celebration, but four days later, in the first night game under the lights at Brooklyn's Ebbets Field, Vander Meer faced the Dodgers. Although he was extremely wild that evening, he didn't allow a hit for eight innings. Dodger supporters, normally the most loyal fans, got caught in the magnitude of the moment and actually started rooting wildly for the Cincinnati pitcher. With 38,748 screaming fans on their feet, Vander Meer loaded the bases in the ninth with only one out. He got Ernie Koy to hit a ground ball to third baseman Lew Riggs, who threw home, forcing out Goody Rosen at the plate. Next, Leo Durocher hit a fly ball to center fielder Harry Craft. Craft caught the ball, ending the game and triggering pandemonium as the Ebbets Field fans saluted Johnny Vander Meer's second consecutive no-hitter.

1939 CINCINNATI REDS

The 1939 National League–champion Cincinnati Reds won 97 games, finishing 5 1/2 games in front of the St. Louis Cardinals. But they were no match for the New York Yankees, losing the World Series in four straight.

During the season, first baseman Frank McCormick led the attack with a .332 batting average, 18 home runs, and a league-leading 128 RBI; at season's end, he was named NL MVP. Right fielder Ival Goodman batted .323 and drove in 84 runs, while Hall of Fame catcher Ernie Lombardi hit .287 with 20 homers and 85 RBI. Ironically, the team's batting-average leader was backup catcher Willard Hershberger, who hit .345. The next season, Hershberger would commit suicide in his hotel room after having a particularly bad game.

The Reds' pitching was superb in '39, as Bucky Walters led the league with 27 wins and an ERA of 2.29. Paul Derringer was almost as good, winning 25 games with a 2.93 ERA.

Beating St. Louis for the pennant was sweet revenge for manager Bill McKechnie, who was fired by the Cardinals when they lost the 1928 World Series to the Yankees in four straight. Fortunately, the Reds owners were more forgiving, and McKechnie returned in 1940 to guide essentially the same group of Reds to another pennant and a World Series victory over the Detroit Tigers.

1939 JOE DiMAGGIO, New York Yankees

Center fielder Joe DiMaggio could do it all. A superb hitter, the Yankee Clipper batted .325 over 13 seasons while averaging 118 RBI per season. Defensively, his graceful fielding was a sight to behold. The three-time American League MVP personified the complete player.

Joe was a 17-year-old shortstop when he joined the

JOE DI MAGGIO

Publisher: TCMA Ltd., Amawalk, NY • Manufacturer: Not Indicated
Type: Chrome • Postmark: Not Used • Value: $10–$15 (recent vintage)

San Francisco Seals of the Pacific Coast League in 1932. Converted to the outfield in '33, he embarked on a 61-game hitting streak. It was a portent of things to come.

While playing with the Seals, Joe suffered a knee injury that frightened away every major league team but the Yankees, who purchased his contract for $25,000 in 1935. By 1936, he was the Yankees' every-day center fielder. He hit .323 with 29 home runs and 125 RBI that rookie season, and came back in '37 to lead the league with a career-high 46 home runs while batting .346 and driving in a career-best 167 runs.

In 1939, Joltin' Joe earned his first MVP award. He also led the Yankees to another pennant and world championship with a career-high .381 batting average to go with 30 home runs and 126 RBI. In '41, he rode a record 56-consecutive-game hitting streak to his second MVP award, edging Boston's Ted Williams, who hit .406 that year. DiMaggio finished the season with a .357 average, a league-leading 125 RBI, and another World Series ring.

After missing three full seasons due to military service, Joe returned to the Yankees in '46 and batted below .300 for the first time in his career, posting a .290/20-homer/95-RBI season. He rebounded the next year with a .315 average, 20 home runs, and 97 RBI, garnering his third MVP award as he led the Yankees to another world championship. In Joe's 13 seasons with the Yankees, the club won nine of 10 World Series.

DiMaggio again performed brilliantly in '48, leading the league with 39 home runs and 155 RBI, but the Yankees finished third behind Cleveland and Boston. A bone spur on his right heel forced Joe to miss more than half of the '49 season, but he still batted .346 while driving in 47 runs. Constant pain and the arrival of his center field successor, Mickey Mantle, brought about DiMaggio's retirement after the 1951 season, but not before he walked away with his ninth championship ring. This postcard, drawn by artist Bruce Stark and published by TCMA, shows Joe in 1939 wearing the Baseball Centennial patch on his sleeve.

1939 HALL OF FAME INDUCTION CEREMONIES

When Stephen C. Clark initially approached the baseball hierarchy about a baseball museum in Cooperstown, New York, National League president Ford Frick was particularly enthusiastic. Frick obtained the backing of commissioner Kenesaw Mountain Landis and American League president William Harridge, and plans were developed for a museum and Hall of Fame honoring the game and its outstanding players. In conjunction with the Baseball Writers of America, a Hall of Fame committee was organized. The rule was established that in order to be inducted to the Hall, a player had to receive votes from 75 percent of the committee's members.

Doubleday Field, Cooperstown, N. Y., Cavalcade of Baseball, June 12, 1939—2

OB-H792

Publisher: C.W. Hughes & Co. Inc., #OB–H792, Mechanicsville, NY • Manufacturer: Curt Teich Co., Chicago, IL • Type: Linen • Postmark: Not Used • Value: $10–$15

When the first HOF elections were held in 1936, five players were elected: Ty Cobb, Babe Ruth, Honus Wagner, Christy Mathewson, and Walter Johnson. Cobb received the most votes, 222 of 225. Ruth and Wagner each received 215, Mathewson received 205, and Johnson received 189. The next year's induction class included Napoleon Lajoie, Tris Speaker, and Cy Young.

Grover Cleveland Alexander was added in 1938, and George Sisler, Eddie Collins, and Willie Keeler in 1939.

The first induction ceremony occurred on June 12, 1939. All the inductees were present at the spectacular event except Keeler, who had died in 1923. Following the induction of the original 12 players, the Hall of Fame's membership has grown steadily over the years.

1940-49

Baseball entered the 1940s on a high note but soon was fighting for its very survival. World War II was raging across Europe and Asia as the decade began, but for the first two years the U.S. was able to remain uninvolved.

In 1940, Cincinnati's Bucky Walters and Paul Derringer were the National League's best pitchers, winning 22 and 20 games, respectively. Offensively, the Reds were led by Hall of Fame catcher Ernie Lombardi and first baseman Frank McCormick, who posted 19 home runs, 127 RBI, and a .309 batting average. In the World Series, the Reds won four games to three over the Detroit Tigers of American League home run and RBI king Hank Greenberg.

The next year, Ted Williams and Joe DiMaggio each had remarkable seasons. DiMaggio set a record that still stands when he batted safely in 56 consecutive games, while Ted became baseball's last .400 hitter, averaging .406. But DiMaggio, who batted .357 and led the AL with 125 RBI, won the MVP award. In the '41 World Series, his Yankees beat the Brooklyn Dodgers in five

games. Second baseman Joe Gordon, who hit .500 with five RBI, and outfielder Charley Keller, who batted .389 and drove in five more runs, led the way.

Soon after that Series ended, on December 7, 1941, the Japanese bombed Pearl Harbor and the U.S. joined the war. Many baseball stars enlisted in the military service, including DiMaggio, Williams, and Cleveland right-hander Bob Feller, to mention a few. Travel was restricted, gas and food were rationed, and there was serious talk of suspending baseball during the war's duration. But President Franklin D. Roosevelt insisted that America needed a healthy diversion from the country's troubles, and so the national pastime played on. The Cardinals and Yankees exchanged World Series championships in 1942 and '43, while the Cardinals defeated the St. Louis Browns for the title in 1944. The only Hall of Famer who participated in that '44 Fall Classic was Cardinal great Stan Musial. Talent was so limited during the war that Pete Gray, a one-armed outfielder, played in 77 games for the Browns in 1945, while the Cincinnati Reds signed Joe Nuxhall, then a 15-year-old high school phenom, to their bullpen.

Paper was another rationed commodity during the war, leading to a decline in postcard production. At the same time, the government encouraged those on the homefront to write to soldiers serving overseas. Product manufacturers like the Kellogg's cereal company offered a solution, adding cut-out postcards to their packaging.

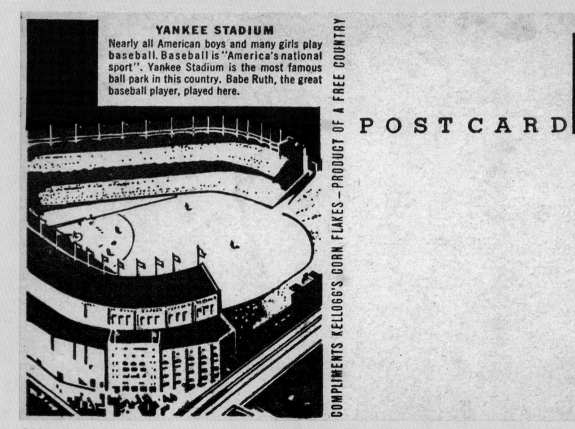

Publisher: Kellogg's Corn Flakes, Battle Creek, MI • Manufacturer: Not Indicated • Type: Red, Green, & White Cereal Box • Postmark: Not Used • Value: $350–$500

Joe Nuxhall—Cincinnati Redlegs

Publisher: Cincinnati Reds • Manufacturer: Not Indicated • Type: Black & White • Postmark: Not Used • Value: $25

Publisher: Val Decker Packing Co., Cincinnati, OH • Manufacturer: Orcajo Photo Art, Dayton, OH • Type: Real Photo • Postmark: Not Used Value: $100–$125

Kellogg's even decorated the cards with line drawings of such American landmarks as Yankee Stadium.

The war ended in '45, and many stars returned to their teams late in the season—including Hank Greenberg, who led the Tigers to the AL pennant and world championship. Baseball quickly returned to normal. In '46, Cleveland right-hander Bob Feller returned to the Indians after four years of naval service, enjoying his finest season. Feller led the AL in wins (26), games (48), games started (42), complete games (36), innings pitched (371), and strikeouts (348). Nevertheless, Cleveland finished 68-86, while the Cardinals defeated the Red Sox in seven games in the 1946 World Series. The Yankees beat the Dodgers in the '47 Series; a year later, Cleveland player/manager Lou Boudreau led the Indians to victory over the Boston Braves in the '48 Classic, earning the AL MVP award for his effort. Finally, in 1949, the Yankees and Dodgers met in the World Series with the usual result: a Yankee victory in five games.

1940 WILLARD HERSHBERGER, Cincinnati Reds

Baseball has had tragedies over the years, but few were more surprising than the suicide of Willard Hershberger, the Cincinnati Reds' backup catcher to Ernie Lombardi. Late in July of 1940, the Reds were on the way to a pennant. Playing the Giants at the Polo Grounds, they were leading 4-1 in the bottom of the ninth inning. With the bases loaded, New York's Harry Danning blasted a grand slam home run to give the Giants a 5-4 victory. Hershberger, who was catching, took responsibility, blaming himself for calling the wrong pitch. His teammates tried to console him, but Hershberger became disconsolate.

Two days later, the Reds were playing a doubleheader with the Braves in Boston. Catching the second game, Hershberger had no hits in five at-bats, and even failed to field a bunt a few feet from home plate. When manager Bill McKechnie rushed out to find out what was wrong, Hershberger said he would discuss it later. McKechnie took him out to dinner and was amazed to hear Hershberger confess that he was contemplating suicide. McKechnie tried to convince his catcher that the best years of his life lay ahead of him, and Hershberger seemed to agree.

The next day, the Braves had another double-header with the Braves. When Hershberger didn't show up, McKechnie sent someone back to the hotel. Hershberger was found dead in his room, his throat slit by a razor blade. His death was a shock to the Reds and to baseball. The 29-year-old had been popular with his teammates, and he showed great promise as a player. Had he maintained his .316 career batting average beyond his three major league seasons, he might one day have been considered for the Hall of Fame.

1940 FRANK McCORMICK, Cincinnati Reds

When the Cincinnati Reds won their second consecutive National League pennant in 1940, first baseman Frank McCormick led the way with 127 RBI, a .309 batting average, an NL-leading 191 hits, and the Most Valuable Player award. The 6-foot-4, 205-pound McCormick was a spectacular defensive first baseman and so agile that he even played second base four times. McCormick had a better season in 1939, batting .332 and leading the league with 128 RBI, but he lost the MVP award to teammate Bucky Walters, a left-handed pitcher who won 27 games. McCormick played 10 seasons with the Reds, was traded to the Phillies in 1946, then to the Braves in 1947. He retired after the Braves won the pennant in 1948.

Publisher: Val Decker Packing Co., Cincinnati, OH • Manufacturer: Orcajo Photo Art, Dayton, OH • Type: Real Photo • Postmark: Not Used
Value: $75–$100

1941 TED WILLIAMS, Boston Red Sox

Ted Williams was given many nicknames: "The Splendid Splinter," "The Thumper," "The Kid." But the nickname most fitting to him, "Teddy Ballgame," he gave to himself. Besides being the greatest natural hitter in the last 50 years, Williams was an intense student of the game. He studied opposing pitchers more closely than did any other player, and as a result, he became baseball's last .400 hitter, batting .406 in 1941. His lifetime .344 batting average stands as the sixth best in baseball history.

As well as Williams played, he was a frequent target of fans who booed because he didn't play even better. Annoyed by such comments, he sometimes showed his displeasure by spitting in the direction of the fans, thereby causing more booing. In his later years, he made peace with the fans and with himself. In his autobiography, *My Turn at Bat,* Williams discussed his love-hate relationship with the fans. "I am sure of one thing, I would never spit at those fans again. Boston fans were the best. I was, in the final analysis, the darling of the fans of Boston. From

Publisher: Prest-O-Lite Batteries, Toledo, OH • Manufacturer: Not Indicated
Type: Black & White • Postmark: Not Used • Value: $150–$200

FAMOUS THRUOUT THE WORLD

VINCENT DI MAGGIO

JOE DI MAGGIO'S RESTAURANT

DOMINIC DI MAGGIO

Fishermen's Wharf

San Francisco, California

Telephone: ORdway 2266 — 205-11 JEFFERSON ST.

Publisher: Joe DiMaggio's Restaurant, San Francisco, CA • Manufacturer: Curt Teich Co., Chicago, IL • Type: Linen • Postmark: Not Used • Value: $100–$150

the earliest days, I was their guy, because I was exuberant, I was natural, I was different. I am sorry I was late finding out, but I'm glad I did find it out."

Considering that Williams missed almost five seasons serving in the military during World War II and the Korean War, his record is remarkable. When he first left in 1943, he had won two consecutive American League batting titles, hitting .406 in 1941 and .356 in '42. He also led the league in home runs both years with 37 and 36, respectively. Williams hit 521 home runs in his career, including one in the last at-bat of his last game in 1960. The 42-year-old Williams finished that final season with a .316 batting average and 29 home runs. Six years later, he was inducted into the Hall of Fame.

1941 JOE, DOM, & VINCE DiMAGGIO

The most famous and probably the best of the brothers who have played baseball were the DiMaggios. They grew up near the San Francisco waterfront, so it's not surprising that they parlayed their fame and money into a popular restaurant on Fisherman's Wharf.

Vince, the eldest of the brothers, was the least successful as a player. He played for 10 years in the National League with Boston, Cincinnati, Pittsburgh, Philadelphia, and New York. He had a .249 career bat-

ting average—his career high was the .289 he compiled in 1940—and led the National League in strikeouts in six of his 10 years.

Dom, the youngest brother, had the misfortune to play in Joe's shadow. Dom spent his entire 11-year career with the Boston Red Sox, where he was considered the second-best center fielder in the American League. Although the Red Sox and Yankees frequently battled for the pennant, Joe and the Yankees usually won. Dom, nicknamed "The Little Professor" for his scholarly appearance, had a .298 career average. In 1950, his best season, he batted .328 and led the AL with 131 runs scored and 15 stolen bases.

Joe, in 13 seasons, compiled a career batting average of .325. In 1941, the Yankee Clipper established a major league record that still stands, hitting safely in 56 consecutive games. After the streak was finally halted by Cleveland's Al Smith and Jim Bagby, Joe went on to hit safely in 17 more consecutive games. His performance and the Yankees' first-place finish earned Joe the year's AL MVP award over Boston's Ted Williams.

JOSH GIBSON

Publisher: Magnum Comics • Manufacturer: Not Indicated
Type: Chrome • Postmark: Not Used • Value: $5 (recent vintage)

1943 JOSH GIBSON, Homestead Grays

Next to Satchel Paige, Josh Gibson was probably the most famous Negro League player of all time. Joining the Homestead Grays in 1930 as an 18-year-old catcher, Gibson played 10 of his 16 seasons with the Grays, who split their home games between Pittsburgh and Washington, D.C. Gibson became known as "the Babe Ruth of the Negro Leagues." He had tremendous power, but he also maintained a high batting average. In 1937, he won his first Negro League batting title, hitting .500 in 42 at-bats, according to *The Baseball Encyclopedia's* Negro Leagues Register.

Unfortunately, Gibson played when most Negro League teams spent as much time barnstorming with semi-pro clubs as they did playing within the league. As a result, his Negro League statistics reflect only a portion of what he did each year. Anecdotes from his contemporaries help flesh out the complete picture. In 1943, he reportedly hit 10 home runs out of spacious Griffith Stadium. According to the records, he hit 16 home runs altogether that year while batting an incredible .517 in 209 at-bats.

Gibson began having recurring headaches in 1942, but continued to play through the 1946 season. He died on January 20, 1947, still a member of the Grays at age 35. He was inducted into baseball's Hall of Fame in 1972.

1944 BOBBY DOERR, Boston Red Sox

Bobby Doerr quietly went about his job as one of baseball's premier second basemen during his 14 years with the Red Sox. Two Hall of Famers, general manager Eddie Collins and manager Joe Cronin, approved Doerr's big-league signing after seeing him in action in 1936 with San Diego, where he led the Pacific Coast League in hits (238). After joining Boston in 1937, he was beaned in an exhibition game, limiting his play that season to 55 games.

In 1938, his first full season, he batted .289 with 5 home runs and 80 RBI. Bobby went on to bat above .300 three times, in 1939 (.318), 1944 (.325), and 1949 (.309). Six times he drove in more than 100 runs, with

Publisher: Boston Red Sox • Manufacturer: Not Indicated
Type: Black & White • Postmark: Not Used • Value: $25 Signed

his best mark (120) coming in 1950. In 1944, Bobby was named Player of the Year by *The Sporting News* after he batted .325 with 15 home runs and 81 RBI while fielding brilliantly. Always among the top fielders in the league, he once handled 414 chances without an error. Red Sox teammate Ted Williams called Bobby "Our Silent Captain."

Though Doerr had only one opportunity to play in the World Series (1946), he performed brilliantly, batting .408 against the Cardinals. A chronic bad back led him to retire after the 1951 season, a year in which he batted .289 with 13 home runs and 73 RBI despite the pain. Bobby was elected to the Hall of Fame in 1986.

1945 CHICAGO CUBS

Over the years, the Chicago Cubs have been adopted by many fans who have never lived near Chicago. Perhaps it's the years of frustrating finishes, often in the second division, that have rallied so many baseball fans to the Cub cause. Perhaps they've heard about the great Cubs teams of the early 1900s and hope for a revival of those achievements. The photograph below shows the Cubs in their last pennant-winning season, 1945. First baseman Phil Cavaretta led the team and the league with a .355 batting average, while center fielder Andy

Pafko powered the Cubbies with 110 RBI. Stan Hack hit .323 and anchored the defense at the hot corner, leading all National League third basemen in putouts (195) and fielding percentage (.975). Right-hander Hank Wyse led the pitching staff with 22 wins and a 2.68 ERA. The club faced the Detroit Tigers in the World Series, losing in seven. Unfortunately for their fans, the Cubs haven't been back to the Fall Classic since.

1946 BOB FELLER, Cleveland Indians

When Bob Feller left his family's Iowa farm in 1936 to join the Cleveland Indians, his blazing fastball was already legendary, having earned him the high school nickname "Rapid Robert." Feller made his debut on July 6, 1936, facing the Cardinals in an exhibition game. In three innings, he struck out eight Cardinal batters. As Feller recalled in *Strikeout Story,* his autobiography, St. Louis pitcher Dizzy Dean, who threw an outstanding fastball of his own, was very impressed. When the photographers asked Dean to pose with Feller, Dean replied, "If it's all right with him, it's all right with me."

Despite losing four prime seasons to military service during World War II, Feller won 266 games over his 18-year career. He also had 2,581 career strikeouts, including a career-high 348 in 1946, when he also led

Publisher: Grogan Photo Co., Danville, IL • Manufacturer: Grogan Photo Co. • Type: Real Photo • Postmark: Not Used • Value: $150–$200

the AL in wins (26), shutouts (10), complete games (36), and innings pitched (371⅓). Feller threw three no-hitters and a record 12 one-hitters before he retired in 1956. He entered the Hall of Fame in 1962.

MICKEY VERNON

Publisher: TCMA Ltd., Amawalk, NY • Manufacturer: Not Indicated
Type: Chrome • Postmark: Not Used • Value: $10 (recent vintage)

Publisher: Van Patrick, Cleveland, OH • Manufacturer: Not Indicated
Type: Real Photo • Postmark: Not Used • Value: $100–$125 Signed

1946 MICKEY VERNON, Washington Senators

First baseman Mickey Vernon ranks among the most popular Washington Senators players in history, winning two American League batting championships during two separate tenures with the team. He won his first batting crown in 1946, averaging .353 as he led the team to its final first-division finish. The 'Nats finished fourth that year with a 76-78 record. Vernon drove in 85 runs in '46, second on the team to Stan Spence, who had 87.

Traded to Cleveland in 1949, Vernon returned to Washington early in the 1950 season. He won his second batting title in 1953, averaging .337. That season, he also led the AL in doubles with 43 and had a career-high 115 RBI. Vernon batted .301 for the Senators in 1955, then was traded to the Red Sox, for whom he

batted .310. Mickey finally played with a contender in 1960, appearing in nine games with the champion Pittsburgh Pirates. In 1961, he became manager of the expansion Senators, a post he held for two seasons and part of a third. In 20 big-league seasons, Vernon batted .286. But on the strength of his two batting titles with a predominantly weak team, he may someday wind up in the Hall of Fame.

1947 JACKIE ROBINSON, Brooklyn Dodgers

The impact of Jackie Robinson on baseball has been thoroughly documented. When he joined the Brooklyn Dodgers in 1947, he became the first African American to play in the major leagues since the turn of the century. Two black brothers, Moses "Fleet" Walker and Welday Walker, played briefly with the Toledo Blue Stockings of the American Association in 1884. However, their careers lasted less than a season because of strong objections from white players.

With the integration of the armed forces after World

War II and a growing black insistence for equality, Dodgers general manager Branch Rickey sensed a change coming and decided to challenge baseball's color line. He knew the first African American to play would be subjected to tremendous abuse, and he needed someone who could withstand that abuse. He selected Jackie Robinson, a four-sport star at UCLA and a Lieutenant in the U.S. Army during the war. Robinson was playing shortstop for the Kansas City Monarchs of the Negro National League when he met Rickey at his office. The Dodger manager asked many tough questions, including how Robinson would react if someone hit him. "Mr. Rickey, do you want a ballplayer who's afraid to fight back?" Robinson asked. Rickey said, "I want a ballplayer with guts enough not to fight back. You've got to do this job with base hits and stolen bases and by fielding ground balls, Jackie, and nothing more." And he did. Robinson signed a Dodgers contract in 1946 and joined the Montreal Royals of the International League where he was an instant success, leading the league with a .349 batting average. In 1947, he joined the Dodgers, becoming a star and leading the National League with 29 stolen bases while hitting .297. In 1949 his .342 average gave him the NL batting title. Robinson retired in 1956 with a career .311 batting average.

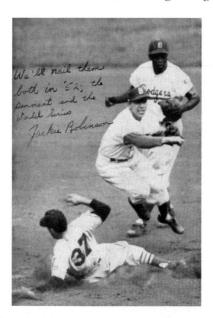

Publisher: Not Indicated • Manufacturer: Not Indicated • Type: Real Photo
Postmark: Not Used • Value: $150–$200

Publisher: Cleveland Indians • Manufacturer: Not Indicated • Type: Real Photo • Postmark: Not Used • Value: $25–$40

1947 LARRY DOBY, Cleveland Indians

Larry Doby did not receive the same fanfare as Jackie Robinson. He quietly broke the American League color line with the Cleveland Indians in 1947. Cleveland owner Bill Veeck purchased Doby from the Newark Eagles of the Negro National League in 1947 and immediately brought him to the Indians. Doby had played college basketball and baseball on predominantly white teams before joining the Indians. Player/manager Lou Boudreau recalled Doby's first appearance. "We talked for quite a while and I told Larry exactly what my plans were for him. I pointed out that because he was the first player of his race to enter the American League, he was bound to be the subject of a great deal of newspaper publicity, and I also thought it would be a good bet he would be reading stories saying I would be prejudiced in my dealings with him. I made it plain that he should pay no attention to such sensationalism and just concentrate on the job of playing ball as well as he knew how." Obviously nervous and under pressure, Doby hardly looked impressive at first. Making only 32 plate appearances in 29 games, he batted .156. It was Boudreau who proposed playing Doby slowly. "Because the pressure on him was tremendous and I was unwilling to let one-half year's playing under such terrific odds spoil his future, I tried to spot him where I thought he would be most likely to come through. In that way, I hoped to assist Larry in gaining the confidence he had to have before he made good in our league."

Boudreau's handling of Doby paid dividends. In 1948, his .301 batting average, 14 home runs, and 66 RBI helped the Indians win the AL pennant. Initially an infielder, he moved to the outfield that season and remained there for most of his career. In 13 major league seasons, Doby compiled a .283 lifetime batting average. He retired in 1959 and was elected to the Hall of Fame in 1998.

1947 JIMMY DUDLEY, Cleveland Indians (broadcaster)

Jimmy Dudley was an outstanding major league broadcaster for more than 20 years. He launched his career in 1947 with the Cleveland Indians, joining former player and longtime Voice of the Tribe Jack Graney. Dudley wound up his big-league broadcasting career with the Seattle Pilots in 1969, thereafter retiring to Arizona.

This colorful card, published by Indians radio sponsor Erin Brew, shows a smiling Dudley beside a billboard promoting the product. The legend on the back of this card reads, "Erin Brew brings you Jimmy Dudley and the Play by Play of the Cleveland Indians—a public service to baseball fans since 1947." Jimmy was elected to the Broadcast Wing of the Baseball Hall of Fame in 1997.

1948 BOSTON BRAVES

"Spahn and Sain and Pray for Rain" was the battle cry of the 1948 Boston Braves as they fought for their first National League pennant since 1914. Fans' hopes were pinned on the pitching of left-hander Warren Spahn and right-hander Johnny Sain. Spahn contributed 15 victories to the pennant-winning season, while Sain led the NL with 24 wins and compiled a 2.60 ERA in 315 innings.

Although the battle cry was a clever way of suggesting that the Braves had a two-man pitching staff, that wasn't entirely true. Rookie right-hander Vern Bickford spoiled the rhyme with his 11 wins and 5 losses. When the 1948 season ended, the Braves had 91 wins and a 6½ game lead over the Cardinals. In addition to good pitching, the Braves had an abundance of good hitters, led by right fielder Tommy Holmes (.325 batting average), left fielder Jeff Heath (.319 average, 20 home runs, 76 RBI), and third baseman Bob Elliott (.283 average,

Publisher: Fine Arts Studio • Manufacturer: Dexter Press, W. Nyack, NY • Type: Chrome • Postmark: Not Used • Value: $25–$35

Boston Braves Baseball Team of 1948

Front L. to R.—Sibby Sisti, Clyde Shoun, Bob Keely, Fred Fitzsimmons, Billy Southworth, Johnny Cooney, Bob Elliott, Red Barrett, Bill Salkeld, Vern Bickford, Phil Masi, Jim Russell.

Second L. to R.—George Young, Frank McCormick, Ernie White, Connie Ryan, John Sain, Bob Hogue, Mike McCormick, Clint Conatser, Jeff Heath, John Antonelli, Warren Spahn, Nelson Potter.

Third L. to R.—Bob Sturgeon, Si Johnson, Earl Torgeson, Al Dark, Tommy Holmes, Bill Voiselle, John Beazley, Al Lyons. Bat Boys L. to R.—Charlie Chronopoulos, Tom Ferguson, Frank McNulty.

Publisher: Tichnor Bros., #78732, Boston, MA • Manufacturer: Tichnor Bros. • Type: Linen • Postmark: Not Used • Value: $35–$50

23 homers, 100 RBI). However, Cleveland's pitchers stopped the Braves in the World Series as the Indians won the championship in six games.

1948 LOU BOUDREAU, Cleveland Indians

When Lou Boudreau was the player/manager of the Cleveland Indians in the 1940s, he led by example. Boudreau's leadership reached its pinnacle in 1948 when the Tribe won the American League pennant in a dramatic one-game playoff with the Boston Red Sox, then went on to beat the Boston Braves in the World Series. Boudreau was fortunate to enjoy a season that many players dream about but very few achieve. He had a .355 batting average with 106 RBI, fielded brilliantly at shortstop, and seemed to make all of the correct managerial decisions. His performance earned him the 1948 AL Most Valuable Player Award.

Boudreau documented this amazing season in his autobiography, *Player-Manager*. Fans could purchase the book by using the postcard pictured here as an order form and mailing it to the publisher.

Boudreau remained with the Tribe through 1950, and later managed the Boston Red Sox, Kansas City Athletics, and Chicago Cubs. He was elected to the Hall of Fame in 1970.

Player - Manager
By LOU BOUDREAU
with
ED FITZGERALD

A Great Baseball Success Story told in the words of the man who lived it.

Please send me _____ copies of PLAYER-MANAGER at $2.75 each.
☐ Charge my account. ☐ Cash enclosed.
Add any city or state tax

Name _____

Address _____

Publisher: Burrows, Cleveland, OH • Manufacturer: Not Indicated • Type: Business Reply Card • Postmark: Not Used • Value: $100–$150

Publisher: Cleveland Indians • Manufacturer: Not Indicated • Type: Real Photo
Postmark: St. Louis, MO, July 27, 1952 • Value: $250 Signed, $100 Unsigned

1948 SATCHEL PAIGE, Cleveland Indians

Leroy "Satchel" Paige was a legend in the Negro Leagues for 22 years before he joined the Cleveland Indians as a 42-year-old rookie in 1948. Although Paige was well past his prime, he contributed greatly to Cleveland's march to the championship, winning 6 and losing only 1. Used primarily in relief for the Tribe, Paige still started seven games and completed three, compiling a fine 2.48 ERA in his 21 appearances. After winning 4 and losing 7 for the Indians in 1949, he was released. But when former Indians owner Bill Veeck bought the St. Louis Browns in 1951, Satchel returned to the bigs. He had his best season in 1952, winning 12 games and losing 10 for the Browns with a 3.07 ERA. Released by the Browns after a 3-9 1953 season, Satchel came back for one appearance with the Kansas City Athletics in 1965, at the age of 59. He worked three innings, giving up one hit and no runs, with no walks and one strikeout.

Satchel acquired his nickname by working as a 7-year-old porter at the Mobile, Alabama, rail depot. A

perpetual showman, Paige developed the "hesitation pitch" that thrilled crowds for years but was outlawed in the major leagues. His major league record was only 28-31, but his untold wins in the Negro Leagues—the records guess at 124 over 17 seasons—earned Paige a spot in the Hall of Fame in 1971.

Publisher: Cleveland Indians • Manufacturer: Not Indicated • Type: Real Photo • Postmark: Not Used • Value: $100 Signed, $50 Unsigned

1948 BILL VEECK, Cleveland Indians

Promotional genius Bill Veeck's enchantment with baseball was natural. His father, William Sr., was president of the Chicago Cubs in the 1920s. In fact, young Veeck planted the ivy that adorns the wall at Wrigley Field. Working around the ballpark as a jack-of-all-trades, Bill learned all the rudiments of baseball operations. In 1940, he bought the financially strapped Milwaukee Brewers, turning them into a moneymaker with imaginative promotions. In 1946, he purchased the Cleveland Indians and, incorporating many giveaways and crowd-pleasing gimmicks, helped set an organization attendance record that stood for nearly 20 years. As owner of the

Publisher: Arch McDonald, Washington, DC • Manufacturer: Not Indicated • Type: Black & White • Postmark: Not Used • Value: $150–$200

Browns, he brought in midget Eddie Gaedel, who walked in his only at-bat. As White Sox owner, Veeck introduced player names on uniforms. Fireworks in exploding scoreboards was another Veeck innovation. This Cleveland postcard of Veeck, issued in 1948, is his prime collectible.

1948 GIL COAN/MICKEY VERNON, Washington Senators

Baseball-wise, 1948 was not a good year for the Washington Senators. Under manager Joe Kuhel, the team won 56 and lost 97, finishing seventh in the American League. But Senators fans remember '48 fondly as the year that Senators broadcaster Arch McDonald and the team's sponsor, Gunther Beer, issued a set of 11 postcards. Except for a card featuring Kuhel, each postcard presented photos of two players, separated by a line running down the card's horizontal center. Kids could cut down the line to create two cards the size of standard baseball cards—and many did, making this an extremely rare postcard set. The card featuring Senators star Mickey Vernon and rookie outfielder Gil Coan is the rarest of the bunch.

Like their team, neither Vernon nor Coan had a particularly good year in '48. Vernon, who had hit .353 two

years earlier to win the AL batting title, hit only .242, some 44 points below his career mark of .286. Coan, playing his first full season in the bigs, was a speedster who finished second to Browns star Bob Dillinger with 23 stolen bases. Gil came into his own in 1950, batting .303 in 104 games before suffering a skull fracture when he crashed into a wall, an injury that sidelined him for the remainder of the season. Although he bounced back in '51 to hit .303 again with a career-high 61 RBI, he was never quite the same after the injury. He never played another full season, finally retiring after 11 big-league years.

1949 BOB DILLINGER, St. Louis Browns

Even though he had a relatively brief major league career, third baseman Bob Dillinger was one of the finest players of his day. During his rookie season with the St. Louis Browns in 1946, he batted a career-low .280. Six seasons later, when he retired after the 1951 season, he had pulled his career average up to .306.

The reverse of the extremely rare postcard on p. 94, probably published by Dillinger himself, lists his impressive history year by year, starting with his 1939 stint in Lincoln, Nebraska. The card's last three entries emphasize Dillinger's outstanding credentials:

Publisher: Bob Dillinger • Manufacturer: Not Indicated • Type: Black & White • Postmark: Not Used • Value: $100

- *1947 St. Louis Browns. BA .294. Led AL 34 stolen bases.*
- *1948 St. Louis Browns. BA .321. Led AL 207 hits. 28 stolen bases.*
- *1949 St. Louis Browns BA .323. Played in All-Star game. Led AL 22 stolen bases.*

The Baseball Encyclopedia disagrees with this card's '49 stats, crediting Dillinger with a .324 batting average and 20 steals, but still acknowledges him as the American League's leader in the latter category. Unlike some lesser players who earned batting titles and the like in the mid-1940s when many of the game's stars were serving in the military, Dillinger performed his feats after players like Ted Williams and Joe DiMaggio had returned to the diamond, proving he could hold his own with all of them.

1949 RALPH KINER, Pittsburgh Pirates

Outfielder Ralph Kiner had a relatively brief major league career beginning in 1946 when he joined the Pittsburgh Pirates. But during his tenure, he was the National League's best home run hitter, leading the NL in that category for seven consecutive years starting in his rookie

season, when he hit 23. In 1947, he hit 51 home runs, had 127 RBI, and batted .313. His statistics that season are even more impressive given that the Pirates finished in last place. Kiner said later, "The hardest thing in the world is to play for a losing team. I always had a strong competitive drive and I hated to lose."

Kiner had his best season in 1949 with 54 homers, 127 RBI, and a .310 average. Despite his success, the Pirates finished sixth in the NL with 71 wins and 83 losses. Undeterred, Kiner continued his home run tear for three more seasons, bashing 47 in 1950, 42 in 1951, and 37 in 1952. A chronic back ailment cut short his career, which ended in 1955 while he was with the Cleveland Indians. In his 10 seasons, Kiner hit 369 home runs, bashing homers in 7.1 percent of his at-bats. Only Babe Ruth and, through 1998, Mark McGwire have higher home run percentages.

Ralph Kiner became a baseball broadcaster for the New York Mets in 1961, and continues in that role today. He was elected to the Hall of Fame in 1975.

Ralph Kiner

Publisher: Pittsburgh Pirates • Manufacturer: Genuine Photo-Film Fotos, New York, NY • Type: Real Photo • Postmark: Not Used Value: $100–$150

The Detroit Tigers 1949

Bottom Row, l to r: Harvey Reibe, C.; Paul Campbell, I.F.; Hal White, P.; Ted Gray, P.; Hoot Evers, O.F.; Ed. Lake, I.F.; Stubby Overmire, P.

Second Row: John Lipon, I.F.; Jim Outlaw, I. F; Hal Newhouser, P.; Ted Lyons; "Red" Rolfe, Mgr.; Dick Bartell; Virgil Trucks, P.; George Kell, I.F.; Neil Berry, I.F.; Lou Kretlow, P.

Third Row: Jack Homel, Trainer; Dick Wakefield, O.F.; A. Robinson, C.; George Vico, I.F.; Bob Swift, C.; Art Houtteman, P.; Marlin Stuart, P.; Vic Wertz, O.F.; Marvin Grissom, P.; Don Kolloway, O.F.

Top Row: Don Lund, O.F.; Saul Rogovin, P.; John Groth, O.F.; Tony Lupien, I.F.; Pat Mullin, O.F.; Fred Hutchinson, P.; Paul Trout, P.

Publisher: Grogan Photo, Danville, IL • Manufacturer: Grogan Photo • Type: Real Photo • Postmark: Not Used • Value: $100–$150

1949 DETROIT TIGERS

The 1949 Detroit Tigers finished in fourth place with a record of 87-67, 10 games behind the New York Yankees, who in that season won the first of five consecutive pennants under Casey Stengel. Meanwhile, former Yankee third baseman Red Rolfe managed the Tigers, led offensively by their own third baseman, George Kell, whose .343 average topped the American League. Among the pitchers, another Hall of Famer, "Prince" Hal Newhouser,

won 18 games and lost 11, while Virgil "Fire" Trucks led the staff with 19 wins, 11 losses, and a team-best 2.81 ERA. Art Houtteman and Fred Hutchinson chipped in with 15 victories each, while Ted Gray won 10, giving the Tigers five pitchers with at least 10 wins. Only the Yankees could also make that claim. Virtually the same team came back in 1950, winning 95 games but still finishing three games behind the Yankees.

1950-59

The 1950s proved to be one of the most eventful decades in baseball history. Mickey Mantle of the Yankees and Willie Mays of the Giants joined Duke Snider of the Dodgers to give New York City three of the best center fielders in history—all future Hall of Famers. The Yankees, who had won the World Series in 1949, tacked on four more championships from 1950–53, giving them an unprecedented five titles in a row. Professor Casey Stengel pulled all the right strings as manager, while Hall of Famers Mantle, Yogi Berra, Joe DiMaggio, Phil Rizzuto, Johnny Mize, and Whitey Ford led the club to victory.

The Yankee spell was broken in 1954, when the Indians set an American League record for wins in a season with 111. The Tribe boasted the best pitching staff in baseball, with Hall of Famers Bob Lemon and Early Wynn leading the American League with 23 victories apiece. But in the World Series against the under-dog Giants, the hitting of New York's Dusty Rhodes, coupled with Mays' defensive brilliance, destroyed the Indians in four straight.

In '55, the Brooklyn Dodgers finally gained a measure of revenge against the Yankees, who had beaten them in all five of their previous World Series meetings. The Dodgers took the championship from their crosstown rivals in seven thrill-packed games. But the Yankees returned the favor in '56, beating Brooklyn four games to three. The Milwaukee Braves won the National League flag in '57 and '58, beating the Yankees in the World Series the first year and losing to them the second. The Braves relied on outstanding hitting from Hall of Famers Hank Aaron, Eddie Mathews, and Red Schoendienst, plus brilliant pitching by Warren Spahn and Lew Burdette.

As you've probably noticed, the Yankees missed only one World Series through 1958. The '59 postseason proved to be the club's second no-show of the decade, as the Go-Go Chicago White Sox took the AL pennant. Sparked by Hall of Famers Louis Aparicio, Early Wynn, and AL MVP Nellie Fox, the Sox finished five games in front of the Cleveland Indians. Wynn led the AL in victories with 22 and innings pitched with 256. But none of that helped the White Sox in the World Series, where

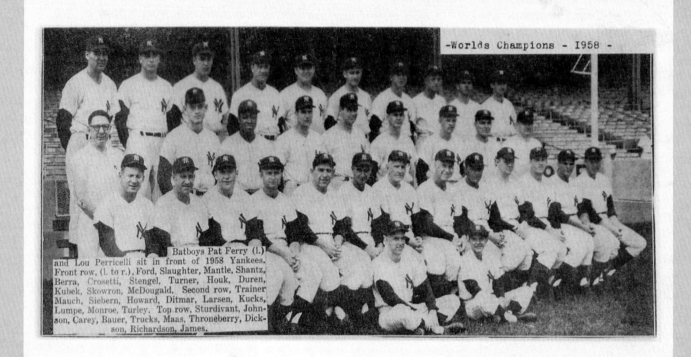

-Worlds Champions - 1958 -

Batboys Pat Ferry (l.) and Lou Perricelli sit in front of 1958 Yankees. Front row, (l. to r.), Ford, Slaughter, Mantle, Shantz, Berra, Crosetti, Stengel, Turner, Houk, Duren, Kubek, Skowron, McDougald. Second row, Trainer Mauch, Siebern, Howard, Ditmar, Larsen, Kucks, Lumpe, Monroe, Turley. Top row, Sturdivant, Johnson, Carey, Bauer, Trucks, Maas, Throneberry, Dickson, Richardson, James.

Publisher: Not Indicated • Manufacturer: Not Indicated • Type: Real Photo • Postmark: New York, NY, Oct. 15, 1958 • Value: $50

Publisher: Louis Dormand, #128 3592, Riverhead, NY • Manufacturer: Not Indicated • Type: Chrome • Postmark: Not Used • Value: $50–$75

Publisher: Cleveland Indians • Manufacturer: Not Indicated • Type: Real Photo • Postmark: Not Used • Value: $50 Signed

the Dodgers—who bounced back from a seventh-place finish in '58 to win the pennant—topped Chicago in six.

The denizens of Brooklyn, though, had less reason to celebrate the Dodgers' second championship than they had the first. That's because between the two, the club had relocated to Los Angeles, one of a series of moves that marked baseball's first city-hopping in 50 years. The Braves went from Boston to Milwaukee in '53, the Browns moved from St. Louis to Baltimore—where they became the Orioles—in '54, and the Athletics relocated to Kansas City in '55. After the '57 season, two of New York's three franchises moved to the West Coast: the Dodgers to L.A. and the Giants to San Francisco. It was arguably the most important event in baseball in half a century. Many baseball purists still abhor the city switch, but it proved to be a big success financially—particularly for the Dodgers, who set all sorts of attendance records. Inarguably, the move changed the face of baseball forever.

1950 LUKE EASTER, Cleveland Indians

Luke Easter was a powerfully built slugger who stood 6 feet 4 1/2 inches, weighed 240 pounds, and could hit the ball a mile. He came up with the Cleveland Indians late in the 1949 season, batting only .222.

But as a starter in 1950, Easter became a feared slugger, blasting 28 home runs, driving in 107 runs, and batting .280. In '51, Luke hit 27 home runs with 103 RBI. He walloped 31 home runs in 1952, driving in 97 runs. In 1953, when he was batting .303 with 311 RBI after 68 games, he suffered a broken foot that virtually ended his major league career. He was only able to play six games in 1954.

Easter appeared on several team-issued postcards during his Cleveland career, which ended in '54 with a lifetime .274 average, 93 home runs, and 340 RBI, compiled in less than four full seasons over six years.

1950 RICHIE ASHBURN,
Philadelphia Phillies

Outfielder Richie Ashburn was an outstanding major league hitter from 1948, his first season with the Phillies, through his final year, 1962, which he spent with the Mets. Richie chalked up two National League batting titles in his 15 years. His prowess was evident from the outset; in his rookie season, he hit .333 and led the league with 32 stolen bases while patrolling center field with the speed and grace of a gazelle. His batting average fell to .284 in '49, but Ashburn bounced back with a .303 mark in 1950, when the Phillies won the pennant, and followed up with a .344 average in '51. After dipping to .282 in 1952, he reeled off four consecutive seasons batting .313 or better, including a .338 mark in '55, when he won his first batting championship. After a subpar .297 season in '57, Ashburn hit a career-high .350 in '58, earning his second batting title.

Ashburn left the Phillies for the Cubs in 1960. After two seasons in Chicago, he wound up his career with the Mets. One of the New York club's few bright spots in its inaugural season, Ashburn batted .306, just two points below his career .308 average. Following his playing days, Richie returned to Philadelphia to broadcast Phillies games, a task he performed until he died in 1997.

In 1995, Ashburn proved that you don't have to be a power hitter to make the Hall of Fame. Through his entire career, he never hit more than seven home runs in a season; his best RBI total was 63, which he compiled in 1951. But leading the league in hitting twice, hits three times, triples twice, and walks four times was enough to earn him induction.

1950 ROBIN ROBERTS, Philadelphia Phillies

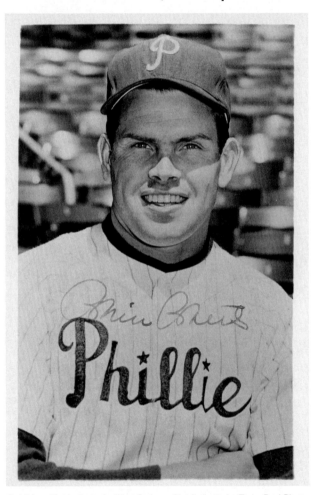

Publisher: Not Indicated • Manufacturer: Not Indicated • Type: Real Photo
Postmark: Not Used • Value: $50–$60 Signed

In 1950, the Philadelphia Phillies won their first pennant since 1915, thanks largely to the exploits of right-handed pitcher Robin Roberts. Two years before, Roberts had joined the club fresh from Michigan State University. The 22-year-old rookie went 7-9 with a 3.15 ERA. In 1949, he evened his record, winning 15 games and losing 15. By 1950, he was ready to establish himself as a star. Making a league-leading 39 starts, Roberts won 20

Publisher: Fine Arts Studios, Cleveland, OH • Manufacturer: Dexter Press, W. Nyack, NY • Type: Chrome • Postmark: Not Used • Value: $50

and lost 11, launching a streak of six consecutive 20-win seasons. He led the National League in wins in four of those years, with 28 victories in 1952 and 23 each in '53, '54, and '55.

Roberts had a high-velocity fastball and exceptional control. During his 19 years in baseball, he struck out 2,357 batters while walking 902; that averages out to a little more than one walk in each of his 676 games. Through the 1950s, Roberts was the Phillies' workhorse, leading the NL in starts six times and in complete games and innings pitched five times each. He also twice led the league in strikeouts. Roberts was named to the Hall of Fame in 1976.

1950 CURT SIMMONS, Philadelphia Phillies

During the Phillies' pennant-winning 1950 season, Curt Simmons was almost the equal of Robin Roberts on the pitching mound. Simmons posted a 17-8 record, and might have won 20 had he not missed the last month of the season—and the postseason—to military service.

Simmons joined the Phillies in 1947, signing a $65,000 bonus contract. He went on to enjoy a fine 20-year pitching career, but early on, he also showed promise as a hitter. While in high school, Simmons once played in a Babe Ruth All-Star game at the Polo Grounds. Dividing his time between the pitching mound and the outfield, Simmons drove in the winning run, prompting Ty Cobb to suggest to him that he switch to the outfield full-time. But Simmons chose to remain a pitcher, without regret.

This postcard was produced by the Pennsylvania Dairy Council, for which Simmons was a spokesman. The back includes a message from the clean-living native of Egypt, Pennsylvania, encouraging fans to drink milk and enjoy good health.

1950 DETROIT TIGERS

The 1950 Tigers pictured on this Grogan postcard won 95 games under manager Red Rolfe—enough wins to earn the pennant in most years. Unfortunately for these Tigers, they had to face one of the great dynasties in baseball history. Detroit finished the season three games behind the New York Yankees, who went on to win the World Series.

The Tigers were led by third baseman George Kell, who batted .340 and drove in 101 runs. Behind Kell, the entire starting outfield of Vic Wertz, Johnny Groth, and Hoot Evers topped .300, batting .308, .306, and .323, respectively. The '50 Tigers were also devastating run scorers. Wertz had a team-leading 123 RBI, while Evers drove in 103 runs. The pitching, too, was outstanding. Detroit had five hurlers each with 10 or more wins: Art Houtteman (19-12), Fred Hutchinson (17-8), Hal New-houser (15-13), Dizzy Trout (13-5), and Ted Gray (10-7). In addition to his 17 wins, Hutchinson contributed at the plate, batting .326 with 20 RBI in 95 at-bats. Two members of this remarkable Tiger team, George Kell and Hal Newhouser, are now in the Hall of Fame.

Publisher: Dairy Council • Manufacturer: Not Indicated • Type: Black & White
Postmark: Not Used • Value: $25–$35

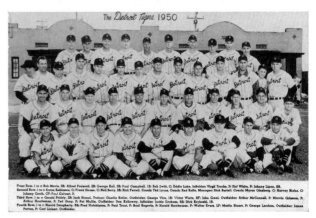

Publisher: Grogan Photo Co., Danville, IL • Manufacturer: Grogan Photo Co. • Type: Real Photo • Postmark: Not Used • Value: $125–$150

Publisher: Louis Dormand, Riverhead, NY • Manufacturer: Not Indicated • Type: Chrome • Postmark: Not Used • Value: $75–$100 Signed

1950 PHIL RIZZUTO, New York Yankees

Phil "Scooter" Rizzuto played 13 seasons with the New York Yankees. During that time, the team won 10 pennants and eight championships. The spark-plug shortstop deserves much credit for the team's success. Turned down by both the Giants and Dodgers because of his size, the 5-foot 6-inch, 150-pound Rizzuto impressed the Yankees enough to be signed on the spot after a workout at Yankee Stadium. General manager Ed Barrow kidded about how Rizzuto became a Yankee: "We signed him for 15 cents—a 10-cent call to his home in Glendale, Long Island, and a nickel for the cup of coffee we gave him when he showed up at the stadium."

In his first season with the Yankees (1941), Phil batted .307, helping the team to the pennant and a World Series victory over the Dodgers. Phil's finest season was 1950, when he batted a career-high .324, drove in 66 runs, and fielded brilliantly on the way to being named American League MVP for his efforts. That fall, the Yankees beat the Phillies in the World Series.

When his career ended following the 1956 season, Phil stepped into the Yankees broadcasting booth, where he began a long career as an announcer. He was inducted into the Hall of Fame in 1994.

1951 NED GARVER, St. Louis Browns

Right-hander Ned Garver—the pride of Ney, Ohio, where he was born and still lives—was one of the American League's best pitchers in 1951, compiling a 20-12 record with the St. Louis Browns. While a 20-win season is hardly unheard of, it's remarkable in this case because the Browns were dead last in the AL that season, winning only 52 games while losing 102. There's no telling how many games Garver might have won for a better team. He started 30 games for the Browns that season, and led the AL with 24 complete games—three more than Hall of Famer Early Wynn pitched for the second-place Cleveland Indians. Garver's outstanding '51 performance brought him so many autograph requests that he had this postcard produced to accommodate fans.

Although Garver never again posted 20 victories in a season, he did return to double digits, winning 11, 14, and 10 games, respectively, from 1953 through '55 for the Detroit Tigers, and 12 and 10 in '58 and '59, respectively, for the Kansas City Athletics. After 14 seasons, nearly all with bad ballclubs, Garver retired with 129 wins, 157 losses, and an ERA of 3.73 to show for his career.

Publisher: Not Indicated • Manufacturer: Not Indicated • Type: Black & White • Postmark: Not Used • Value: $50–$75

1951 BILLY GOODMAN, Boston Red Sox

Billy Goodman was an outstanding major league infielder who retired after 16 seasons with an even .300 batting average. Take away his last four seasons, over which he averaged .250, and his batting would have looked even better.

In his prime years with the Red Sox, Goodman was one of the finest—and most versatile—players in the game. Primarily a second baseman, he spent time at every other infield position and even saw duty as an outfielder. Offensively, Goodman had his best season in 1950, when he led the American League with a .354 batting average, his personal best, and drove in a career-high 68 runs. Aside from that high point, Goodman was consistent at the plate, hitting between .293 and .313 every year from 1948 through 1958.

While Goodman may have been all but forgotten by many baseball fans, his postcard is of particular interest to collectors because it's a U.S. Postal card. Some Red Sox players sent these cards to fans in response to fan mail; no other major league team had players who used these cards. Besides Goodman, other Red Sox known to use U.S. Postals to respond to fan mail were Walt Dropo, Mickey McDermott, and Johnny Pesky. This particular specimen was sent to a fan in 1951, a year in which Goodman hit .297 while scoring 92 runs.

Publisher: Not Indicated • Manufacturer: Not Indicated Type: U.S. Government Postal • Postmark: Not Used • Value: $25–$35

THE 1951 WASHINGTON SENATORS

Publisher: Eastern Air Advertising Service, Washington, DC • Manufacturer: Not Indicated • Type: Black & White • Postmark: Not Used • Value: $250–$300

1951 WASHINGTON SENATORS

The 1951 Washington Senators finished seventh in the eight-team American League, winning only 62 games while losing 92 under Hall of Fame manager Bucky Harris. Despite the dismal record, there were a few bright spots that season. First baseman Mickey Vernon, a two-time American League batting champ, led the league in fielding with a .994 average. He also batted .293, second only to left fielder Gil Coan's .303 performance. Sam Mele, who later managed the Minnesota Twins to the 1965 AL pennant, was the RBI leader with 94. Third baseman Eddie Yost led the league with 203 putouts, while center fielder Irv Noren was the putout leader at his position with 420.

Connie Marrero led the pitching staff with 11 wins against 9 losses. Right-hander Bob Porterfield, who would lead the AL with 22 wins in 1953, was 9-8 with a team-best 3.24 ERA in his first year as a Senator after coming from the New York Yankees in a trade.

Of that '51 roster, only Bucky Harris made the Hall of Fame, although Mickey Vernon remains a future possibility.

1951 GRIFFITH STADIUM, Washington Senators

This is the only known commercially produced postcard of Griffith Stadium. It shows a capacity crowd at opening day of the 1951 season. The Washington Senators generally faded into the oblivion of the second division by June or July of each year. "First in War, First in Peace, and Last in the American League" was a common expression among fans. A more positive tradition was established in the nation's capital on opening day in 1910, when President William Howard Taft threw out the first baseball to mark the beginning of the new season.

GRIFFITH STADIUM OPENING DAY

Publisher: Eastern Air Advertising Service, Washington, DC • Manufacturer: Not Indicated • Type: Black & White • Postmark: Not Used • Value: $200–$250

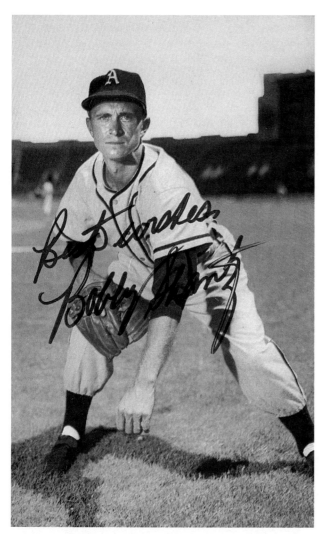

Publisher: Fine Arts Studio, #63501, Cleveland, OH • Manufacturer: Dexter Press, W. Nyack, NY • Type: Chrome • Postmark: Not Used • Value: $50

1952 BOBBY SHANTZ, Philadelphia Athletics

In 1952, right-hander Bobby Shantz of the Philadelphia Athletics was the finest pitcher in baseball. With a record of 24-7, he led the league in victories and winning percentage (.774), earning the AL MVP award for his brilliance. Almost single-handedly, he propelled the Athletics into the first division; the team finished fourth with a record of 79 wins and 75 losses.

Shantz's '52 performance wasn't exactly a fluke; he posted an 18-10 record in '51. But Shantz also pitched 279 $^2/_3$ innings in '52, a Herculean effort that took its toll on the diminutive right-hander. Standing just 5 feet 6 inches and weighing only 139 pounds, Shantz could throw remarkably hard. But he suffered arm trouble in both '53 and '54, and was never the same pitcher thereafter.

Nevertheless, he tenaciously hung on until 1964, switching to the bullpen and becoming a fine relief pitcher. With the New York Yankees in 1957, he won 11 and

lost only 5 as a starter/reliever, leading the league with a 2.45 ERA. Shantz pitched in the majors for 16 seasons in all, compiling a record of 119 wins and 99 defeats. In addition to his remarkable regular-season performances, Shantz pitched one inning of a rain-abbreviated All-Star Game at Philadelphia, striking out the side. Bobby appears on postcards as an Athletic and a Yankee.

1952 HOYT WILHELM, New York Giants

Knuckleballer Hoyt Wilhelm became the first relief pitcher in history to make the Hall of Fame when he was inducted in 1985. During his 20-year major league career, he appeared in more games than any pitcher in history (1,070). Hoyt won 143 major league games, including a record 124 from the bullpen. However, his finest performance came as a starter with the Baltimore Orioles on September 20, 1958, when he no-hit the Yankees. His best year as a starter was 1959, when he won a career-high 15 games while compiling a league-leading 2.19 ERA.

But while a starting pitcher could work only every

Publisher: Not Indicated • Manufacturer: Not Indicated • Type: Real Photo Postmark: Dobbs Ferry, NY, July 7, 1953 • Value: $50–$75 Signed

four or five days, Hoyt could be used as a reliever almost every day. And that's why Hoyt Wilhelm pitched in 1,070 games, most ever in the major leagues.

Trivia buffs, take note: In his first major league at-bat, with the New York Giants on April 23, 1952, Hoyt hit his first and only home run. Slugger he was not. Knuckleballing genius he was.

1952 ERNIE HARWELL, broadcaster

Ernie Harwell is the only major league broadcaster ever to have been traded for a baseball player. The longtime voice of the Detroit Tigers and Hall of Fame member developed an outstanding reputation as a broadcaster for Earl Mann's Atlanta Crackers of the Southern Association. Harwell attracted the attention of Brooklyn general manager Branch Rickey, who wanted to hire him as the Dodgers' announcer. Mann didn't wish to stand in Harwell's way. However, he considered himself to be in a good bargaining position. Always looking for good players, Mann requested that Rickey send catcher Cliff Dapper to Atlanta in exchange for the release of Harwell from his Crackers contract.

Harwell broadcast Dodgers games for a few years, then was hired by the New York Giants at a higher salary. This postcard shows Harwell broadcasting for radio station WMCA at the Polo Grounds during a Giants game in the early 1950s. Note the two packages of Chesterfield cigarettes visible in the bottom right-hand corner of the photograph. Harwell has never been a smoker, but Chesterfield sponsored the broadcasts.

In 1954, Ernie became the first announcer for the Baltimore Orioles. In 1960, he went to Detroit as the Tigers announcer, holding the post until the end of the 1991 season. In 1992, he began broadcasting CBS Radio's Game of the Week.

1953 COUNTY STADIUM, Milwaukee Braves

When Milwaukee's $5 million County Stadium was nearing completion in 1953, it was scheduled to become the home of the American Association's Milwaukee Brewers. The Brewers were the top minor league farm club of the Boston Braves, who owned the Milwaukee franchise. The Braves had lost more than $1 million during the previous three seasons in Boston due to dwindling attendance at Braves Field. The completion of County Stadium brought an immediate response from the Perini brothers, who owned the Braves and the Brewers. On March 18, 1953, while the Braves were at spring training, the Perinis announced that the franchise would immediately relocate to Milwaukee. This dual illustration

Publisher: Not Indicated • Manufacturer: Not Indicated • Type: Real Photo • Postmark: Not Used • Value: $50–$75

1953 Home
of the "Brewers"
Milwaukee County
Municipal Stadium

Borchert Field,
Home of
Milwaukee
"Brewers"
Baseball Club
1902 - 1952.

Publisher: E.C. Kropp Co., #4953N, Milwaukee, WI • Manufacturer: E.C. Kropp Co. • Type: Black & White • Postmark: Not Used • Value: $200–$250

includes an artist's sketch of County Stadium, the first known view. It also shows Borchert Field, home to the minor league Brewers for more than 50 years.

1953 WARREN SPAHN, Milwaukee Braves

Some say Hall of Famer Warren Spahn is the finest left-hander in baseball history, citing his 363 wins as proof. Considering Spahn didn't get his first major league victory until 1946, when he was 25 years old, his achievements are that much more remarkable. The Cy Young award, given to baseball's best pitcher, didn't begin until 1956; by that time, Warren already had six 20-victory seasons under his belt. His finest season was undoubtedly 1953, when he won 23, lost 7, and led the National League with a career-low 2.10 ERA. When he won his first and only Cy Young award in 1957, he notched a league-high 21 wins in leading the Milwaukee Braves to their only world championship.

From 1956 through 1961, Spahnie won 20 or more games; after winning 18 in 1962, he came back in '63 to tie his career-best 23 wins. Consistency was Spahn's hallmark, as his lifetime 3.09 ERA attests. Teammate Johnny Sain—a fine pitcher in his own right and later an outstanding pitching coach—attributed much of Spahn's success to his intelligence, calling him "one of the smartest men ever to play the game." Basically a power pitcher early in his career, Spahn adjusted well when his fastball lost some of its steam, evidenced by his 23-7 record for the Braves in 1963 at the age of 42.

Publisher: Bill & Bob, #28169, Bradenton, FL • Manufacturer: Not Indicated
Type: Chrome • Postmark: Not Used • Value: $150 Signed

Publisher: Photo by Requina, #66888 • Manufacturer: Not Indicated
Type: Chrome • Postmark: Not Used • Value: $15

1953 WHITEY FORD, New York Yankees

Much of the credit for the success of the New York Yankees during the 1950s and 1960s must go to left-handed pitcher Whitey Ford. During his 16 seasons with the club, the Yankees won 11 pennants and seven World Series. When he retired in 1967, Ford had won 236 games and lost only 106, compiling a .690 winning percentage that stands as the third-best in the history of baseball.

At 5 feet 10 inches tall and 178 pounds, Ford was not an overpowering pitcher. He had superb control, excellent breaking pitches, and a fine change-up. He kept batters off-balance by changing speeds and sending the ball exactly where he wanted it to go. In his rookie season, 1950, Ford endeared himself to Yankee fans by winning 9 games and losing only 1, then winning 1 game in the World Series against the Philadelphia Phillies. Returning from two years of military service in 1953, he won 18 games and lost 6. In 1955, he was the American League's top pitcher with 18 wins and 7 losses, with 2 more victories in the World Series. He was the top pitcher in 1961 with 25 wins and 4 losses and again

in 1963 with 24 wins and 7 losses. Ford's lifetime World Series record of 10 wins and 8 losses stands as the most of each ever by one pitcher. The ultimate finesse pitcher, Ford was nicknamed "Slick" and "Chairman of the Board." He made the Hall of Fame in 1974.

1954 HANK AARON, Milwaukee Braves

As baseball's all-time home run king, it's fitting that Hank Aaron's name is the first one listed in *The Baseball Encyclopedia's* Player Register. In 23 years, Hammerin' Hank walloped 755 home runs.

In 1952, at the age of 18, Aaron signed with the NL's Milwaukee Braves, having previously played for all-black teams in Alabama and Indiana. He was only 20 when he reached the major leagues, where he quickly established himself as one of baseball's finest players. Aaron played most of his major league career with the Braves—in Milwaukee from 1954–65 and in Atlanta from 1966–74—then returned to Milwaukee with the Brewers of the American League for the 1975 and 1976 seasons.

Publisher: Bill & Bob, Bradenton, FL • Manufacturer: Not Indicated
Type: Chrome • Postmark: Not Used • Value: $100

Aaron had a lifetime batting average of .305. Besides holding the lifetime home run record, he tops the major league's all-time RBI list with 2,297 and the total bases list with 6,856. He did all this in 12,364 at bats (second all-time) in 3,298 games (third) with 3,771 hits (also third). His league-topping 1,477 extra base hits include 624 doubles, good for eighth all-time. Still, Aaron's best-remembered feat occurred on April 8, l974, when he surpassed Babe Ruth's lifetime record of 714 homers.

1954 BOBBY THOMSON, Milwaukee Braves

On October 3, 1951, Bobby Thomson fired the "Shot Heard 'Round the World," slamming a dramatic home run off Brooklyn right-hander Ralph Branca. Thomson's heroics in the final inning of the third playoff game decided the National League championship, giving the New York Giants the pennant. His three-run blast barely made the left field seats at the Polo Grounds, some 315 feet from home plate, but to Bobby and the Giants it traveled a mile. Amazingly, the Giants were 13½ games behind the Dodgers as late as August 11, but finished the season winning 39 of their last 47 games to bring about the playoff.

Thomson's home run is one of the most famous moments in baseball, still talked about nearly 50 years later. It was no fluke that Thomson hit the home run; he led the Giants that season with 32 round-trippers, the best total of his 15-year career. His .293 batting average in '51 was the second-best full-season mark of his career, exceeded only by a .309 mark in 1949. Seven other times, Bobby had 20 or more homers; he drove in 100 or more runs four times.

Publisher: Spic & Span Dry Cleaners, Milwaukee, WI • Manufacturer: Not Indicated • Type: Black & White • Postmark: Not Used • Value: $50

Thomson was born in Glasgow, Scotland, in 1923—one of the few major league players born in Europe during the 20th century—hence his nickname, the Staten Island Scot. This advertising postcard, issued by Spic & Span Cleaners of Milwaukee, shows Bobby in a Braves uniform. He joined the Braves in 1954. Thomson also played with the Cubs, Red Sox, and Orioles before retiring following the 1960 season with a career .270 batting average and a storied place in baseball history.

1954 GIL HODGES, Brooklyn Dodgers

Publisher: Louis Dormand, #129 3593, Riverhead, NY • Manufacturer: Not Indicated • Type: Chrome • Postmark: Not Used • Value: $350

When the Brooklyn Dodgers moved to Los Angeles in 1958, Gil Hodges had been a member of the team longer than any other player. Hodges first played with the Dodgers in 1943, seeing action as a third baseman in one game. In three trips to the plate, he drew a walk and struck out twice. It was hardly an auspicious debut for a player who would become one of the finest first basemen of his time.

After spending a few years in military service during World War II, Hodges rejoined the Dodgers on a permanent basis in 1947 and was used primarily as a catcher. In 1948, he was converted to first base, where he remained for the bulk of his career.

This photograph by Louis Dormand was taken in 1954, one year before the Dodgers brought Brooklyn its only world championship. Hodges played well in that World Series, though teammate Duke Snider led the offense. It was Hodges' turn to lead in 1959, when the relocated Dodgers faced the White Sox in the World Series. During the regular season, he had batted .276 and led the team with 25 home runs, two more than

Snider. In the series, Hodges batted .391 as the Dodgers won in six.

Hodges later managed the expansion Washington Senators and New York Mets, whom he led to the world championship in 1969. Hodges' Dormand postcard is the rarest of the set, generally selling for more than $300 today.

1954 PEE WEE REESE, Brooklyn Dodgers

Publisher: Louis Dormand, #127 3591, Riverhead, NY • Manufacturer: Not Indicated • Type: Chrome • Postmark: Not Used • Value: $75–$100

Pee Wee Reese earned his nickname shooting marbles as a youngster in Louisville, Kentucky. He earned his Hall of Fame credentials as a star shortstop for 16 years with the Brooklyn and Los Angeles Dodgers. Pee Wee captained the Dodgers and was a big reason the club won seven pennants during his 15 years in Brooklyn. His lifetime .269 batting average doesn't begin to tell the story, as his fielding and leadership on and off the field are intangibles that can't be measured.

Reese was a scrappy competitor who frequently sparked the Dodgers' offense without swinging his bat. In 1954, he led the National League with 104 walks, in 1949 he was tops with 132 runs, and in 1952 he led all National Leaguers with 30 stolen bases. Coincidentally, the Dodgers were NL champs all three years.

Reese retired after the 1958 season, the Dodgers' first in Los Angeles. Following retirement, Reese served as a network baseball commentator and representative for Hillerick & Bradsby, manufacturers of Louisville slugger bats. He entered the Hall of Fame in 1984.

1954 LEO DUROCHER, New York Giants

Nice Guys Finish Last is the title of Leo Durocher's autobiography and a motto he lived by as both player and manager. Leo the Lip, as he was known for his outspoken personality, was a light-hitting shortstop who became a winning manager during his nearly 50 years in baseball. Durocher broke in with the Yankees

Publisher: Not Indicated • Manufacturer: Not Indicated
Type: Black & White • Postmark: Flushing, NY, Sept. 18, 1954
Value: $100–$125 Signed

for two games in 1925, going 0 for 1 in his only at-bat. He came back in '28 and stuck, batting .270 as the Yanks played their way to the world championship.

Only two years later, in 1930, Durocher found himself in Cincinnati, from where he was dealt to St. Louis in 1933. With the Cardinals, Durocher found himself on his second world championship team in 1934. Two years after that, he posted his highest batting average, .286.

Durocher's managerial career began in 1939 with the Brooklyn Dodgers, with whom he continued to play through 1945, though on a very limited basis for his final three seasons. Leo guided the Dodgers to the National League pennant in 1941. Suspended from baseball in '47 because of his friendship with gamblers, Durocher returned to manage the Dodgers for the first half of the '48 season before suddenly becoming manager of Brooklyn's hated rivals, the New York Giants. With the Giants, Durocher enjoyed his greatest success, leading the club to NL pennants in 1951 and '54 and a world championship in '54. Durocher also managed the Chicago Cubs from 1966 until '72 and the Houston Astros from the last part of '72 through '73. A colorful character his entire career, Durocher was inducted into the Hall of Fame in 1994.

Publisher: J.D. McCarthy, Oak Park, MI • Manufacturer: Not Indicated
Type: Black & White • Postmark: Montgomery, AL, Nov. 6, 1956
Value: $25–$35 Signed

1954 DUSTY RHODES, New York Giants

New York fans will always fondly remember pinch-hitter extraordinaire James "Dusty" Rhodes, who played a prominent role in the Giants' 1954 world championship season. Appearing in 82 games during the regular season, Rhodes batted .341—a career high—with 15 home runs and 50 RBI, also career marks. In the World Series against the heavily favored Cleveland Indians, who had set an American League record with 111 wins, Dusty was even more amazing. In three games, he batted .667 with four hits in six at-bats and led the team with four RBI and two home runs to almost single-handedly crush the Indians.

Rhodes had another fine season in '55, batting .305 in 94 games with 6 home runs and 32 RBI. The rest of his career was unremarkable. Rhodes completed his seven-year stint as a utility outfielder in 1959, with a .253 lifetime batting average. But he left with the knowledge that for one shining season, Dusty Rhodes had been the toast of baseball.

1954 BOBBY AVILA, Cleveland Indians

Mexico native Roberto "Bobby" Avila remains one of the finest players from that country to reach the majors. For 11 seasons, Avila was one of baseball's top second basemen. Joining the Cleveland Indians in 1949, he played with the Tribe for 10 seasons, winding up his career in 1959 with three different teams: the Baltimore Orioles, Boston Red Sox, and Milwaukee Braves.

Publisher: Cleveland Indians • Manufacturer: Not Indicated • Type: Real Photo • Postmark: Not Used • Value: $20

When the Indians won the '54 American League pennant, Avila led the league with a .341 batting average and notched career highs in home runs (15) and RBI (67). He had batted .300 or better previously in 1951 and 1952. Lifetime, he accrued a .281 average. One of the slickest fielders in the game, Avila saw action in several All-Star games. He is a member of the Mexican Baseball Hall of Fame. Pins, exhibit cards, and postcards are all prime Avila collectibles.

1954 MIKE GARCIA, Cleveland Indians

The 1954 Cleveland Indians ran roughshod over their American League opponents, winning an AL-record 111 games and finishing eight games in front of the defending world champion Yankees. The Tribe ended a string of five straight Yankee pennants and World Series championships. Under manager Al Lopez, the team's brilliant pitching, fine defense, and power hitting had them in first place by May 10.

Burly right-hander Mike Garcia, known as "The Big

Bear," played a key role in the Indians' success. Garcia led the AL with a 2.64 ERA while winning 19 games and losing only 8. He had won 20 games in 1951 and 22 in '52. When his career ended in 1961, he had posted a career total of 142 wins and 92 losses with a 3.27 ERA.

Cleveland was the favorite to win the '54 World Series, but the underdog National League–champion New York Giants upset the Indians in four straight games. Garcia started Game 3 and suffered the 6-2 loss. This photograph shows the 195-pound Big Bear putting all of his weight behind a fastball.

1954 BOB LEMON, Cleveland Indians

Right-hander Bob Lemon began his baseball career as a third baseman, joining the Indians in that capacity for five games in both 1941 and '42. But while serving in the military for three years during World War II, Lemon began to experiment as a pitcher. He pitched against Ted Williams, who was so impressed with Lemon's slider that he told Cleveland manager Lou Boudreau that

Publisher: Cleveland Indians • Manufacturer: Not Indicated • Type: Real Photo • Postmark: Not Used • Value: $40 Signed

Publisher: Cleveland Indians • Manufacturer: Not Indicated • Type: Real Photo Postmark: Cleveland, OH, Aug. 16, 1952 • Value: $40 Signed

Lemon was being wasted as an infielder. Thus when Lemon returned from the war in 1946, he pitched in 32 games, largely as a reliever, winning 4 and losing 5 with a 2.49 ERA. The next season, he went 11-5. In '48, when Cleveland won the pennant and World Series, Lemon led the way with 20 wins against 14 losses, plus two more victories in the World Series. Bob won 20 or more games seven times, producing a league-high 23 in 1950 and 1954. Lemon's 13-year big league totals of 207 wins versus 128 losses helped him to a spot in the Hall of Fame in 1976.

1954 RAY NARLESKI, Cleveland Indians

Right-hander Ray Narleski was an extremely effective relief pitcher for the Cleveland Indians from 1954 through 1958, finishing his six-year major league career with the Detroit Tigers in 1959. An elbow injury in 1956 hampered his effectiveness, although he was able to come back in '57 and '58, winning 11 and 13 games, respectively. In 1959, however, he won only 4 games

while losing 12. His record as a reliever with Cleveland was 39-21, but the 12 losses in '59 left his career totals at 43-33.

This real-photo postcard of Narleski is unique. It's an advertising card to promote Cleveland Indians Jeans, which were available only in a Cleveland department store in 1954 and '55.

1954 EARLY WYNN, Cleveland Indians

In 1954, Cleveland's "Big Three" pitching staff—Mike Garcia, Bob Lemon, and Early Wynn—was considered the best in baseball. The right-handed Wynn was probably the toughest, most competitive bird of the bunch. Famed for brushing back batters, Wynn was once asked if he would throw at his grandmother. "Only if she was digging in," he replied. But as fierce as he was to opponents, he was equally loyal to teammates. In 1949, while pitching for Cleveland, Wynn watched a Detroit pitcher throw twice at Indians outfielder Larry Doby, the American League's first black player. When the

Publisher: Cleveland Indians Jeans • Manufacturer: Not Indicated • Type: Real Photo • Postmark: Not Used • Value: $30–$40

Publisher: Cleveland Indians • Manufacturer: Not Indicated • Type: Real Photo • Postmark: Cleveland, OH, Aug. 9, 1956 • Value: $50 Signed

Publisher: Baltimore Orioles • Manufacturer: Not Indicated • Type: Real Photo • Postmark: Not Used • Value: $250–$300

pitcher came to bat, Wynn knocked him down four times on four straight pitches.

Wynn pitched for 23 seasons, seeing action in four decades. He began with the Washington Senators in 1939, was sent to the minors for the '40 season, then returned to the Senators from 1941–48. Arriving in Cleveland in '49, he soon became the Indians' workhorse, leading the AL in innings pitched twice and in starts three times over nine seasons. In 1954, he won a career-high 23 games, tying teammate Lemon for the AL lead.

Wynn was traded to the Chicago White Sox in 1958. In '59, at age 39, he won the Cy Young award, leading the AL with 22 wins, 37 starts, and $255^{1}/_{3}$ innings pitched. That year, the White Sox won their first pennant since 1919. Wynn returned to Cleveland in 1963 to earn his 300th win, then retired. Named to the Hall of Fame in 1972, he passed away on Easter Sunday 1999.

1954 MEMORIAL STADIUM, Baltimore Orioles

April 15, 1954. It was an important day in the history of Baltimore. For the first time since its original American League franchise had moved to New York in 1902, the city had its own major league club. As shown in this photograph, a crowd of 46,354 eager fans came to see

the Orioles beat the Chicago White Sox, 3-1. Unfortunately, the Orioles quickly sank into oblivion, ending the season with 54 wins and 100 losses, the second-worst record in the American League.

Despite the poor showing, the Orioles drew 1,060,910 fans during that initial season. The previous year, when the franchise was in St. Louis where it had been called the Browns, attendance was only 297,238. Owner Bill Veeck, beleaguered by cash-flow problems and debt, had been forced to sell the franchise to a group of Baltimore businessmen headed by Clarence W. Miles and James Keelty Jr.

1954 BOB TURLEY, Baltimore Orioles

If the 100-loss Orioles had a bright spot in their first season in Baltimore, it was flame-throwing right-hander Bob Turley. "Bullet Bob," as he was called, pitched the entire opening day game against the White Sox, striking out nine in the 3-1 win. Turley led the American League in strikeouts that year with 185, while giving Baltimore's fans 14 wins and 15 losses. Many of the losses can be classified as "heartbreakers." For example, in the first night game at Memorial Stadium, the Orioles were ahead of the Cleveland Indians 1-0 as Turley carried a no-hitter into the ninth. After getting the first out, Turley

Publisher: Baltimore Orioles • Manufacturer: Not Indicated • Type: Real Photo • Postmark: Not Used • Value: $60–$75

gave up a double to Al Rosen and a home run to Larry Doby for a 2-1 loss. He lost many well-pitched games because his teammates failed to produce many runs.

The following year, Turley went to the New York Yankees as part of a 17-player trade. He had success in New York, becoming the American League's first Cy Young award winner in 1958. That season, he led the AL in wins (21), winning percentage (.750), and complete games (19), and finished third in strikeouts with 168. He went on to become MVP of the '58 World Series, winning two games as the Yankees beat the Milwaukee Braves.

Converted to relief toward the end of his career, Turley retired in 1963—nine years after this photograph was taken in Yuma, Arizona, during the Orioles' first spring training.

TED KLUZEWSKI

Publisher: TCMA Ltd., Amawalk, NY • Manufacturer: Not Indicated • Type: Chrome • Postmark: Not Used • Value: $10 (recent vintage)

1954 TED KLUSZEWSKI, Cincinnati Reds

Ted Kluszewski was one of the most feared batters in baseball during his 15-year career, from 1947–1961. His lifetime .298 batting average was lowered considerably in the last five years. Klu batted .302 or better in five consecutive seasons with Cincinnati, from 1952–56, with a .326 average in 1954 standing as his best mark. That season was his best overall, as he led the National League with 49 home runs and 141 RBI.

In 1958, the Reds traded Ted to the Pirates, who in turn sent him to the Chicago White Sox late in the '59 season. It turned out to be a big break for Chicago, as the Sox won the pennant thanks largely to Klu's .297 average in 31 games. Getting a chance to play in his only World Series, Big Klu was at his best, hitting .391 with 3 home runs, 5 runs, and 10 RBI in Chicago's losing cause.

Publisher: Louis Dormand, #8023, Riverhead, NY
Manufacturer: Not Indicated • Type: Chrome • Postmark: Not Used
Value: $75–$100 Signed

Publisher: Louis Dormand, #113 65433, Riverhead, NY
Manufacturer: Not Indicated • Type: Chrome • Postmark: Not Used
Value: $150–$200 signed

1954 ENOS SLAUGHTER, New York Yankees

When this photograph was taken, Enos "Country" Slaughter was a New York Yankee with the best years of his career behind him. He was 38 years old and had been in the major leagues since 1938, when he joined the St. Louis Cardinals. Slaughter played baseball only one way—all out. In the eighth inning of Game 7 of the 1946 World Series, Slaughter's dash from first base to home plate gave the Cardinals a 4-3 win and the world championship. A decade later, he helped the Yankees win the 1956 Series, batting .350 with four RBI.

Slaughter bounced between New York, Kansas City, and Milwaukee in his final years. The gentleman farmer from North Carolina retired from baseball in 1959 with a career .300 batting average. He was inducted into the Hall of Fame in 1985.

1954 CASEY STENGEL, New York Yankees

The New York Yankees were the dominant team in baseball during the 1950s, winning the American League pennant every year except 1954 and 1959. Manager Casey Stengel was largely responsible for this success. Born Charles Dillon Stengel in Kansas City, Missouri, he acquired his nickname from the abbreviation of his hometown. Stengel was also dubbed "The Old Professor" for his ability to teach baseball. An avid student of the game, he devised the platoon system that employs right-handed batters against left-handed pitchers and vice versa. Extremely intelligent, Stengel was a dental school graduate who never practiced dentistry. He had a marvelous ability to tell stories, and crafted a language of double talk that became known as "Stengelese."

Stengel played for 14 years with the Dodgers, Pirates, Phillies, Giants, and Braves, ending his career in 1925 with a .284 lifetime batting average. He seemed to thrive in postseason play. In 12 games during three

Publisher: J.E. Tetrick, #SK 8208, Kansas City, MO • Manufacturer: Colour Picture, Boston, MA • Type: Chrome • Postmark: Not Used • Value: $20

different World Series, Stengel compiled a .393 batting average. However, it was his success as a manager that placed him in the Hall of Fame.

Stengel began managing in 1934 with the Brooklyn Dodgers. In 1938, he took over as skipper of the Boston Braves. In nine years of managing, Stengel never had a team finish higher than fifth place. Fired by the Braves after the 1943 season, he took a job managing the Oakland Oaks in the Pacific Coast League.

When Bucky Harris was fired as Yankees manager after the 1948 season, the 59-year-old Stengel was named to succeed him. The result was instant success. The Yankees won five consecutive World Series. The run came to an end in 1954, when the Indians won 111 games to capture the AL pennant. Ironically, Stengel's Yankees won 103 games that season, the most of any team he managed.

1955 MUNICIPAL STADIUM,
Kansas City Athletics

The state of Missouri lost its American League franchise before the 1954 season, when the St. Louis Browns moved to Baltimore and became the Orioles. Apparently the baseball gods could not abide such a void, for later that year, Chicago industrialist Arnold Johnson purchased the Philadelphia Athletics from Connie Mack

and prepared to move the team to Kansas City. The western Missouri metropolis proved ready for the team, showing excellent fan support. Despite the A's 63-91 record and sixth-place finish, 1,393,054 fans attended the games; only 304,666 bought tickets in the A's final season in Philadelphia.

The late-year sale of the team gave Kansas City just a few months to come up with a place for the A's to play. Johnson, who also owned the American Association's Kansas City Blues and its ballpark, sold Blues Stadium to the city for $500,000. Work immediately began on refurbishment. By Opening Day 1955, the capacity of the renamed Municipal Stadium was expanded from 17,000 to more than 30,000, enabling 32,844 fans to see President Harry Truman throw out the first pitch on April 2 and watch the A's beat the Detroit Tigers, 6-2. This postcard, featuring an artist's sketch, is the first issued for the stadium.

1955 AL KALINE, Detroit Tigers

Al Kaline jumped from Baltimore's Southern High straight into the majors with the Detroit Tigers in 1953. Two years later, at age 20, he was the American League batting champion with a .340 mark and a league-topping 200 hits. That same season, he socked 27 home runs and drove in 102 runs. Kaline was a model of

Publisher: Not Indicated • Manufacturer: Not Indicated • Type: Real Photo
Postmark: Detroit, MI, Sept. 6, 1956 • Value: $75–$100 Signed

consistency throughout his 22-year career, which he concluded in 1974 with a .297 lifetime average. He batted .304 or better nine times and topped 100 RBI three times, with 128 in 1956 his best effort. His final hit came off fellow Hall of Famer Jim Palmer, giving him a career total of 3,007.

A superb fielder with a powerful throwing arm, Kaline was named to the AL All-Star team 18 times. He got his only World Series chance in 1968 and made the most of it, giving a typical clutch performance with a .379 average, 2 home runs, and 8 RBI as he led the Tigers to victory in a seven-game thriller against the St. Louis Cardinals. His performance was overshadowed only by left-hander Mickey Lolich's three victories.

Al was elected to the Hall of Fame in 1980. Since his retirement, Kaline and fellow Hall of Famer George Kell have been sharing the Tigers television booth, where both display the same excellence they did as players.

1955 YOGI BERRA, New York Yankees

Lawrence Peter "Yogi" Berra was unquestionably one of the finest catchers in baseball history. His 19-season career began in 1946 and continued until 1965, when he appeared in four games as a player/coach with the New York Mets. Except for those four games, Berra played his entire career with the New York Yankees, whose dynastic run of championships in the 1950s can be attributed directly to their starting catcher. Berra appeared in a record 14 World Series with the Yankees; the team won all but four of them. In 1951, '54, and '55, Berra was named American League MVP. His contributions to his team's success, along with his career .285 batting average and 358 home runs, earned him induction into the Hall of Fame in 1972.

Yogi grew up in the Hill District of St. Louis, where he lived across the street from Joe Garagiola, another future major league catcher. Berra acquired his nickname from boyhood friend Jack McGuire. In a motion picture, McGuire saw a Hindu fakir—a disciple of

Publisher: Photo by Requina, #69891, New York, NY • Manufacturer: Not Indicated • Type: Chrome • Postmark: Not Used • Value: $35 Unsigned

Yoga—sit motionless with arms and legs folded and a strong facial expression. He decided the man looked like his pal Berra. From that time on, Berra was known as Yogi. Years later, a caricature of Berra's face became the inspiration for the cartoon character Yogi Bear.

1955 JIM KONSTANTY, New York Yankees

Publisher: Louis Dormand, #138 12821, Riverhead, NY • Manufacturer: Not Indicated • Type: Chrome • Postmark: Not Used • Value: $125–$150 Signed

Right-hander Jim Konstanty achieved a unique distinction in 1950, becoming the first relief pitcher in major league history to win the MVP award. Appearing in 74 games for Philadelphia, all in relief, Konstanty won 16, lost only 7, and saved 22 while compiling an ERA of 2.66. He was the principal reason the Phillies won their first pennant since 1915. Pressed into a starting role in the World Series when Curt Simmons departed for military service, Konstanty lost a 1-0 heartbreaker to the New York Yankees. Ironically, Konstanty joined the Yankees late in the '54 season and became a standout reliever for New York in 1955, compiling a 7-2 record.

1956 GEORGE KELL, Baltimore Orioles

This illustration of third baseman George Kell was issued by the Orioles when he joined the team in 1956, at the end of an outstanding American League career. Kell began in the majors in 1943 with the Philadelphia Athletics, was traded to the Detroit Tigers in 1946, went to the Boston Red Sox in 1952, then to the Chicago White Sox in 1954, and lastly to the Orioles in 1956. Everywhere he went, Kell found success. In 1949, with the Tigers, he won the AL batting title with a .343 batting average. The next year, he batted .340 with a career-best 101 RBI.

In 1956, Orioles manager Paul Richards welcomed Kell both for his performance with bat and glove and for his teaching skills. Richards needed someone to tutor an outstanding young third base prospect named Brooks Robinson. Kell worked tirelessly with Robinson, teaching him the tricks of the hot corner. When Kell retired after the 1957 season, he knew his protégé was ready to take over. Both Kell and Robinson were eventually elected to the Hall of Fame.

GEORGE CLYDE KELL
(GEORGE)

Publisher: Baltimore Orioles • Manufacturer: Not Indicated • Type: Real Photo • Postmark: Not Used • Value: $50 Signed

Publisher: Baltimore Orioles • Manufacturer: Not Indicated • Type: Real Photo • Postmark: New York, NY, July 3, 1956 • Value: $35 Signed

1956 GEORGE ZUVERINK, Baltimore Orioles

The last player listed in *The Baseball Encyclopedia,* right-hander George Zuverink was one of the better relief pitchers of the 1950s. He led the American League in appearances in two consecutive seasons, pitching in 62 games in 1956 and 56 in 1957, both with the Orioles. He also led the AL in saves with 16 in 1956 while posting a 7-6 record. The next year, Zuverink had his best overall season, winning a career-high 10 games against 6 losses, compiling a career-best 2.15 ERA, and notching 9 saves.

Zuverink broke in with the Indians in 1951, returned to the minors in '52, and saw duty with the Reds and Tigers before heading to Baltimore early in the '55 season. His eight-year totals show 32 wins, 36 losses, and an ERA of 3.54.

1956 HARMON KILLEBREW, Washington Senators

Harmon Killebrew has the unique distinction of being the only member of the Baseball Hall of Fame to sign a major league contract based on the recommendation of a U.S. Senator. Playing high school and semi-pro ball in his hometown of Payette, Idaho, Killebrew gained the attention of Idaho senator Herman Welker. Speaking with his friend, Washington Senators owner Clark Griffith, Welker urged the Senators to offer a contract to the 17-year-old Killebrew, claiming Harmon would become better than Mickey Mantle. Well, Killebrew never did match Mantle's foot speed or batting average, but he did hit more home runs than The Mick.

Following up Welker's recommendation, Senators farm director Ossie Bluege went to Idaho to see Killebrew and returned impressed. He advised signing the youngster to a bonus contract of $30,000, the highest paid by the Senators to that date. Initially, Killebrew struggled at the plate, but he eventually achieved his potential and enjoyed a 22-year major league career with the Senators, Minnesota Twins, and Kansas City

Publisher: Don Wingfield, Alexandria, VA • Manufacturer: Not Indicated
Type: Chrome • Postmark: Not Used • Value: $50 Unsigned

Royals. In 1959, his first season as a full-time player, "Killer" smacked 42 home runs to lead the American League. He went on to win or share the AL home run title five more times, belting 40 or more in eight seasons. In all, he hit 573 home runs in his career—good for fifth on the all-time list—while playing third base, outfield, and first base.

This is the only color postcard produced by photographer Don Wingfield. It was taken in 1959, the only year Killebrew's team wore zip-up jerseys that read "Senators" on the front.

1956 DON LARSEN, New York Yankees

Publisher: J.D. McCarthy, Oak Park, MI • Manufacturer: Not Indicated
Type: Black & White • Postmark: New York, NY, Aug. 12, 1956 • Value: $35

On October 8, 1956, facing the Brooklyn Dodgers, right-hander Don Larsen was immortalized forever. That was the date Larsen pitched the only perfect game in World Series history. In fact, Larsen excelled in 10 World Series appearances over five different years, winning 4 and losing 2 while compiling a fine 2.75 ERA. Overall, however, his 14-year career with eight different teams—the Browns, Orioles, Yankees, Athletics, White Sox, Giants, Astros, and Cubs—was generally unproductive. Larsen's career regular-season record was 81 wins and 91 defeats, 21 of the latter coming with Baltimore in 1954, when he led the league in losses.

Traded to the Yankees after the '54 season along with Bob Turley in a multiplayer deal, Larsen turned his career around, going 9-2, 11-5, and 10-4 the next three years with New York. Larsen suffered an elbow injury in 1958 and was never the same thereafter. But his perfect game in the '56 World Series will keep his name alive forever in baseball annals. The most sought-after Don Larsen collectible is a plate commemorating that remarkable feat.

1956 MICKEY MANTLE, New York Yankees

As he did in center field at Yankee Stadium, Mickey Mantle followed in the footsteps of Joe DiMaggio by lending his name to a restaurant. The Dugout Lounge at the Holiday Inn in Joplin, Missouri, may not have had the glamour of San Francisco's Fisherman's Wharf, where DiMaggio's restaurant was located. But the experience gave Mantle the background that would help years later when he lent his name to a restaurant in New York City, which remains open today, years after his death in 1995.

When The Mick first joined the Yankees in 1951, manager Casey Stengel hailed him as Babe Ruth, Lou Gehrig, and DiMaggio all rolled into one. At first, Mantle struggled to live up to the billing. But by 1956, when he won the AL triple crown with a .353 batting average, 52 home runs, and 130 RBI, Mantle had proven himself.

Despite an arrested case of osteomyelitis, numerous injuries, and frequent surgery on his knees—which bothered him throughout his career—Mantle is remembered

Publisher: Holiday Inn, #2DK 33, Joplin, MO • Manufacturer: Curt Teich Co., Chicago, IL • Type: Chrome • Postmark: Not Used • Value: $30–$40

as a speedy base runner who also hit some of the longest home runs in baseball. Mantle hit one homer 565 feet out of Washington's Griffith Stadium. After 18 years, all with the Yankees, Mantle had 536 home runs and a .298 lifetime batting average. He retired after the 1968 season and was a first-ballot Hall of Fame inductee in 1974.

1957 LEW BURDETTE, Milwaukee Braves

Publisher: Bill & Bob, #48136, Bradenton, FL • Manufacturer: Not Indicated
Type: Chrome • Postmark: Not Used • Value: $75–$100 Signed

In the late 1950s, the Milwaukee Braves won two pennants (1957 and '58) and finished second in the National League three times ('56, '59, and '60). The team's success was due in no small part to pitchers Warren Spahn, Bob Buhl, and Lew Burdette—the Big Three.

Right-hander Lew gave no indication of his later success when he came up with the Yankees in 1950. He had no wins or losses his first two seasons in the big leagues. With Boston in 1952, he finally broke into the win column, but wound up with 11 losses to go along with his 6 victories.

Things improved dramatically for Burdette in 1957

when the Braves won their first pennant in Milwaukee. Lew became the Braves' World Series hero, defeating the Yankees three times in three starts to help his team to the championship. When the Braves won another pennant in '58, Burdette won 20 games for the first time, losing 10 as he compiled the NL's best winning percentage (.667) that season. In '59, when the Braves finished second to the Dodgers, Lew led the league with 21 victories.

After a 1967 campaign in which he pitched in 19 games and compiled a 1-0 record for the California Angels, Burdette finally retired with 203 victories against only 144 defeats, plus 4 more wins in the World Series.

1957 FRED HANEY, Milwaukee Braves

This colorful Bill and Bob postcard shows Milwaukee manager Fred Haney, who led the Braves to back-to-back National League pennants in 1957 and '58 and a world championship in '57. Both times, the Braves faced the New York Yankees, and each Series went the entire seven games.

Haney took the reins of the Braves from Charley

Publisher: Bill & Bob, #28170, Bradenton, FL • Manufacturer: Not Indicated
Type: Chrome • Postmark: Milwaukee, WI, Sept. 12, 1957
Value: $75 Unsigned

Grimm 46 games into the 1956 season, overseeing a surge in which the Braves won 68 games and lost 40. The spurt propelled the club to second place, one game behind the defending-champion Dodgers. Haney left the Braves following the '59 season to become general manager of the expansion California Angels, who began play in the American League in 1961.

Prior to his brilliant success with the Braves, who never finished lower than second during his four years as skipper, Haney managed bad teams. In six years—three with the St. Louis Browns and three with the Pittsburgh Pirates—he never had a team come close to a winning season. Overall, Haney's 10-year managerial record shows 629 wins and 757 losses.

1957 EDDIE MATHEWS, Milwaukee Braves

When the Braves moved from Boston to Milwaukee in 1953, third baseman Eddie Mathews hit 47 home runs to lead the National League, immediately winning the hearts of Milwaukee fans. The previous year, in his rookie season

at Boston, Mathews hit 25 home runs. The move to Milwaukee, where the left field fence was 17 feet closer than it had been in Boston, helped improve Eddie's power hitting. When he retired in 1968, he had 512 career home runs—enough to earn him election to the Hall of Fame in 1978.

In 1957, Mathews helped the Braves win their first pennant in Milwaukee, batting .292 with 32 home runs and 94 RBI. The team went on to win the World Series that year. Mathews and Hank Aaron helped bring the city another pennant in '58, but the Braves lost the championship to the Yankees, four games to three.

This photograph, shot in Bradenton during spring training, was released on a Spic and Span Dry Cleaners promotional postcard.

1957 ROY CAMPANELLA, Brooklyn Dodgers

In the '50s, baseball's most dominant catchers both made their homes in New York. Yogi Berra of the Yankees was the top catcher in the American League, while Brooklyn's Roy Campanella was the best catcher in the

Publisher: Bill & Bob, #13503, Bradenton, FL • Manufacturer: Not Indicated
Type: Chrome • Postmark: Reensburg, WI, April 10, 1956
Value: $175–$200 Signed

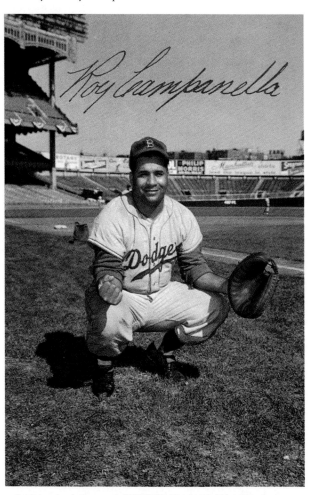

Publisher: Louis Dormand, #125 3590, Riverhead, NY • Manufacturer: Not Indicated • Type: Chrome • Postmark: Not Used
Value: $175–$200 Unsigned

BALTIMORE ORIOLES—1957

Publisher: Baltimore Orioles • Manufacturer: Not Indicated • Type: Black & White • Postmark: Not Used • Value: $250

National League. The pair's careers had other similarities. Each was named Most Valuable Player three times, both were outstanding handlers of their pitchers, and both had an ability to produce timely base hits in important situations.

Born in 1921, Campanella signed a professional baseball contract with the Baltimore Elite Giants of the Negro National League when he was only 15 years old. He soon became one of the league's stars. After the major leagues were integrated in 1947, Campanella joined Jackie Robinson on the Dodgers' roster. In 1948, his first season, he batted .258 in 83 games. It was an inauspicious beginning to a superb 10-year career that ended all too abruptly. Early in 1958, weeks before spring training was set to open, Campanella's car skidded on a slick road and crashed into a telephone pole. Campy broke his back and became a paraplegic. Lesser men might have become bitter because of the tragedy, but Campanella maintained a marvelous attitude. In 1969, when he was inducted into the Hall of Fame, he recalled one of his favorite expressions: "There's a bit of little boy in every good ballplayer." Campy's "little boy" attitude helped him to overcome his problems. He maintained his positive outlook until he died in 1993.

1957 BALTIMORE ORIOLES

In 1957, the Orioles enjoyed their best season since their departure from St. Louis, where they had played as the Browns until 1954. Under manager Paul Richards, the team reached the .500 mark, finishing 76-76. First baseman Bob Boyd led the team in batting with a .318 average, while one-time batting champ Billy Goodman hit .308 in a utility role. Most of the club's power came from catcher Gus Triandos, who supplied 19 home runs and 72 RBI, and left fielder Bob Nieman, with 13 homers and 70 RBI. Third baseman George Kell batted .297 while tutoring his protégé, Brooks Robinson. Robinson appeared in 50 games that season, and though he batted only .239, he still played excellent defense. Even with the team's mediocre finish, four pitchers managed double-digit win totals: Connie Johnson (14), Billy Loes (12), Ray Moore (11), and George Zuverink (10), who also appeared in a league-high 56 games. This team-issued real-photo postcard is extremely hard to find and brings $250 or more today.

1957 ROY SIEVERS, Washington Senators

ROY SIEVERS - WASHINGTON NATIONALS
Copyright 1955 - Don Wingfield
Griffith Stadium, Washington, D. C.

Publisher: Don Wingfield, Alexandria, VA • Manufacturer: Not Indicated
Type: Real Photo • Postmark: Mt. Rainier, MD, Aug. 17, 1955 • Value: $60–$75

Roy "Squirrel" Sievers was an excellent outfielder/first baseman for 17 big-league seasons. Sievers broke in with his hometown St. Louis Browns in 1949 but was traded in 1954 to Washington, where he enjoyed his finest seasons. From 1954 through 1959, he never hit fewer than 21 home runs for the Senators. In 1957, he led the American League in that category, hitting 42 home runs, while also driving in an AL-best 114 runs and compiling a career-high .301 batting average. Sievers also topped 100 RBI in 1954 (102), '55 (106), and '58 (108).

Sievers was traded to the Chicago White Sox in 1960, to the Phillies in '62, and back to the Senators in '64, remaining in Washington until he retired in '65. His 318 career home runs testify to his ability to hit with power. Today, a 1955 Don Wingfield postcard of Sievers commands $75 in mint condition.

1957 JIM BUNNING, Detroit Tigers

Right-hander Jim Bunning amassed 224 major league wins almost equally divided between the American League (118 with the Detroit Tigers) and the National League (106 with the Phillies, Pirates, and Dodgers). He won 20 in a season only once, in 1957, but won 19 games four times in the 1960s. Jim was also his league's strikeout king three times—with the Tigers in '59 and '60, when he recorded 201 Ks in each season, and in '67, when he struck out 253 for the Phillies. He notched a career-best 268 Ks in 1966, but finished fourth in strikeouts behind Sandy Koufax, who had 382 that year.

As his strikeout records show, Bunning was one of the hardest throwers in the game. After 17 seasons, he retired, eventually entering politics. In fact, Bunning was representing his native Kentucky in Congress when he was elected to the Hall of Fame in 1996.

Publisher: Graphic Art Service, Cincinnati, OH • Manufacturer: Not Indicated
Type: Black & White • Postmark: Not Used • Value: $25 Unsigned

Publisher: J.D. McCarthy, Oak Park, MI • Manufacturer: Not Indicated
Type: Black & White • Postmark: Not Used • Value: $30

1958 ERNIE BANKS, Chicago Cubs

Ernie Banks played his entire 19-year major league career in Chicago; he is fondly remembered as "Mr. Cub." Purchased from the Kansas City Monarchs of the Negro League in 1953 for $25,000, Banks immediately established his big-league credentials with a .314 batting average in 10 games. Originally a shortstop, Ernie converted to first base when bad knees began to hamper his mobility. The problem didn't hamper his bat, which pounded out an average of 27 home runs per season. Banks established his home run hitting credentials in only his second full season in 1955, when he blasted 44. During his peak home run years, 1957–1960, he walloped 43, 47 (still the record for a shortstop), 45, and 41.

Although Banks never played on a championship team, he won back-to-back NL MVP awards in '58 and '59. Those were the only full seasons that he batted above .300 (.313 with 129 RBI in '58, .304 and 143 RBI

in '59), but he drove in 102 or more runs six other times.

Ernie's sunny disposition made him perhaps the most popular player in Cubs' history. He was elected to the Hall of Fame in 1977 with 512 career home runs and a lifetime .274 batting average.

Publisher: Falstaff Brewing Corp., St. Louis, MO • Manufacturer: Not Indicated • Type: Chrome • Postmark: Not Used • Value: $100

1958 SAN FRANCISCO GIANTS

For New York baseball fans, 1958 is a year that will live in infamy. That was the year the Giants and Dodgers moved to California, bringing major league baseball to the West Coast. This Giants advertising postcard, published by the team's new radio and television sponsor, shows the initial San Francisco club, which finished third in the league behind Milwaukee and Pittsburgh with a record of 80 wins and 74 losses. Center fielder Willie Mays led the Giants with a .347 batting average, second in the National League behind Richie Ashburn's .350 mark for Philadelphia. Mays' team-leading .583 slugging average was second in the NL to Ernie Banks' .614. Mays also shared the team lead in RBI with first baseman Orlando Cepeda, who batted .312; each drove in 96 runs. Although the Giants had no 20-game winners that year, left-hander Johnny Antonelli finished sixth in the NL with 16 victories, while Stu Miller was the NL's ERA leader with a 2.47 mark. Four years later many of the same players would lead the Giants to the NL pennant.

1958 WILLIE MAYS, San Francisco Giants

Willie Mays was one of the most exciting players in baseball. The multitalented "Say Hey Kid" was able to do everything required in the game. He had great speed, could hit with power, and was able to catch almost every fly ball hit to center field, where he ranked as one of the best defensive outfielders.

If Mays were to be remembered for only one play, it would be his catch of a 450-foot drive by Cleveland's Vic

Wertz in the first game of the 1954 World Series. Playing at the Polo Grounds, the Giants and Indians were tied 2-2 in the eighth inning, with two Cleveland runners on base. Wertz sent a tremendous drive into deep center field. Mays began running at the crack of the bat and caught the ball over his shoulder in front of the wall while running at full speed. Baseball writer Fred Leib, who had covered World Series games for more than 50 years, called it the greatest catch that he had ever seen. Most important for the Giants, the catch prevented a triple by Wertz and kept the winning run from scoring. That play was the climax of an outstanding season in which Mays batted a league-high .345, hit 41 home runs, and had 110 RBI, earning the Most Valuable Player award. After the Giants moved to San Francisco in 1958, Mays batted .347 and led the NL with 121 runs scored. This card shows Mays in a New York Mets uniform, which he wore in 1972 and '73 before retiring. He was inducted into the Hall of Fame in 1979.

Publisher: Ford Motor Co., Dearborn, MI • Manufacturer: Not Indicated
Type: Chrome • Postmark: Not Used • Value: $100

1958 ROCKY COLAVITO, Cleveland Indians

Power-hitting Rocky Colavito probably will never make the Hall of Fame. Nevertheless, he was one of baseball's most feared power hitters in his day. Over 14 excellent years, Colavito compiled a .266 batting average with 374 home runs and 1,159 RBI.

A free-swinging slugger who broke in with the Indians in 1955, Rocky became an instant fan favorite in Cleveland. In 1958, he batted .303, topping .300 for the first and only time in his career, while slamming 41 home runs and driving in 113 runs. Although his average dipped to .257 in '59, he drove in 111 runs and led the American League with 42 homers.

Traded in 1960 to Detroit, where this postcard photo was taken, Colavito continued his prodigious slugging with the Tigers. He belted 35 home runs his first year in Detroit. Unfortunately, his career-best 45 homers and

Publisher: J.D. McCarthy, Royal Oak, MI • Manufacturer: Not Indicated
Type: Black & White • Postmark: Not Used • Value: $20 Unsigned

140 RBI in '61 got lost in the noise surrounding Roger Maris' surpassing of Babe Ruth's single-season home run record. In 1962, Rocky had 112 RBI along with 37 home runs. After his production fell to 22 homers and 91 RBI in '63, the Tigers traded him to the Kansas City Athletics. Rocky bounced back with 34 home runs and 102 RBI in '64. In 1965, he was traded back to Cleveland, where he socked 26 home runs and led the league with 108 RBI and 93 walks. Thereafter, he served short stints with the White Sox, Dodgers, and Yankees before retiring in 1968.

1958 BROOKS ROBINSON, Baltimore Orioles

Recognized by many as the finest defensive third baseman ever to play the game, Brooks Robinson is also one of the nicest guys ever to put on a major league uniform. He's arguably the most popular player in Baltimore Ori-

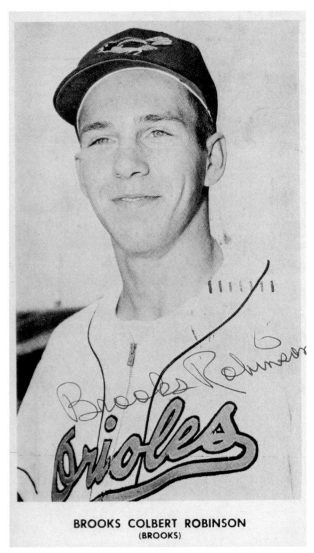

BROOKS COLBERT ROBINSON
(BROOKS)

Publisher: Baltimore Orioles • Manufacturer: Not Indicated • Type: Black & White • Postmark: Baltimore, MD, July 26, 1957 • Value: $50

oles' history, earning the title "Mr. Oriole" during his 23 years with the Birds. "Brooksy" was beloved not only for his tenure with the team and competitive fire, but for his on-field accomplishments, which included winning the 1964 American League MVP award with career highs in batting average (.317), home runs (28), and RBI (118); winning 16 Gold Gloves, a major league record Robinson shares with pitcher Jim Kaat; appearing in 16 All-Star Games, including the 1966 mid-summer classic, where he won the All-Star MVP award; and being named MVP of the 1970 World Series, when his one-man display of offensive and defensive mastery derailed Cincinnati's Big Red Machine. Robinson batted .429 in the Orioles' five-game triumph while earning the title "Human Vacuum Cleaner" for his dazzling play in the field.

Robinson first came up with the Orioles for six games in 1955. Originally a shortstop, he was brought up from the minors again in '56 and '57 to study third base–play under Hall of Famer George Kell. Robinson became the Orioles' regular hot corner–man in '58 and retained the post until his retirement in '77. He was elected to the Hall of Fame in 1983, his first eligible year. This team-issued postcard from 1957 is the first of many featuring the Oriole Hall of Famer.

1959 BOB BUHL, Milwaukee Braves

Right-hander Bob Buhl joined the Braves in 1953, the club's initial season in Milwaukee. He proved to be a big factor in the team's rise to the top, which culminated in back-to-back pennants in 1957 and '58. Though he was frequently overshadowed by teammates Warren Spahn and Lew Burdette, Buhl had the National League's best winning percentage in 1957 with a .720

Publisher: Baltimore Orioles • Manufacturer: Not Indicated • Type: Black & White • Postmark: Baltimore, MD, July 26, 1957 • Value: $50

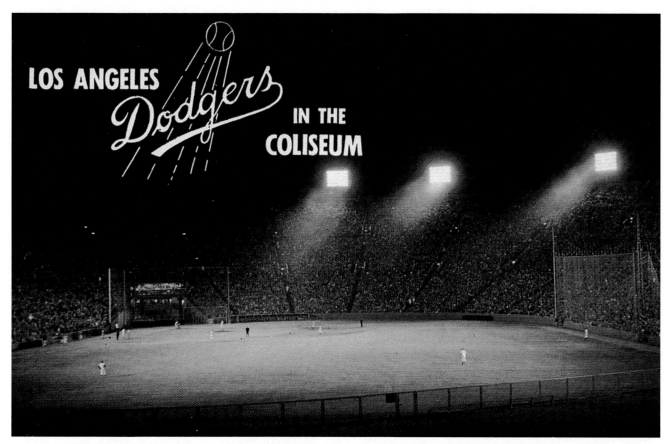

Publisher: Souvenir Color Card Co., #LA 1126, Los Angeles, CA • Manufacturer: H.S. Crocker Co., Los Angeles, CA • Type: Chrome
Postmark: Not Used • Value: $20–$25

(18-7) mark. He had gone 18-8 the year before, as Milwaukee finished a game behind the Dodgers in the NL pennant race.

Buhl developed arm trouble in '58, winning only five games while losing two. He bounced back to win 15 games in '59 and 16 in '60. Traded to the Cubs in 1962, Buhl won 57 games over his last six seasons. After spending 1967 with the Phillies, he concluded his impressive 15-year career with a record of 166 wins and 132 losses.

1959 COLISEUM, Los Angeles Dodgers

This postcard, featuring a photograph taken at Los Angeles' Coliseum on May 7, 1959, shows the largest crowd in the history of major league baseball. The event was not a regular season game but an exhibition to honor Dodgers catcher Roy Campanella, who had been paralyzed in an automobile accident the year before. The Dodgers played the Yankees before 93,103 fans, with the proceeds going to help pay Campy's huge hospital expenses. Even the vast Coliseum could not accommodate everyone who wanted a ticket; 15,000 fans were turned away because the stadium was filled to capacity. With the modern trend toward smaller baseball parks with capacities limited to

50,000 or less, we can assume a crowd of this size will not be topped anytime soon.

This picture, taken from a high position in the left center field seats, shows the short distance between the left field stands and home plate—only 250 feet. It also shows the vast space in right center field, stretching 440 feet from home.

1959 DUKE SNIDER, Los Angeles Dodgers

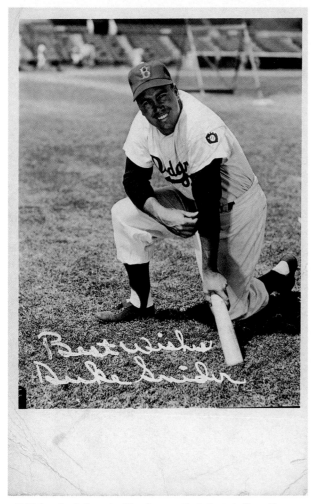

Publisher: Not Indicated • Manufacturer: Not Indicated • Type: Chrome
Postmark: Not Used • Value: $75 Unsigned

Dodger right fielder Duke Snider was a fan favorite in Brooklyn who became equally popular in Los Angeles, his hometown. Snider had been a member of the club for 12 years when this photograph was taken in 1959. That year, he led the Dodgers with a .308 batting average and 88 RBI, helping them win the 1959 pennant.

Fine as his season was, it didn't top Snider's 1955 performance, when he batted .309 with 42 home runs and led the National League with 136 RBI and 126 runs scored. That year, the Dodgers won both the pennant and their first World Series. Snider was a big part of the team's success on both coasts.

1959 DON MOSSI, Detroit Tigers

Left-hander Don Mossi pitched 12 seasons in the majors, proving to be one of the top relief pitchers of his era as well as a successful starter. With Cleveland, for whom he pitched his first five years, he was used almost exclusively in relief. When he went to the Tigers in 1959, Detroit used him primarily in a starting role. Mossi came up with the Indians in their pennant-winning '54 season. Appearing in 40 games, all but five of them in relief, he went 6-1 with a 1.94 ERA, the lowest of his career. The 111-win Indians finished the season a heavy favorite to beat the New York Giants in the World Series. Despite the Indians' record season and Mossi's strong performance—he didn't allow an earned run in three games—the Giants socked the Tribe in four straight.

Mossi worked his way into the Indians' rotation in

Publisher: Ford Motor Co., Dearborn, MI • Manufacturer: Not Indicated
Type: Chrome • Postmark: Not Used • Value: $75–$85 Signed

'57, starting 22 times and finishing 11-10. Traded to Detroit in '59, he started in 30 of his 34 games, winning a career-high 17 while losing only 9. Retaining a starting role, he went 15-7 for the Tigers in 1961. When he retired after the '65 season with Kansas City, his career totals showed 101 wins and 80 defeats. Mossi appears on postcards with both Cleveland and Detroit.

1959 NELLIE FOX, Chicago White Sox

In 1959, the Chicago White Sox were called the "Go-Go Sox" for their speed and daring on the bases and their superb defensive ability. The combination enabled the team to overcome relatively weak hitting and win the American League pennant. Nellie Fox personified the go-go spirit, igniting rallies by getting on base, driving in key runs, and ending opponents' rallies with remarkable fielding. Fox led the 1959 White Sox with a .306 batting average and was second on the team in RBI with 70 to catcher Sherman Lollar's 84. The quick-fielding Fox also led all AL second basemen in putouts and assists, forming a superb double-play combination with shortstop Luis Aparicio. Fox was rewarded with the 1959 AL Most Valuable Player award. In the World Series, Fox batted .375, connecting nine times in 24 at-bats. Despite his heroics, the Sox lost to the Dodgers, four games to two.

Fox retired in 1965 with a .288 career batting average. Five times in his 19 seasons, he led the American League in base hits. Despite his great play, he was overlooked for years by baseball writers who vote on Hall of Fame inductees. Thanks to public statements by baseball authorities like Ted Williams, Fox was voted into the Hall by his peers in 1997.

Publisher: Nellie Fox Bowl, Chambersburg, PA • Manufacturer: Not Indicated
Type: Black & White • Postmark: Not Used • Value: $20–$25 Unsigned

1960-69

The 1960s were a turbulent period in American history, what with the Vietnam war, war protests, race riots, and the assassinations of President John F. Kennedy, Robert Kennedy, and Martin Luther King. All of these events had an effect on baseball, but the game emerged from the turmoil in surprisingly good health.

In 1960, the Yankees returned to the World Series after missing out in '59, only to be upset by the Pittsburgh Pirates on Bill Mazeroski's dramatic home run in the bottom of the ninth inning of the seventh game. Soon after, for the first time since before the turn of the century, baseball expanded from 16 to 18 teams as the American League added new teams in Washington and Los Angeles. The Washington franchise replaced the original Senators, who moved to Bloomington, Minnesota to become the Twins before the 1961 season. In Los Angeles, former cowboy star Gene Autry headed up the group that owned the Angels. The National League followed suit the next year, adding the New York Mets and Houston Colt 45s for the '62 season.

Just prior to that, the '61 season had a Hollywood finish as Yankee outfielder Roger Maris earned his second consecutive MVP award and broke Babe Ruth's single-season home run record of 60 by hitting 61. Maris battled Mickey Mantle most of the year for the record, but late-season injuries took The Mick out of the race. The Yankees beat the Cincinnati Reds in the '61 World Series, then beat the San Francisco Giants the following year in seven games played over 13 days because of torrential rain in California. Ralph Terry was the Yankee hero in '62, winning two of his three games, including the finale.

Hall of Fame pitchers Don Drysdale and Sandy Koufax stymied the Yankee bats in the '63 Series as the Dodgers won in four. In '64, Cardinals Hall of Famer Bob Gibson won two Series games as St. Louis outlasted the Yankees in seven. The Dodgers returned to the Fall Classic in '65, beating Minnesota four games to three in the Twins' first World Series appearance. Koufax got his final World Series victory in the seventh game that year, tossing a three-hit shutout.

Pitching continued to decide the World Series throughout the decade. In '66, the Dodgers were stunned by the Baltimore Orioles, who swept them in four games as Jim Palmer, Wally Bunker, and Dave McNally pitched shutouts and Moe Drabowsky added a win in relief of McNally. The next year, the Cardinals' Gibson proved too much for the Red Sox, winning three games without a loss, while

Publisher: Digree Photographers, Minneapolis, MN • Manufacturer: Dexter Press, W. Nyack, NY • Type: Chrome • Postmark: Not Used • Value: $100–$125

"BOOG" POWELL/AMERICAN LEAGUE/ COPYRIGHT PRO STAR PROMOTIONS INC.
Printed in Canada

Publisher: Pro Star Promotions, Canada • Manufacturer: Not Indicated
Type: Color Lithograph • Postmark: Not Used • Value: $5–$8

Boston's Cy Young winner, Jim Lonborg, won two but ran out of gas in the final, losing to Gibson. Denny McLain won a phenomenal 31 games during the regular season to get the Tigers into the '68 Series, where he was picked up by teammate Mickey Lolich. The lefty won three games against the Cardinals, beating Gibson in the seventh game. In 1969, Gil Hodges' Miracle Mets stunned the Orioles four games to one, thanks to two wins by Jerry Koosman and one each by Tom Seaver and Gary Gentry, along with a save by Nolan Ryan.

Off the field, collecting baseball mementos became a legitimate hobby as the '60s rolled along. The same boys who made baseball cards an American staple in the 1950s grew up, and many of them maintained their interest in collectibles related to their heroes. The Hartland Plastics Co. of Hartland, Wisconsin, met the memorabilia demand, producing a series of baseball statues designed by Frank Fulop. Today, the original 11 figures—all of which depicted future Hall of Famers—sell for at least $200 each.

1960 DICK GROAT, Pittsburgh Pirates

Dick Groat was an all-American baseball and basketball player at Duke University who went on to spend 14 seasons as a major league shortstop, compiling a .286 lifetime batting average. He had his best year in 1960, when his .325 average led the National League and helped the Pirates win the pennant en route to a World Series championship. Groat's best RBI season came the year after he was traded away from the Pirates, 1963, when he drove in 73 runs for the St. Louis Cardinals. He also batted .319 that season. Groat was instrumental in the Cardinals' 1964 pennant-winning season, batting .292 and driving in 70 runs. Although Dick batted only .192 in the '64 World Series, the Cardinals beat the Yankees in seven games. An outstanding fielder as well as a timely hitter, Groat stands a slim chance of someday being admitted to the Hall of Fame.

Publisher: Pittsburgh Pirates • Manufacturer: Not Indicated • Type: Black & White • Postmark: Not Used • Value: $25 Signed

1960 BILL MAZEROSKI, Pittsburgh Pirates

Bill Mazeroski is responsible for one of the great moments in baseball history. His leadoff home run off Yankee right-hander Ralph Terry in the bottom of the ninth inning of the seventh game of the World Series gave the Pirates the 1960 championship. For pure drama, the moment will live forever in baseball lore.

Maz spent all 17 of his big-league seasons with the Pirates, compiling a .260 lifetime batting average and earning recognition as one of the finest defensive second baseman in history. Longtime rival Pete Rose paid him the ultimate compliment when he said, "Maz was the best I ever saw at turning the double play."

Offensively, Mazeroski was consistent throughout his career. His best-remembered year, 1960, was one of his better seasons, as he batted .273 and drove in 64 runs to help the Pirates grab the pennant. He batted his career high, .283, in 1957, his first full season in the majors, bashed a career-best 19 home runs the next year, and drove in a lifetime-high 82 runs in 1966.

Well past his peak by 1971, Mazeroski still was able to contribute to another Pirates pennant and world championship. One of the most popular players in

Publisher: Pittsburgh Pirates • Manufacturer: Not Indicated • Type: Black & White • Postmark: Not Used • Value: $25 Signed

Publisher: Falstaff Brewing Co., St. Louis, MO • Manufacturer: Not Indicated • Type: Chrome • Postmark: Not Used • Value: $100

Pirates history, Mazeroski watched as his number 9 was retired on August 7, 1987.

1961 LOS ANGELES ANGELS

In 1961, the American League expanded for the first time, putting teams in Los Angeles and Washington. The advertising postcard pictured at the bottom of the facing page, published by the Angels' radio and TV sponsor, shows the initial California team. The 1961 Los Angeles Angels played better than expected under manager Bill Rigney, finishing eighth in the new 10-team set-up, winning 70 and losing 91. No future Hall of Famers graced the Angels' lineup, but right-hander Ken McBride was fifth in the AL that season with 180 strikeouts and 6.70 strikeouts per nine innings pitched.

As a team, the Angels flashed surprising power, as five players hit at least 20 home runs. The five were outfielders Leon Wagner (28), Ken Hunt (25), and Lee Thomas (24), catcher Earl Averill (21), and first baseman Steve Bilko (20). Individually, though, their totals were not as impressive as those of Roger Maris and Mickey Mantle, who belted 61 and 54, respectively.

1961 FRANK ROBINSON, Cincinnati Reds
1966 FRANK ROBINSON, Baltimore Orioles

Frank Robinson holds the unique distinction of being the only player in baseball history honored as the MVP in both the American and National leagues. He was first honored in 1961, when he led the Cincinnati Reds to the National League pennant. Then, after being traded to Baltimore for the 1966 season, he led the Birds to their first World Championship, surprising the Los Angeles Dodgers four games to none. Robinson also was named World Series MVP.

Breaking in with the Reds in 1956, he immediately began to realize his potential, batting .290 with 38 home runs and 83 RBI. Before his career ended 20

FRANK ROBINSON

Publisher: Baltimore Orioles • Manufacturer: Not Indicated
Type: Chrome • Postmark: Not Used • Value: $5–$8 Unsigned

years later, he would have 586 home runs, 1,812 RBI, and a career batting average of .294. In his MVP season of 1961, Robinson batted .323 with 37 home runs and 124 RBI. In 1962, Frank did even better, hitting .342 and driving in 136 runs, both career highs. In his first year with the Orioles, he batted .316, blasted 49 home runs, and had 122 RBI, all his best marks in the American League.

In September 1974, Robinson joined the Cleveland Indians in a trade with California. On October 4, the day after the season ended, he became baseball's first black manager. He was player/manager for the Indians in 1975 and 1976 and manager exclusively in 1977. He also managed the San Francisco Giants (1981–1984) and the Orioles (1988–1991). Robinson entered the Hall of Fame in 1982.

FRANKIE ROBINSON
Cincinnati Reds

Publisher: Cincinnati Reds • Manufacturer: Not Indicated • Type: Black & White • Postmark: Not Used • Value: $20

Publisher: Sam's Restaurant, Sacramento, CA • Manufacturer: Not Indicated
Type: Chrome • Postmark: Not Used • Value: $75–$100

1961 ROGER MARIS, New York Yankees

Roger Maris will be forever remembered as the man who broke Babe Ruth's single-season record of 60 home runs by slamming 61 in '61. The final blast occurred on October 1 of that year, at Yankee Stadium, off Jack Fisher of the Baltimore Orioles. Maris battled teammate Mickey Mantle all year for the honor of setting the new mark. Mantle finished with 54, making the M & M boys the most prolific pair of single-season home run hitters ever to share a team.

Although Maris has not been elected to the Hall of Fame—and may never be—he had a better-than-average 12-year career, accentuated by that remarkable '61 season, which included a .269 batting average and a league-leading 142 RBI and 132 runs scored. His career marks include a .260 average and 275 homers.

This advertising postcard for Sam's Restaurant in Sacramento, California, shows Roger with restaurant owner Sam Gordon displaying the historic 61st home run ball. The back reads, "Slugger Roger Maris of the New York Yankees examines the famous baseball he hit

for his 61st home run, breaking Babe Ruth's 34-year-old Major League record, after receiving it from Sam Gordon in a ceremony at Sam's Original Ranch Wagon in Sacramento. Gordon, restauranteur and fan, purchased the ball for $5,000 from Sal Durante, [the] young Brooklyn spectator who caught it at Yankee Stadium on October 1, 1961. Gordon brought Maris and Durante and his bride Rosemary to Sacramento in November for this memorable occasion."

1962 DON DRYSDALE, Los Angeles Dodgers

For 14 seasons with the Brooklyn and Los Angeles Dodgers, hard-throwing right-hander Don Drysdale was an intimidating presence on the mound. Standing 6 feet 6 inches and weighing more than 200 pounds, "Big D" was an intense, sidearming competitor who frequently brushed batters back in establishing his turf. Don's only manager, fellow Hall of Famer Walt Alston, said he never saw a pitcher so unafraid of batters. Drysdale parlayed his intimidating style, live fastball, and sweep-

Publisher: Los Angeles Dodgers, #P02130 • Manufacturer: Colour Picture, Boston, MA • Type: Chrome • Postmark: Not Used • Value: $10–$15

ing curve into 209 wins, 2,486 strikeouts, and a Hall of Fame berth in 1984. Drysdale's finest season was 1962, when he led the league with 314 ⅓ innings and a career-high 25 wins, earning the Cy Young award. Nevertheless, he may be best remembered for his performance in 1968 when he pitched six straight shutouts over 58 consecutive scoreless innings.

In 1965, Drysdale won 23 games as he helped the Dodgers to the world championship. In seven World Series appearances over five Series, Don was 3-3 with an ERA of 2.95—identical to that of his career. Drysdale died of a heart attack on July 3, 1993, while pursuing his second successful career as a Dodger broadcaster.

1962 SANDY KOUFAX, Los Angeles Dodgers

Brooklyn native Sanford "Sandy" Koufax didn't play baseball with his high school team until his senior year. As a youth, he was better known for his basketball prowess. Koufax won a basketball scholarship to the University of Cincinnati, but he also played baseball

Publisher: Los Angeles Dodgers • Manufacturer: Colour Picture, Boston, MA • Type: Chrome • Postmark: Not Used • Value: $15–$20 Unsigned

and attracted the attention of major league scouts with his fastball. In his freshman year, Koufax struck out 51 batters in only 32 innings. During the summers, he played sandlot baseball for the Parkviews in a Coney Island league.

In September 1954, Koufax worked out at Ebbets Field and was offered a contract and a place on the 1955 team. He was one of the few players who did not play in the minor leagues. Yet Koufax was not an immediate success at the major league level; in his early days, he lacked fastball control. Over his first six seasons, he won 36 games and lost 40. He began to show what he was capable of in 1961, going 18-13 and setting a new National League record with 269 strikeouts, surpassing the record of 267 set by the Giants' Christy Mathewson in 1903.

For the next six years, Koufax was baseball's dominant pitcher, winning 129 games. In 1966, with 165 career wins and 2,396 strikeouts to his credit, he had to retire from baseball due to arthritis in his left elbow. Koufax was elected to the Hall of Fame in 1972.

1963 LOS ANGELES DODGERS

Publisher: Los Angeles Dodgers, #P55773 • Manufacturer: Colour Picture, Boston, MA • Type: Chrome • Postmark: Not Used • Value: $25–$35

The 1963 world champion Los Angeles Dodgers came within one game of 100 victories. Manager Walter Alston led the team to a 99-63 record, calling on an arsenal of weapons to forge the club's success. Left fielder Tommy Davis was the National League batting champ with a .326 average, and his 88 RBI topped the team. Shortstop Maury Wills, who batted .302, led the NL with 40 stolen bases. In addition, the '63 Dodgers were a terrific defensive ball club. Ron Fairly topped all first basemen with a .995 fielding average. But Dodger pitching was the dominant force. Sandy Koufax's 25 wins versus only 5 defeats earned him the first of three consecutive Cy Young awards. His win total topped the NL, as did his brilliant 1.88 ERA. Don Drysdale won 19 but suffered 17 defeats, even with an ERA of 2.63.

Publisher: Houston Sports Association • Manufacturer: Not Indicated • Type: Chrome • Postmark: Not Used • Value: $75–$100

Reliever Ron Perranoski had 21 saves and topped all pitchers with an .842 winning percentage on 16 wins against only 3 losses.

In the '63 World Series, the Dodgers beat the New York Yankees in four straight, with Koufax winning two and Drysdale and Johnny Podres one each. During the regular season, Podres won 14 and lost 12. Alston, Drysdale, and Koufax all went on to the Hall of Fame.

1965 BASEBALL GREATS

To find a Hall of Famer pictured on a postcard is always a pleasure, but to find three on the same card is pure delight. This card shows Dodger great Don Drysdale on the left, along with 1964 Cy Young winner Dean Chance of the California Angels. Drysdale won the Cy Young himself in '62 and was elected to the Hall of Fame in 1984. The right panel shows Dodger ace Sandy Koufax, who won the Cy Young award three times (1963, '65, '66), joining the Hall in '72, and Willie Mays, inducted in 1979 after a memorable 22-year career with the New York and San Francisco Giants and New York Mets. Although Chance is unlikely to ever receive Hall of

Fame recognition, he had a fine career, winning 128 and losing 115 while compiling an outstanding 2.92 ERA over 11 years. In his Cy Young year, Chance won 20 and lost 9 while posting a career-best 1.65 ERA. In '67 with the Minnesota Twins, he won 20 while losing 14.

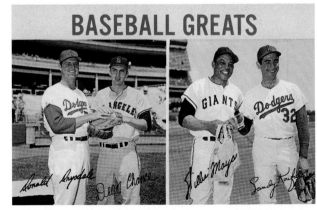

Publisher: Mitock & Sons, Sherman Oaks, CA • Manufacturer: Colour Picture, Boston, MA • Type: Chrome • Postmark: Not Used • Value: $25–$35

1965 HOUSTON ASTROS

When the Houston Astrodome opened in 1965, it was billed as the Eighth Wonder of the World. It's magnificence was universally recognized—largely because the Astros did everything possible to promote the indoor stadium. Their efforts included a series of postcards documenting virtually every inch of the place, top to bottom, inside and out.

The ballclub also issued a 5x7-inch postcard (facing page) showing the first Astros team to play in the dome. The team was hardly an artistic success, finishing ninth in the 10-team National League with a record of 65 wins and 97 losses under manager Lum Harris. Only the hapless New York Mets, with a 50-112 record, were worse.

Despite the Astros' dismal record, 2,151,479 fans poured through the Astrodome gates to watch center fielder Jimmy Wynn lead the team with a .275 batting average, 23 home runs, and 73 RBI. Second baseman Joe Morgan batted .271, while up-and-coming outfielder Rusty Staub finished second to Wynn in homers (14) and RBI (63). Right-hander Dick Farrell led the pitching staff in victories with 11 wins. Meanwhile, second baseman Nellie Fox, in the final season of a Hall of Fame career, appeared in 21 games, batting .268 and sharing his immense knowledge with Morgan, who also would one day attain Hall of Fame status.

1967 RED SCHOENDIENST,
St. Louis Cardinals

Red Schoendienst was born in Germantown, Illinois, only 40 miles east of St. Louis, the city where he eventually became a Hall of Fame second baseman. In 1942, after he attended their tryout camp, the Cardinals signed 19-year-old Schoendienst to a minor league contract. By 1945, he had reached the majors. That proved to be the first of 48 consecutive seasons that Red wore a big-league uniform as a player, coach, or manager.

Red played the outfield his first season and led the league in stolen bases with 26. In 1946, manager Eddie Dyer converted him to second base, where he sparkled for many years. HOF teammate Stan Musial said Red had the best hands he ever saw and that his fine speed enabled him to reach nearly everything hit his way.

At the plate, Red's first .300 season (.303) came in 1952, and was followed by his finest year ever, when he compiled a .342 average. Altogether, Red batted .300 or more seven times and led NL second basemen in fielding seven times. After a brief stint with the Giants, Schoendienst was traded to the Braves. He helped the club win its first pennant and World Series in '58. Championships were old hat to Red. He played for the '46 Cardinals, who beat the Red Sox in that year's Series. He also managed the Cardinals to a world

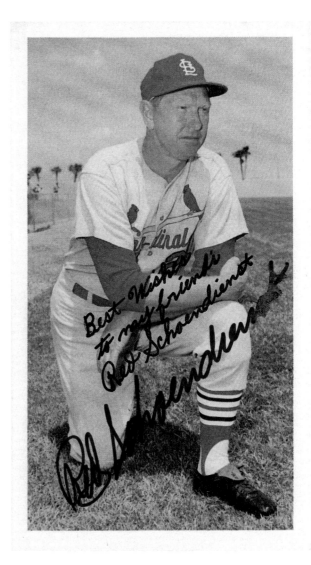

Publisher: St. Louis Cardinals • Manufacturer: Not Indicated • Type: Chrome • Postmark: Not Used • Value: $25–$35 Signed

championship in 1967, again beating the Red Sox. The Cardinals won the pennant again in '68, only to lose the Series to the Detroit Tigers in seven games. Red was inducted into the Hall of Fame in 1989 with a career .289 batting average.

**BOSTON RED SOX
1967 AMERICAN LEAGUE CHAMPIONS**

BACK ROW: Gary Waslewski, Jose Santiago, Gary Bell, Dave Morehead, Jerry Stephenson, Jim Lonborg, Darrell Brandon, Russ Gibson, Sparky Lyle, John Wyatt, Bill Landis, Lee Stange, Hank Fischer

MIDDLE ROW: Billy Rohr, Joe Foy, Mike Andrews, Ken Harrelson, Elston Howard, Mike Ryan, George Thomas, Dalton Jones, Norm Siebern, Jose Tartabull, Batboy Jimmy Jackson, Dan Osinski, Equipment Manager Vince Orlando

FRONT ROW: Batboy Keith Rosenfield, Tony Conigliaro, Carl Yastrzemski, Rico Petrocelli, Coach Sal Maglie, Coach Bobby Doerr, Manager Dick Williams, Coach Eddie Popowski, Coach Al Lakeman, Reggie Smith, George Scott, Traveling Secretary Tom Dowd, Trainer Buddy LeRoux, Equipment Manager Don Fitzpatrick

INSERT: Jerry Adair

Publisher: Boston Red Sox • Manufacturer: Not Indicated • Type: Real Photo • Postmark: Not Used • Value: $75–$100

1967 BOSTON RED SOX

It was the year of the Impossible Dream. In 1967, the Red Sox won their first American League pennant since 1946. Led by AL MVP Carl Yastrzemski and Cy Young winner Jim Lonborg, the BoSox rose from seventh place the previous year to capture the flag. Yaz won the triple crown that season with a .326 average, 44 home runs, and 121 RBI. But he was hardly a one-man offense. First baseman George Scott batted .303 with 19 homers and 82 RBI, while Tony Conigliaro blasted 20 dingers and drove in 67 runs. Lonborg was equally brilliant on the mound, leading the majors with 22 wins against only 9 losses and leading the AL with 246 strikeouts. Relief pitcher John Wyatt was second in the league in saves with 20.

The only damper on the season came when the club lost the World Series to the St. Louis Cardinals in seven games. Yaz batted .400 in the World Series, while Lonborg won his first two starts before losing the seventh and deciding game to Cardinals ace Bob Gibson, who won three games, going the distance in all.

Publisher: Jerry Buckley, #K19575, Boston, MA • Manufacturer: Tichnor Bros., Boston, MA • Type: Chrome • Postmark: Not Used • Value: $25–$35 Signed

Publisher: Jerry Buckley, #K19266, Boston, MA • Manufacturer: Tichnor Bros., Boston, MA • Type: Chrome • Postmark: Not Used
Value: $50–$75 Signed

1967 JIM LONBORG, Boston Red Sox

When the Boston Red Sox won the 1967 American League pennant, right-hander Jim Lonborg was largely responsible. Jim won 22 and lost only 9 that season, leading the AL and posting career highs in both victories and strikeouts (246). His performance earned him the Cy Young award as the AL's best pitcher. He was almost as brilliant in the World Series, winning two games before getting tagged for the loss in the seventh and deciding game.

Although Jim went on to enjoy a fine career that lasted until 1979, he never again achieved the same success he had in '67. His arm never seemed to be the same, and he had to rely more on cunning than on his flaming fastball. Traded to the Milwaukee Brewers in 1972, he went 14-12. The next season, he joined the Philadelphia Phillies, where he won 17 in 1974 and 18 in '76. Lonborg's totals over 15 seasons in the majors include 157 wins, 137 losses, and a lifetime ERA of 3.86.

1967 CARL YASTRZEMSKI, Boston Red Sox

Hall of Fame outfielder Carl Yastrzemski was the complete package for the Boston Red Sox. An outstanding hitter and superb defensive outfielder, he won seven Gold Glove awards for his fielding prowess. Yaz was at his best in 1967, leading the Red Sox to the American League pennant as he captured the league's MVP Award. In a dream year, he batted .326, tied for the AL home runs title with 44, and drove in 121 runs to lead the league in all three categories.

During Yastrzemski's 23 major league seasons, he compiled a .285 batting average, batted better than .300 six times, and made the American League All-Star team 17 times. A great clutch hitter throughout his career, he batted .350 in two World Series appearances, hitting .400 in '67 and .310 in '75. The Red Sox lost each Series in seven games.

Yaz signed with the Red Sox off the Notre Dame campus. He actually began his career as a shortstop, but was converted to the outfield when he joined Boston in 1961. When his career finally ended after the '83 season, he had 452 career home runs and a total of 3,308 hits. He reached base via a hit or walk 5,264 times, trailing only Pete Rose and Ty Cobb on the all-time major league list.

1968 ST. LOUIS CARDINALS

The 1968 Cardinals were defending world champs after beating the Red Sox in the '67 World Series. The Cards won the National League pennant for the second straight year as former Cardinal star Red Schoendienst managed them to 97 victories in '68, only four fewer than they won the year before. Cy Young–winner Bob Gibson was outstanding, leading the league with 22 wins against only 9 losses, compiling an incredible 1.12 ERA, striking out 268, and hurling 13 shutouts—all league bests.

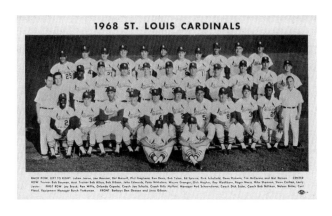

Publisher: St. Louis Cardinals • Manufacturer: Not Indicated
Type: Black & White • Postmark: Not Used • Value: $35–$45

The '68 Cardinals were not a heavy-hitting team. No one had more RBI than third baseman Mike Shannon's 79. Outfielder Curt Flood's .301 batting average was the highest mark on the team. The Cardinals relied on pitching, strong defense, and speed for their success in the World Series. Flood's 386 putouts were the best among NL center fielders, while left fielder Lou Brock led the NL with 62 stolen bases. Unfortunately for St. Louis fans, the Cards came up against the superb pitching of Detroit's Mickey Lolich, who won three games, beating Gibson in the seventh and final one. Denny McLain, who earned the AL Cy Young award that year with 31 wins, got the other Tiger victory.

1968 BILL FREEHAN, Detroit Tigers

Michigan photographer J.D. "Charley" McCarthy produced thousands of postcards of major league baseball players, all but two of them in black and white. The exceptions are a card of Tigers Hall of Famer Al Kaline

and this one of All-Star catcher Bill Freehan.

A University of Michigan graduate, Freehan spent just over a year in the minors before becoming the Tigers' starting catcher in 1963. He held the job until he retired in 1976. During his 15-year career, Freehan was consistently one of the best catchers in the game, both offensively and defensively. Freehan played in 11 All-Star Games, starting for the American League seven consecutive times from 1966 through 1972. He was a brilliant handler of pitchers and won five consecutive Gold Gloves (1965-1969) for defensive excellence. And he was no slouch with the bat, as his career .262 batting average indicates. In his prime, Freehan averaged about 20 home runs per year, knocking a career-best 25 in 1968 to go with 84 RBI—another career high—as he helped Detroit to the AL pennant and world championship. His power numbers fell off after he underwent back surgery in 1972, but based on his career statistics, there's a chance Freehan could someday join his HOF teammate Kaline in Cooperstown.

Publisher: J.D. McCarthy • Manufacturer: Not Indicated • Type: Chrome Postmark: Not Used • Value: $50

Publisher: J.D. McCarthy • Manufacturer: Not Indicated • Type: Black & White • Postmark: Not Used • Value: $25–$30 Unsigned

DENNY McLAIN

1969 Dodge Charger

Look who's pitching Dodge Fever!

Mickey Lolich
Detroit 3-game winner
in the 1968 World Series.

Publisher: Chrysler Corporation, Detroit, MI • Manufacturer: Not Indicated • Type: Black & White • Postmark: Not Used • Value: $35–$45

1968 MICKEY LOLICH, Detroit Tigers

Left-hander Mickey Lolich was one of the finest pitchers of his era. His shining moment came in the 1968 World Series, when his three victories enabled the Tigers to claim the world championship. During the regular season, his 17-9 record was overshadowed by the astonishing 31-6 performance of teammate Denny McLain. But the Series belonged to Lolich, who hurled three complete-game victories, besting Hall of Famer Bob Gibson 4-1 in the seventh and deciding game. In the 27 innings he worked, Lolich struck out 21 and compiled a 1.67 ERA.

Mickey enjoyed his finest season in 1971, leading the American League with a career-high 25 wins and 308 strikeouts. In '72, he was almost as good, winning 22 and striking out 250 while posting a career-best 2.50 ERA. After 16 years, mostly with the Tigers, Lolich retired with 217 wins against 191 defeats.

1968 DENNY McLAIN, Detroit Tigers

For two remarkable seasons, in 1968 and '69, right-hander Denny McLain was the finest pitcher in baseball. He remains the last man to have won 30 games, posting a 31-6 record in the Tigers' world championship season of '68. That year, he led the American League in wins,

winning percentage (.838), and complete games (28) while compiling a career-low 1.96 ERA. He followed that performance with a league-leading 24-9 record in '69 to capture his second consecutive Cy Young award.

The world was McLain's oyster during those heady seasons. For a while, he seemed indestructible, pitching 336 innings in '68 and 325 in '69. But the huge workload took a terrible toll on his arm, and he never really recovered. Traded to Washington in 1971, he led the AL with 22 losses. Nevertheless, he retired with a respectable 131-91 record.

Unfortunately, in recent years, his personal life has become a disaster. In 1970, he was suspended from baseball for gambling. Since his playing days ended in 1972, McLain has twice spent time in a federal prison. In the mid-1980s, he served 29 months in jail after being convicted of racketeering and drug possession. He was released when an appeals court determined that he hadn't received a fair trial. In 1996, he was convicted of money laundering, conspiracy, theft, and mail-fraud for taking money from a meatpacking company's pension fund.

JUAN MARICHAL/NATIONAL LEAGUE/ COPYRIGHT PRO STAR PROMOTIONS INC.
Printed in Canada

Publisher: Pro Star Promotions, Canada • Manufacturer: Not Indicated
Type: Color Lithograph • Postmark: Not Used • Value: $10–$15 Unsigned

1969 JUAN MARICHAL, San Francisco Giants

Juan Antonio Marichal was one of the first and best players from the Dominican Republic to reach the major leagues, and the first to be enshrined in the Hall of Fame. Marichal spent all but two of his 16 seasons with the San Francisco Giants, where he won 238 of his 243 career victories. A six-time 20-game winner, he led the National League in victories twice, compiling 25 wins in 1963 and 26 in '68. Juan lost the Cy Young award to Sandy Koufax in '63 and to Bob Gibson in '68, but finally won the honor in '69, winning 21 games and leading the NL with a 2.10 ERA.

While his Hall of Fame contemporaries like Koufax, Gibson, and Steve Carlton relied on blazing fastballs for their success, Marichal relied mostly on finesse. What the 6-foot, 185-pound right-hander lacked in power, he made up for with outstanding control. Marichal never walked more than 90 batters in a single season. In all but five seasons, he issued fewer than 50 walks—a remarkable feat for a pitcher who worked an average of 220 innings per year. He was elected to the Hall in 1983.

1969 FRANK HOWARD & TED WILLIAMS, Washington Senators

During my years broadcasting major league baseball, I met many great players, some of whom remain good friends to this day. But the two nicest were Brooks Robinson and Frank Howard. I met Howard for the first time in 1969, while the Senators were training in Pompano Beach, Florida, when I was preparing to broadcast their games. Frank was one of those people you couldn't help but like, friendly and down-to-earth. Even though he was one of baseball's superstars, it never affected his personality. When the Senators' rookies came up from the minor leagues in September, Frank made it a point to take all of them out to dinner, letting them get a taste of life in the big leagues even though many would never make the grade. Some of today's players could learn from his example.

How good was "Hondo" with the Senators? The

Publisher: Washington Senators • Manufacturer: Not Indicated • Type: Black & White • Postmark: Not Used • Value: $30–$35 Unsigned

records speak for themselves. He led the American League in home runs in '68 and '70 with 44 each season, and in '69 he hit a career-high 48. His best RBI total came in 1970 when he drove in 126 runs. Senators manager Ted Williams had a major impact on Howard, getting him to be much more selective at the plate and thus cutting down his strikeouts. On a flight back to Washington from Detroit, where Frank had hit one of his tape-measure home runs, Williams said to me, "Ron, I always thought Jimmy Foxx hit the ball harder than anyone I ever saw until I saw Frank. I'm convinced Frank hits it even harder than Jimmy."

This postcard showing the two sluggers was published by the Senators in 1969 as a ballpark giveaway. Ted Williams, in his first year managing, led the Senators to an 86-76 record, the best in the expansion club's history. Frank made the great season possible with a .296 batting average, 48 home runs, and 111 RBI.

1970-79

In 1970, the Baltimore Orioles won their second consecutive American League pennant, while Cincinnati's Big Red Machine won the National League flag. In the World Series, the Orioles won in five games as Baltimore third baseman Brooks Robinson put on a one-man show offensively and defensively. He batted .429 with 2 home runs, 5 runs scored, and 6 RBI, while making some defensive plays that still make the highlight reels.

The next season, 1971, was a year of finales. Washington, D.C., marked its last year as home to a ballclub; after the season, the expansion Senators moved to Arlington, Texas, to become the Rangers. (Many one-time 'Nats fans, myself included, are still rankled by that move.) The Orioles made the last of three straight World Series appearances, losing to Pittsburgh in seven. The Pirates were led by outfielder Roberto Clemente, who hit .414 in the Series. Sadly, it would be his last appearance in the Fall Classic. The Pirates lost the NL pennant to Cincinnati in '72, and after the season, Clemente died in a plane crash while on a mission of mercy.

Things looked brighter on the West Coast, where 1972 marked the beginning of the Oakland A's' reign as world champs. Combining the great pitching of Hall of Famers Catfish Hunter and Rollie Fingers and the outstanding hitting of Reggie Jackson, Sal Bando, Joe Rudi, and Gene Tenace, the A's beat the Reds, Mets, and Dodgers in '72, '73, and '74. In the three championships, Hunter won four games without a loss.

In 1975 and '76, Cincinnati's Big Red Machine rolled

Publisher: New York Yankees • Manufacturer: Dexter Press, W. Nyack, NY
Type: Chrome • Postmark: Not Used • Value: $10–$15

into high gear, beating the Red Sox and Yankees, respectively, in the World Series. Pete Rose, George Foster, and Hall of Famers Johnny Bench and Joe Morgan led the attack, while reliever Rawly Eastwick won two games in '75 and a third in '76 and left-hander Don Gullett picked up a win in each series. The back-to-back championships capped an eight-year run in which the Reds took five division championships and four NL pennants, while four members of the lineup captured six NL MVP awards: Bench in 1970 and '72, Rose in '73, Morgan in '75 and '76, and Foster in '77. But not even the addition of Tom Seaver, who won the NL Cy Young award in 1973 and '75, could stave off the end of Cincinnati's dynasty.

The Yankees returned to the World Series in '77, beating the Dodgers in six as Mike Torrez won a pair of complete games and Reggie Jackson and Thurman Munson led the attack. The two teams met again in '78, with similar results.

The postseason of 1979 saw a replay of the '71 World Series between Baltimore and Pittsburgh, and the result was identical: Pirates in seven. Hall of Famer Willie Stargell was the Pirates hero, batting .400 with three home runs, seven runs, and seven RBI, while reliever Kent Tekulve saved three games for Pittsburgh. Down three games to one, the Pirates rallied to win the last three and their third world championship in three tries since 1960.

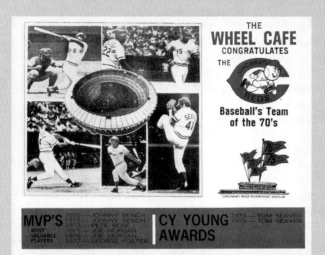

Publisher: The Wheel Cafe, Cincinnati, OH • Manufacturer: Not Indicated
Type: Chrome • Postmark: Not Used • Value: $25–$35

Publisher: Montreal Expos, #11 • Manufacturer: SNS, Montreal, Quebec, Canada • Type: Chrome • Postmark: Not Used • Value: $15 Unsigned

1970 RUSTY STAUB, Montreal Expos

Known as "Le Grand Orange" for his red hair when he played in Montreal, Rusty Staub became one of the most popular players in Expos history. Originally signed by the Houston Astros as a bonus baby right out of a New Orleans high school, Staub stayed with the Astros from 1963 through 1968, when he was selected by the Expos in the expansion draft. With Houston, Staub had a career high .333 batting average in 1967, when he led the NL with 44 doubles. In '69, his first year with the Expos, Staub captured the hearts of Canadian fans by batting .302. He followed that two years later with a .311 average.

Staub was traded to the New York Mets after the '71 season and was a mainstay there for four years. Dealt to the Detroit Tigers before the season of '76, he continued to excel. In fact, his 121 RBI for the Tigers in 1978 was a career high.

Staub returned to Montreal briefly in '79, then went on to Texas in 1980, where he batted .300. Returning to the Mets in '81, Staub hit .317 in 70 games. He closed

out his career in New York in 1985, finishing with a career .279 batting average, 292 home runs, and 1,466 RBI over 23 major league seasons. A gourmet cook, Rusty opened a restaurant in New York City while still with the Mets. It remains popular to this day.

1970 EARL WEAVER, Baltimore Orioles

Some of the best managers in major league history never played in the majors. Earl Weaver is a case in point. For 13 years, Earl toiled in the minor leagues as a second baseman, never getting the chance to play in the bigs. But the experience he acquired as a player during those 13 seasons and his subsequent 12 years as a minor league manager paid handsome dividends. Weaver became the Orioles' manager in 1968, replacing Hank Bauer midway through the season. He kept the job for 17 years, guiding the Birds to four pennants and one world championship (1970) while winning 1,480 games against 1,060 losses. His .583 regular-season winning percentage ranks sixth among those who have managed 10 or more seasons in the 20th century. Weaver was inducted into the Hall of Fame in 1996.

EARL WEAVER

Publisher: Baltimore Orioles • Manufacturer: Not Indicated
Type: Chrome • Postmark: Not Used • Value: $25 Signed

Publisher: Cincinnati Reds, #72173-D • Manufacturer: Dexter Press, W. Nyack, NY • Type: Chrome • Postmark: Not Used • Value: $15–$20 Unsigned

1970 JOHNNY BENCH, Cincinnati Reds

Johnny Bench was an important cog in Cincinnati's Big Red Machine as well as one of the best catchers in major league history. Defensively, he was superb, with a strong throwing arm and catlike quickness. When bad knees curtailed his activity behind the plate, Johnny played third, first, and the outfield to keep his hitting and leadership ability in the lineup. In 17 seasons, all with the Reds, he compiled a .267 career average while slamming 389 home runs and driving in 1,376 runs.

Bench was the National League's MVP in both '70 and '72, his best all-around seasons. In '70, he batted .293 while leading the NL with 45 home runs and 148 RBI, both career highs. He also led the league in homers and RBI in '72—with 40 and 125, respectively—while compiling a .270 average.

This postcard of Bench, with its facsimile autograph on the front, was produced to accommodate his many fan requests. It contains the following message on the back:

Dear Fan,

Thank you for your recent letter. It was nice to hear from you. One of the most pleasant things about my own base-ball career is having the chance to meet—sometimes only by mail—people like yourself who share my love for this great game. Thank you for your interest. Hit 'em hard.

Best regards,

Johnny Bench

Johnny was inducted into the Hall of Fame in 1989, the first year he was eligible.

1971 VIDA BLUE, Oakland A's

Vida Blue was a flame-throwing left-hander who won the MVP and Cy Young award with the Oakland A's in 1971—his first full season—winning 24, losing 8, striking out 301 batters, and leading the league with a 1.82

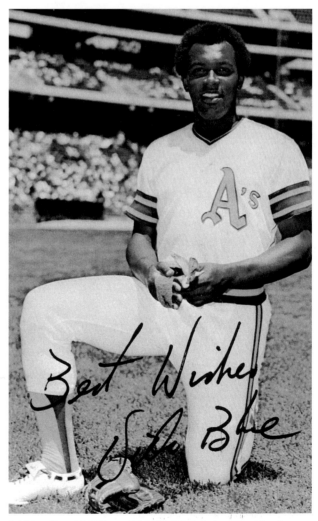

Publisher: Doug McWilliams, #T1-8 KV3509, Berkeley, CA • Manufacturer: Kolor View, Los Angeles, CA • Type: Chrome • Postmark: Not Used
Value: $10 Unsigned

ERA. Even though those numbers proved to be personal highs, Blue had many more outstanding seasons during a 17-year career that left him with 209 wins and 161 defeats. Blue went 20-9 in '73 and 22-11 in '75. After posting a disappointing 14-19 record in 1977, Vida found new life with the San Francisco Giants in '78, winning 18 and losing 10. He never won that many games again, although he did post 14 victories for the Giants in '79 and '80, then went 13-12 for the Kansas City Royals in 1982. After two seasons with the Royals, Blue went back to the Giants for two final seasons in '85 and '86, winning 10 and losing 10 his final year. He threw smoke right up to the end, fanning 100 batters his last season. Yet he never carried his success into the postseason. Appearing in three different World Series for the A's, Vida was 0-3, losing one game each in '72, '73, and '74. Nevertheless, Oakland proved victorious in each of those Series.

1971 JOE TORRE, St. Louis Cardinals

Publisher: Pro Star Promotions, Canada • Manufacturer: Not Indicated
Type: Color Lithograph • Postmark: Not Used • Value: $10–$15 Unsigned

Joe Torre had an outstanding 18-year National League playing career, retiring in 1977 with a lifetime .297 batting average. He came up with the Milwaukee Braves in 1960 for two games, joining his older brother Frank. Joe was extremely versatile, exhibiting great skill as a catcher, first baseman, and third baseman, not to mention a couple of games as an outfielder. In 1964 with Milwaukee, he batted .321 with 20 home runs and 109 RBI. When the Braves moved to Atlanta in '66, Joe batted .315, hit a career-high 36 home runs, and drove in 101 runs.

He was traded to the Cardinals in '69 and went on to enjoy even greater success. In 1970, he batted .325 with 21 home runs and an even 100 RBI. The next season,

he was the NL MVP, leading the league with a .363 batting average, 230 hits, and 137 RBI.

Chronic back problems limited Joe's success thereafter, but he managed to play through 1977, when he became manager of the Mets. He had more success managing the Braves from 1982–84, and did well with the Cardinals from 1990–95. But Torre the manager will be best remembered for helping the Yankees to two world championships, in 1996 and 1998, and for guiding New York to the major league record for victories in a season in 1998. There's a strong possibility that Joe will someday wind up in the Hall of Fame for his success as a player and his astute managing.

1972 FERGUSON JENKINS, Chicago Cubs

Canadian-born Ferguson Jenkins was one of baseball's top pitchers for 19 seasons, winning 284 games while losing 226. Fergie broke in with the Phillies in 1965, but the 6-foot 5-inch, 205-pound right-hander was traded to the Cubs the following year. Jenkins went 6-8 with the

Publisher: Not Indicated • Manufacturer: Not Indicated • Type: Black &
White • Postmark: Not Used • Value: $15 Unsigned

Cubs in 1966, but launched a series of six consecutive 20-win campaigns in 1967 with a 20-13 mark. Toward the end of the stretch, in 1971, Jenkins led the National League with 24 wins. He also led the league in complete games that season, one of four in which he accomplished that feat.

After a subpar 14-16 season in '73, Jenkins was traded to the Texas Rangers. The change of scenery proved beneficial, as he went on to lead the American League with a career-high 25 wins, earning Comeback Player of the Year honors. That proved to be his final 20-victory season, but Jenkins remained a top-flight pitcher for the rest of his career. Fittingly, he returned to the Cubs to finish his career, winning 14 games in '82 and 6 in his final season. Jenkins retired in 1983 and was elected to the Hall of Fame in 1991.

1972 BILLY WILLIAMS, Chicago Cubs

Outfielder Billy Williams played 18 excellent years, primarily with the Chicago Cubs, beginning in 1959. In his career, Williams batted .301 or better five times, including 1972, when he led the National League with a career-high .333 batting average and a personal-best .606 slugging average; he also socked 37 home runs and posted 122 RBI. This performance topped his previous banner year, 1970, when he led the league in hits with 205 and runs with 137, batted .322, and drove in a career-best 129 runs.

For most of his career, Williams played with poor teams. After 16 seasons with the Cubs, he was traded to Oakland, where he was able to get his first taste of postseason play. He retired after the 1976 season with a .290 lifetime batting average. Williams was inducted into the Hall of Fame in 1987.

1972 GAYLORD PERRY, Cleveland Indians

Right-hander Gaylord Perry is the only pitcher in history to win Cy Young awards in both leagues, earning the

Publisher: H.F. Gardner, Chicago, IL • Manufacturer: Not Indicated
Type: Chrome • Postmark: Not Used • Value: $15–$20 Unsigned

Publisher: Cleveland Indians • Manufacturer: Calo, Crane, Howard Fine Line, Cleveland, OH • Type: Chrome • Postmark: Not Used
Value: $25–$35 Signed

honor in 1972 while with the Cleveland Indians and in 1978 with the San Diego Padres. With the Indians in '72, Perry won 24 and lost 16 with an ERA of 1.92. With the Padres in '78, he went 21-6 with a 2.72 ERA. All told, Perry won 314 games and struck out 3,534 batters.

By his own admission, Perry threw a spitter, doctoring the ball with saliva, slippery elm, baby oil, and Vaseline. Perry acknowledged using illegal pitches in his autobiography, *Me and the Spitter,* but claimed he never used them after the book came out in 1974. He said he wanted batters to think he was adept at throwing the pitch to psyche them out, fooling them completely when he threw something else—such as his forkball, which is considered one of the best ever.

Perry struggled after coming up briefly with the San Francisco Giants in '61 and '62, relegated mainly to bullpen mop-up duty. His big break came on May 31, 1964, when he came in from the bullpen in the 13th inning of a 6-6 tie against the Mets. Perry, who had been working on the spitter since spring training, used it for the first time and hurled 10 scoreless innings. Perry went on to win 21 games for the Giants in '66, the first of five seasons in which he reached 20. He led the National League with 23 wins in 1970, then reached his career-high 24 in '72 following his trade to the Indians.

Perry was elected to the Hall of Fame in 1991. Trivia note: Gaylord's older brother Jim was a fine pitcher in his own right, winning 215 games and a Cy Young award of his own.

1972 STEVE CARLTON, Philadelphia Phillies

Steve "Lefty" Carlton was one of baseball's great pitchers and remained so for three decades, winning 329 games in 24 seasons and earning four Cy Young awards in the process. Although he began his career with the St. Louis Cardinals in 1965 and won 20 games for the Red Birds in 1971, he enjoyed his greatest success with the Philadelphia Phillies, to whom he was traded prior to the '72 season. Lefty's first year in Philly was the best of his career. He posted a 27-10 record, leading the National League in wins as well as ERA (1.97), complete games (30), innings pitched ($346^{1}/_{3}$) and strikeouts (310), all career highs. He earned his first Cy Young award that season; he was accorded the honor again in '77 when he went 23-10, in 1980 when he was 24-9, and in '82 when he won 23 and lost 11. In all four of those Cy Young seasons, he led the NL in victories and strikeouts. His four Cy Young awards mark the top total in the National League, a record Carlton shares with Greg Maddux. Steve was inducted into the Hall of Fame in 1994, firmly established as one of the finest pitchers in baseball history.

GREAT **phillies** MOMENTS

Steve Carlton

Publisher: Perez-Steele Galleries, Fort Washington, PA • Manufacturer: Not Indicated • Type: Color Lithograph • Postmark: Not Used • Value: $5 Unsigned

1972 ROBERTO CLEMENTE, Pittsburgh Pirates

In the Pirates' final game of 1972, outfielder Roberto Clemente doubled off Jon Matlack of the New York Mets for his 3,000th career hit. No one suspected it would be his last. The 38-year-old Clemente died in a New Year's Eve plane crash while on a charitable mission to help earthquake victims in Nicaragua. He left behind a legacy of excellence that made him one of Pittsburgh's all-time baseball heroes.

Clemente was a complete ballplayer, a skilled batter and speedy defender with a rifle arm. A career .317 hitter, Clemente won the National League batting title four times—the last time in 1967 with a career-high .357 average. He appeared in two World Series with the Pirates, excelling in both. When the Pirates beat the Yankees in seven games in 1960, Clemente batted .310. In 1971 against the Baltimore Orioles, he almost single-handedly led the Pirates to victory, batting .410 with 2 homers and 2 doubles and earning the World Series

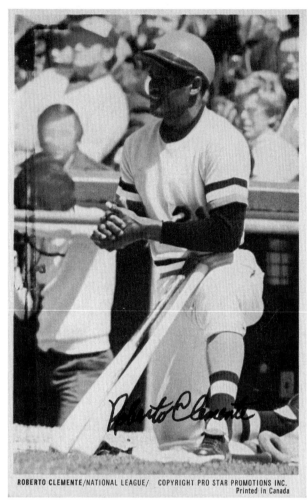

ROBERTO CLEMENTE/NATIONAL LEAGUE/   COPYRIGHT PRO STAR PROMOTIONS INC.
Printed in Canada

Publisher: Pro Star Promotions, Canada • Manufacturer: Not Indicated
Type: Color Lithograph • Postmark: Not Used • Value: $15–$20 Unsigned

MVP award. Clemente had at least one hit in each of his 14 Series games.

Because of his untimely, heroic death, baseball writers held a special election in 1973, admitting Clemente to the Hall of Fame without the customary five-year wait.

Many postcards were issued during Clemente's career, and numerous cards have been produced since, paying tribute to his brilliant play and humanitarian efforts.

1973 REGGIE JACKSON, Oakland A's

They called him "Mr. October" because he always played his best in the Fall Classic. In the 1977 World Series, Reggie Jackson led the New York Yankees to the world championship over the Los Angeles Dodgers with a performance that has yet to be equalled. Jackson slammed five home runs in 20 at-bats, drove in 8 runs, and scored 10 times; he was unanimously voted the World Series MVP. The following year, the Yankees again topped the Dodgers thanks in large part to Jackson's .391 batting, 2 home runs, and 8 RBI.

Jackson laid the groundwork for those amazing exhi-

bitions with the Oakland A's, earning his first World Series MVP title in 1973. Six years earlier, Kansas City Athletics owner Chuck Finley had signed Jackson out of Arizona State University. Jackson had little impact that first season, batting .178 in 35 games. But when the A's moved to Oakland the following season, Jackson began to assert himself, belting 29 home runs with 74 RBI. He enjoyed a banner season in 1969, leading the American League with a .608 slugging average and 123 runs scored while posting career highs in home runs (47) and RBI (118). Reggie the superstar had arrived.

In 1973, Jackson led Oakland to its first world championship, topping the AL in slugging average (.531), home runs (32), runs scored (99), and RBI (117) and winning the AL MVP award. In the Series, he batted .310 with 6 RBI as the A's topped the New York Mets. In all, Jackson appeared in five World Series, compiling the highest composite Fall Classic slugging average ever recorded: .755.

Publisher: Doug McWilliams, #72-14 KV4500, Berkeley, CA • Manufacturer: Kolor View, Los Angeles, CA • Type: Chrome • Postmark: Oakland, CA, June 13, 1973 • Value: $20 Unsigned

After the Yankees lost the 1981 World Series, Jackson signed with the California Angels as a free agent. He saw little postseason activity thereafter, but remained with the team until 1987, when he returned to Oakland for one final season. Jackson reached the Hall of Fame in his first year of eligibility, 1993.

1973 JIM PALMER, Baltimore Orioles

JIM PALMER

Publisher: Baltimore Orioles • Manufacturer: Not Indicated • Type: Chrome
Postmark: Baltimore, MD, April 10, 1974 • Value: $20–25 Signed

Right-hander Jim Palmer remains the greatest pitcher in Orioles history, winning 268 games for Baltimore from 1965 through 1984. His excellence was universally recognized when he won three Cy Young awards in a four-year span ('73, '75, and '76). In addition, Palmer's lifetime ERA of 2.86 is fourth among pitchers who threw 3,000 or more innings in their careers. Palmer was a 20-game winner eight times during 19 seasons with the Orioles, 23 victories in '75 being his career high. When he was only 20 years old, in 1966, Palmer became the youngest pitcher ever to throw a shutout in the World Series. When he won his final World Series game in 1983, he became the first pitcher in major league history to post a Series victory in each of

three decades. Palmer was the winning pitcher in the first four pennant-clinching games for the Orioles and was 8-3 in postseason competition. He was elected to the Hall of Fame on the first ballot in 1990. Since his retirement, he has enjoyed a successful career as a broadcaster.

1973 PETE ROSE, Cincinnati Reds

Pete Rose is unquestionably one of the greatest players in baseball history, but his propensity to gamble may have cost him a spot in the Hall of Fame. He was suspended from baseball for life back in 1989 and as long as that suspension is in effect, he has no chance for enshrinement. But his records will stand forever.

In 24 seasons, Rose, nicknamed "Charley Hustle," amassed 3,562 hits, more than any major leaguer in history. The immortal Ty Cobb held the previous record of 3,034, which stood until Rose broke it in 1985. Most of Pete's years were spent with the Cincinnati Reds, where he was an integral part of the Big Red Machine. Rose won National League batting titles with the Reds in 1968, '69, and '73 with marks of .335, .348, and .338.

Publisher: Pete Rose Ballpark Cafe, Boca Raton, FL • Manufacturer: Not Indicated • Type: Chrome • Postmark: Not Used • Value: $10 Unsigned

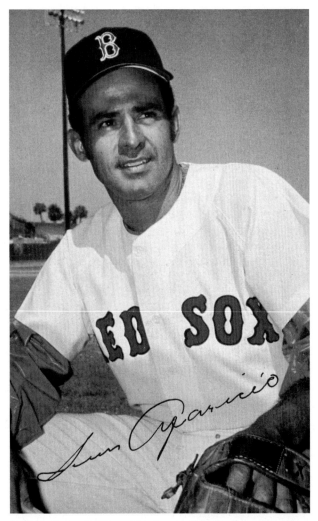

Publisher: Boston Red Sox • Manufacturer: Not Indicated • Type: Chrome
Postmark: Not Used • Value: $10 Unsigned

1973 LUIS APARICIO, Boston Red Sox

In 1984, smooth-fielding shortstop Luis Aparicio became the first Venezuelan native to be elected to the Hall of Fame. Aparicio personified the Go-Go White Sox, who won the American League pennant in 1959. After joining the Sox in 1956, he proceeded to lead the league in stolen bases for nine straight years, pilfering 56 in Chicago's pennant-winning season. After being traded to Baltimore in 1963, Aparicio led the AL in steals two more years, including a career-high 57 in 1964. In 1966, when the Orioles won their first American League pennant and world championship, "Little Looie" generated many rallies with his superb speed and 25 stolen bases.

As a fielder, Aparicio had few equals. To this day, he still holds shortstop records for most games (2,581), chances (12,564), and double plays (1,553). Besides tremendous speed and exceptional range, he had a strong, accurate arm. A starter for 18 seasons with the White Sox, Orioles, and Red Sox, Luis batted a respectable .261 lifetime. But his true value lay in his running and fielding skills, among the best in the history of the game. Postcards dominate Aparicio memorabilia. This Red Sox postcard shows him as he looked in 1973, his final major league season.

1973 BERT BLYLEVEN, Minnesota Twins

Curve-tossing right-hander Bert Blyleven had an outstanding 22-year career, winning 287 games while losing 250. Although he did not win 300 games, the fact that he came close and was at his best in big-game situations may eventually land the Netherlands native in the Hall of Fame.

Seven times he led the NL in hits, and he was the league's MVP in '73. Never a power hitter, Rose relied on speed and hustle to accomplish his feats. His career-high RBI total was 82 in 1969, the same year he topped the NL in runs scored with 120—the first of four seasons in which he copped this honor.

After the 1978 season, Rose signed with the Phillies as a free agent and promptly batted .331. In 1980, when the Phillies won their only world championship, Pete led the NL in doubles with 42. He came back the next season to top the NL in hits with 140.

Rose started 1984 with the Montreal Expos, then returned to the Reds as player/manager for the last 41 games of the season, holding the post until he agreed to the lifetime ban in '89 following an investigation into his gambling activities. An investigation spearheaded by the commissioner's office found that Rose bet on baseball games while he was managing. Rose obviously used poor judgment off the field, but his performance on the diamond can never be questioned.

Publisher: Doug McWilliams, #KVB 10320, 77-94, Berkeley, CA
Manufacturer: Kolor View Press, Los Angeles, CA • Type: Chrome
Postmark: Not Used • Value $10

Blyleven came up with the Minnesota Twins in 1970, winning 10 and losing 9 his rookie year. In 1973, he became a 20-game winner for the only time, going 20-17. He went from the Twins to the Texas Rangers in 1976, then to the Pittsburgh Pirates in 1978. When the Pirates won the '79 pennant, Bert won 12 and lost 5, then went 1-0 against Cincinnati in the National League Championship Series and 1-0 against Baltimore in the World Series as Pittsburgh took the championship. Blyleven went to Cleveland in 1981, then rejoined the Twins in 1985. He won two games without a loss in the '87 ALCS against Detroit, then went 1-1 in Minnesota's World Series victory over St. Louis.

1974 NATIONAL LEAGUE ALL-STARS

Publisher: Bob Bartosz, Pennsauken, NJ • Manufacturer: Not Indicated
Type: Black & White • Postmark: Not Used • Value: $10

This postcard of the 1974 National League All-Stars, shot by gifted photographer Bob Bartosz, is the only known postcard of a major league All-Star squad. The depicted team won the All-Star Game 7-2 before a capacity crowd of more than 50,000 at Pittsburgh's Three Rivers Stadium. The hero of the squad was Dodgers first baseman Steve Garvey, who had a double and a single, drove in a run, scored a run, and made several outstanding defensive plays. The American Leaguers were limited to only four hits by Andy Messersmith, Ken Brett, Jon Matlack, Lynn McGlothen, and Mike Marshall. The NL manager was Yogi Berra of the Mets.

Marshall and Garvey both had sensational seasons for the Dodgers, winning the Cy Young and MVP awards, respectively, at the conclusion of the '74 campaign. Dodger luck turned sour in the World Series, though, as the club lost to the Oakland A's in five games, although both Garvey and Marshall performed exceptionally well. Garvey batted .381, while Marshall posted a 1.00 ERA over nine innings, but was the unfortunate loser in the fifth and final game.

1974 JIM HUNTER, Oakland A's

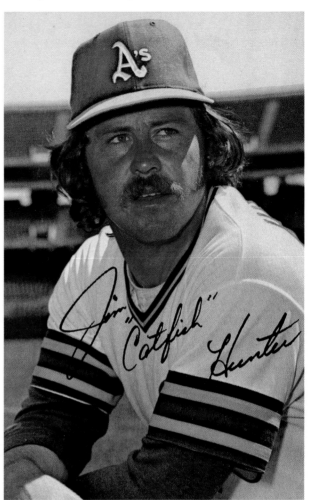

Publisher: Doug McWilliams, #73-29 KV5639, Berkeley, CA • Manufacturer: Kolor View Press, Los Angeles, CA • Type: Chrome • Postmark: Not Used Value: $20 Unsigned

Right-hander Jim "Catfish" Hunter enjoyed HOF success with pinpoint control, a sneaky fastball, an outstanding slider, and the ability to pitch his best in pressure situations. "Catfish" was the moniker bestowed upon him by Charley Finley, the Kansas City Athletics owner who signed him to a $75,000 bonus contract in 1964 at the Hunter family farm in Hertford, N.C. When the team moved to Oakland in 1968, Hunter became the bellwether of the staff, winning 21 games for the first time in 1971 as the A's won the first of five straight division titles. It proved to be the first of four consecutive seasons in which Catfish won 21 or more games with the A's.

Catfish won the Cy Young award in 1974 after leading the league in wins and ERA with 25 and 2.49, respectively. But he had a falling out with Finley and went to the New York Yankees in '75, winning a league-high 23 and helping the team to the American League pennant.

In his second season with the Yankees, Hunter began having shoulder problems. His chronic injuries forced him to retire in 1979 at the relatively young age of 33. But he had proven his mettle. In six different World Series appearances, Catfish won 5 and lost 3 while compiling a 3.29 ERA—almost identical to his lifetime ERA of 3.26. He was elected to the Hall of Fame in 1987. In 1999, sadly, Hunter was stricken with Lou Gehrig's disease.

1974 HANK AARON, Atlanta Braves

Publisher: Atlanta Braves, #6666 • Manufacturer: Multiple Photos, Los Angeles, CA • Type: Chrome • Postmark: Not Used • Value: $20 Unsigned

One of baseball's great moments occurred in Atlanta on April 8, l974, when Hank Aaron slammed his 715th career home run, breaking Babe Ruth's all-time record. This postcard shows Hank just after he connected. The legend on the back of the card tells the complete story:

Before an Opening Night crowd of 53,775, Hank Aaron blasted his 715th home run, surpassing Babe Ruth and becoming the home run king of baseball. Aaron's fourth-inning homer came on a 1-0 pitch from Los Angeles pitcher Al Downing.

After this remarkable achievement, Hammerin' Hank

went on to hit 40 more homers. He finished his 23-year career in the city where it started—Milwaukee, where Hank played his last two seasons with the Brewers. Aaron retired with a career batting average of .305 to go with his all-time record 755 home runs and 2,297 RBI. Not surprisingly, he was inducted into the Hall of Fame in 1982, the first year he was eligible.

1974 AL DOWNING, Los Angeles Dodgers

Al Downing is best remembered for being in Atlanta on April 8, 1974, where he served up the pitch that Hank Aaron belted for his record-setting home run. Nevertheless, the left-hander had a fine 17-year career, winning 123 and losing 107 while compiling a solid 3.22 ERA. Beginning his career with the New York Yankees in 1961, Downing had a five-year stretch from 1963 through 1967 in which he never won fewer than 10 games, notching a high of 14 wins in '67. He was extremely fast in those days, leading the American League in strikeouts with 217 in 1964 while going 13-8. After a 5-13 season with Oakland and Milwaukee in 1970, Downing resurrected his career with the Los Angeles

Publisher: Los Angeles Dodgers #86155 • Manufacturer: Dexter Press, W. Nyack, NY • Type: Chrome • Postmark: Not Used • Value: $15 Signed

Dodgers in '71, winning 20 games for the first and only time. He remained in L.A. for the rest of his career, becoming a reliever in 1975, then retiring after the '77 season.

1974 STEVE GARVEY, Los Angeles Dodgers

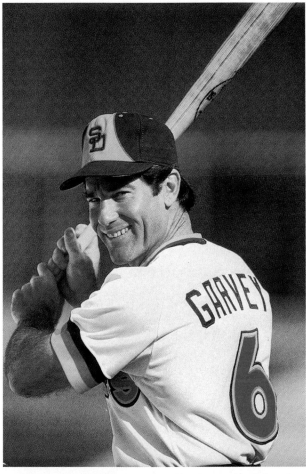

Publisher: Barry Colla, Berkeley, CA • Manufacturer: Not Indicated
Type: Chrome • Postmark: Not Used • Value: $10

The same year that Mike Marshall earned the Cy Young award (1974), teammate Steve Garvey posted a National League MVP season, batting .312 with 21 home runs and 111 RBI. Those numbers proved to be prototypical as Garvey became one of the league's most consistent performers.

Although he began his career as a third baseman, Garvey spent most of his 19-year career playing first, where he won consecutive Gold Gloves from 1974–77 and earned trips to the All-Star game from 1974–81.

After 14 seasons as a Dodger, Garvey joined the San Diego Padres in 1983. Wearing a uniform like the one in the picture above, he helped the team to the NL pennant in '84, batting .284 with 86 RBI.

Throughout his career, Garvey was a big-game player. In five League Championship Series appearances—four with the Dodgers and one with the Padres—he batted

.356. In his five World Series appearances, he hit .319. But he will be best remembered for his every-day play. His .294 career batting average includes seven seasons in which he hit .304 or better. That and his 1,308 RBI—including five years with 106 or more—could one day land him in the Hall of Fame.

1974 DICK BOSMAN, Cleveland Indians

Publisher: Cleveland Pro Sports Entertainment, Cleveland, OH
Manufacturer: Dynacolor Graphics, Miami, FL • Type: Chrome
Postmark: Not Used • Value: $15 Signed

Right-hander Dick Bosman was the most successful pitcher in the history of the expansion Washington Senators. His 2.19 ERA in 1969 topped the American League, while his 16-win total in 1970 was not only a personal high but stands as the record for the expansion club in its 1961–71 history.

As his lifetime average of two walks allowed per game attests, Bosman was a great control pitcher throughout his career, which began with the Senators in 1966 and ended with the Oakland A's in 1976. After the Senators moved to Texas to become the Rangers in '72,

Dick won 8 and lost 10. Traded to Cleveland during the '73 season, he went on to pitch a no-hitter against the defending champion Oakland A's on July 19, 1974. The performance prompted the A's to trade for Bosman in '75. He went 11-4 for Oakland in 22 games, helping them win another AL West title. Bosman's career totals include 82 wins, 85 losses, and a 3.67 ERA.

1975 ROLLIE FINGERS, Oakland A's

Publisher: Doug McWilliams, #73-36 KV5607 • Manufacturer: Kolor View Press, Los Angeles, CA • Type: Chrome • Postmark: Not Used Value: $25–$30 Signed

Right-hander Rollie Fingers is the only pitcher in the Hall of Fame with a losing record. During his 17 seasons in Oakland, San Diego, and Milwaukee, he won 114 games and lost 118. But as a relief pitcher—and particularly a closer—Fingers is second to none. At the time of his retirement in 1985, his save total of 341 was the highest in major league history.

Fingers' debut with the A's in 1968 was hardly the stuff of greatness. In his only appearance, he pitched $1\frac{1}{3}$ innings and gave up four runs on four hits and a walk to

compile an astronomical 27.00 ERA. Back with the club in '69, Fingers showed flashes of things to come. Although his overall record for the year was 6-7, as a reliever he went 4-3 with 12 saves. He remained a part-time starter until 1972, when he pitched entirely out of the bullpen, appearing in 65 games and finishing 11-9 with 21 saves. He then became a staple in Oakland's push for the world championship, pitching in six games during the World Series; he won 1, lost 1, and saved 2.

Fingers remained with the A's through their three title years and on through 1976, after which he joined the San Diego Padres as a free agent. He promptly led the National League in saves with 35, then led the league again in 1978 with 37 saves. In 1981, Fingers returned to the AL, joining the Milwaukee Brewers. He saved 28 games, leading the American League in that category for the first time. That feat, coupled with his 6-3 record and 1.04 ERA, earned him the league MVP award. Fingers retired after the 1985 season, joining the Hall of Fame in 1992.

1975 DENNIS ECKERSLEY, Cleveland Indians

DENNIS ECKERSLEY   **CLEVELAND INDIANS**

Publisher: Cleveland Indians • Manufacturer: Not Indicated • Type: Real Photo • Postmark: Not Used • Value: $10 Unsigned

Publisher: New York Mets Hall of Fame, New York, NY • Manufacturer: Not Indicated • Type: Color Chrome • Postmark: Not Used • Value: $10

Dennis Eckersley began his career rather auspiciously as a starter for the Cleveland Indians in 1975, winning 13 and losing 7 with an excellent 2.60 ERA. In three seasons with the Tribe, he never won fewer than 13 games. Traded to Boston prior to the '78 season, Eck enjoyed his best year with a 20-8 record while compiling a 2.99 ERA. He followed that with a 17-10 mark in '79. Although he won 12 games with the Red Sox in '80, he suffered a losing record for the first time with 14 defeats. His 9 wins in '81—the first season he failed to reach double digits in victories—was followed by 13-13 and 9-13 records. After going 4-4 through the first part of the 1984 season with Boston, Eck was traded to the Chicago Cubs, where he went 10-8. He was 11-7 with the Cubs in '85, but slipped to 6-11 in '86.

Just when Eckersley's career appeared over, he was traded to the Oakland A's (1987). Manager Tony LaRussa moved him to the bullpen, where he became one of baseball's premier closers. In 1992, his 7-1 record and 51 saves earned him both the Cy Young award and American League MVP honors. In 1997, at age 43, he saved 36 games for the St. Louis Cardinals. Chances are good that Eckersley will wind up in the Hall of Fame.

1975 TOM SEAVER, New York Mets

Tom Seaver was the epitome of the complete pitcher. He had a terrific fastball, marvelous control, a wonderful slider, and a competitive spirit second to none. In 20 seasons, he won 311 games while losing only 205 and compiling an ERA of 2.86. He almost single-handedly turned the New York Mets from the laughingstock of baseball into world champions. In 1967, after winning 16 games, he was named National League Rookie of the Year. Two years later, with Seaver winning a career-high 25 games, the once lowly Mets upset the Baltimore Orioles in the World Series. His performance earned him the first of three Cy Young awards; others followed in 1973, when he led the NL in ERA, strikeouts, and complete games, and in 1975, when he won 22 games and struck out 243 batters, both league highs.

Seaver is the only pitcher in history to strike out at least 200 batters in nine straight seasons (1968–1976). On April 22, 1970, his 19 strikeouts tied the all-time single-game record set by Steve Carlton. Though that mark has since been broken, Seaver's single-game record of 10 consecutive strikeouts has yet to be matched. His career total of 3,640 strikeouts ranks fourth on the all-time list. No pitcher has thrown more strikeouts in the NL than the 3,272 Seaver hurled from 1968–83. When his NL career ended after a mediocre 9-14 season in 1983, Seaver bounced back, winning 15 and 16 games with the Chicago White Sox in 1984 and '85. While Tom is most associated with the Mets, he enjoyed significant success with the Cincinnati Reds, tossing his only no-hitter when the team faced St. Louis on June 16, 1978, and helping the Reds win their division in 1979 when he posted a 16-6 record.

Seaver's nickname, "Tom Terrific," was acknowl-edged in 1992 when he was inducted into the Hall of Fame after being named on 98.8 percent of the voting committee's ballots. Seaver's percentage of votes eclipsed the all-time highest mark of 98.2 earned by Ty Cobb in 1936, the Hall's first year.

1976 JIM KAAT, Philadelphia Phillies

JIM KAAT

Publisher: Tres Joli Studio, #P1596, Pennsauken, NJ • Manufacturer: Dynacolor Graphics, Miami, FL • Type: Color Lithograph • Postmark: Not Used • Value: $10–$15 Unsigned

Publisher: Los Angeles Dodgers, #P46521 • Manufacturer: Dynacolor Graphics, Miami, FL • Type: Chrome • Postmark: Not Used • Value: $10–$15 Unsigned

Jim Kaat was perhaps the best fielding pitcher in baseball history, winning 16 Gold Gloves, a record he shares with Hall of Fame third baseman Brooks Robinson. During Jim's 25 major league seasons, he won 283 games while losing 237, enjoying some exceptional years. His best came with the Minnesota Twins in 1966, when he led the AL with a 25-13 record while striking out 205 in 304.2 innings. His win and innings-pitched totals led the league and were personal highs. But even at his peak, Kaat gave up a lot of hits, leading the American League in that cate-gory for three consecutive years—1965, '66, and '67—with 267, 271, and 269, respectively.

Traded to the Chicago While Sox in 1973, Kaat won 21 for the Sox in '74 and 20 in '75. He enjoyed less suc-cess during his three-year stint with the Phillies, when this postcard was produced. Kaat's 12-win 1976 season was his best with Philadelphia. Jim finished his career as a relief pitcher with the St. Louis Cardinals, helping them to the world championship in 1982 with a 5-3 record in 69 games, all but two in relief. Since his play-ing days ended, he has been highly successful as a television analyst. On the strength of his 283 career victories and superb fielding, it would not be surprising to see Jim inducted into the Hall of Fame one day.

1977 TOM LASORDA, Los Angeles Dodgers

Left-hander Tom Lasorda pitched 28 games over three seasons with the Brooklyn Dodgers (1954, '55) and the Kansas City Athletics (1956). His totals showed no wins and 4 losses (all with Kansas City). Yet he is one of the most recognized names in baseball due to his outstanding record as manager of the Los Angeles Dodgers. He managed the team for four games in 1976, then became full-time boss in '77. He won NL pennants in his first two seasons, then led the Dodgers to NL West division titles in 1981, '83, '85, and '88, with NL pennants and world championships in '81 and '88. Lasorda consistently pushed his team to win until he was forced out of his managerial role in 1996 following health problems. He was elected to the Hall of Fame in 1997.

1977 WILLIE McCOVEY, San Francisco Giants

Willie "Stretch" McCovey was a 6-foot-4, 225-pound slugger who walloped 521 home runs during his 22 seasons in the majors. That puts him tops among National League left-handed hitters and 10th overall. His 18 career grand slams rank second only to those of Lou Gehrig of the Yankees, who had 23. Willie was NL home run king three times, with 44 in '63, 36 in '68, and 45 in '69. He also won the RBI championship twice, with 105 in 1968 and a career-high 126 in 1969.

Willie showed signs of his greatness in his very first

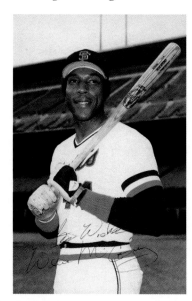

Publisher: Doug McWilliams, #77-95 KVB10358, Berkeley, CA
Manufacturer: Kolor View Press, Los Angeles, CA • Type: Chrome
Postmark: Not Used • Value: $15 Unsigned

game with the San Francisco Giants in 1959, going 4 for 4 with 2 triples and 2 singles, accounting for 3 runs and 2 RBI. He continued his devastating performance all season, batting .354 and slamming 13 home runs with 38 RBI in only 52 games, good for Rookie of the Year honors. Ten years later, he won National League MVP honors with a .320 average and career highs in home runs (45) and RBI (126).

After 15 years with the Giants, Willie was traded to the San Diego Padres, where he played for three seasons. In 1977, McCovey was back with the Giants. With 28 homers and 86 RBI along with a .280 average, he was named Comeback Player of the Year. Willie was named to the Hall of Fame in 1986.

1977 GREG LUZINSKI, Philadelphia Phillies

Greg Luzinski was one of the most feared sluggers in baseball from the day he joined the Philadelphia Phillies in 1970 until he retired from the Chicago White Sox after the 1984 season. Greg left the big leagues with a .276 batting average, 307 home runs, and 1,128 RBI. Affec-

GREG LUZINSKI

Publisher: Bob Bartosz, Pennsauken, NJ • Manufacturer: Not Indicated
Type: Color Lithograph • Postmark: Not Used • Value: $10 Unsigned

tionately known as "The Bull," Luzinski had 30 or more homers four times, once with the White Sox and three times with the Phillies—including his career-best 39 in 1977. That same year, he drove in 130 runs—a career high but not enough to lead the NL in RBI as he did with 120 in 1973, when he also hit 34 round-trippers.

When the Phillies won the World Series in 1980, "The Bull" had 100 RBI during the season but batted just .228, a career low. Nevertheless, the American League's designated hitter rule extended Greg's career. He did exceptionally well in that role after joining the White Sox in '81. In '82, Luzinski had 18 homers and 102 RBI. In '83, he blasted 32 home runs and drove in 95 runs as he helped the Sox to a division title.

This Bob Bartosz postcard shows Luzinski ready to intimidate another pitcher, which he did successfully for 15 years.

1977 GEORGE FOSTER, Cincinnati Reds

Publisher: George Foster • Manufacturer: Not Indicated • Type: Black & White • Postmark: Not Used • Value: $15–$20 Signed

ROD CAREW
MINNESOTA TWINS

Publisher: Minnesota Twins • Manufacturer: Asco Inc., Winona, MN
Type: Chrome • Postmark: Not Used • Value: $15 Unsigned

As this postcard indicates, George Foster was a highly religious person. An integral part of Cincinnati's Big Red Machine, Foster achieved the ultimate honor in 1977, when he was named the National League's MVP. That season, he batted a career-high .320 and led the NL in home runs (52), runs (124), and RBI (149), all personal highs. But Foster was hardly a one-year wonder. He led the NL in RBI in 1976 and 1978 with 121 and 120, respectively. His 40 home runs in '78 also topped the league.

Foster originally came up with the San Francisco Giants in 1969 for nine games and again in '70 for nine more. After 36 games of the '71 season, he was traded to the Reds. It took Foster a few years to break into the Reds' powerful starting lineup, but once he did, he became one of the team's best players. Foster batted .300 for the first time in 1975 and hit .306 in '76 before reaching his blockbuster '77 season. George batted better than .300 for the last time in '79, hitting .302. But his ability to hit 20 or more home runs per year kept him in the majors awhile longer. Foster went to the Mets in 1982 and remained there until midway through the '86 season, when he was traded to the White Sox. After 15 games in Chicago, Foster retired.

1977 ROD CAREW, Minnesota Twins

As a pure hitter, Rod Carew ranks among the best of all time, winning seven batting titles with the Minnesota Twins. In 1977, Carew flirted with the magic .400 mark for most of the season. He finished with a .388 average, good enough to earn him the American League MVP award. He was just the third Twin to be so honored, and no Twin has won the award since.

Carew's graceful hitting stroke enabled him to compile a .328 career batting average over 19 seasons while topping .300 for 15 consecutive years—from 1969, when he won his first batting title with a .332 average, through 1983. Carew played five of those seasons with the California Angels, to whom he was traded prior to the 1979 season for four players.

Carew came up with the Twins as a second baseman in 1967. He switched to first base in 1976 and remained there for the remainder of his career. Never a power hitter, Carew notched career highs in home runs (14) and RBI (100) during his fabulous '77 campaign. He also established career bests—and led the AL—with 239 hits, 16 triples, and 128 runs scored. The speedy Carew stole a lifetime-best 49 bases in 1976. He retired in 1985 after reaching 3,053 hits, and was inducted into the Hall of Fame in 1991.

1979 KEITH HERNANDEZ & WILLIE STARGELL

In 1979, for the first and only time in major league history, two players shared an MVP award: Keith Hernandez of the St. Louis Cardinals and Willie Stargell of the Pittsburgh Pirates. Both were first basemen, and obviously both had outstanding seasons. Hernandez had the better individual season, leading the National League with a .344 batting average, 48 doubles, and 116 runs scored. He also had a career-high 105 RBI. Stargell batted .281 with 32 home runs and 82 RBI. As the leader of the Pirates, he was instrumental in leading them to the NL pennant and a World Series title.

Over a 21-year career, Stargell compiled a .282 batting average. He twice led the league in homers, with 48 in 1971 and 44 in 1973. Five times, he had better than 100 RBI, with 125 in '79 his best ever, though his 119 RBI in '73 was the NL's best mark that season. He was elected to the Hall of Fame in 1987.

Hernandez, who played 17 years with the Cardinals, Mets, and Indians, finished his career with a .296 batting average. He's a longshot to follow Stargell into the Hall, but in 1979, the two were equal in the eyes of baseball writers.

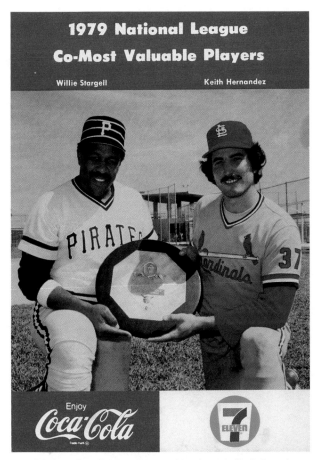

1979 National League Co-Most Valuable Players

Willie Stargell   Keith Hernandez

Publisher: Coca-Cola/7-11 Stores • Manufacturer: Not Indicated
Type: Chrome • Postmark: Not Used • Value: $20 Unsigned

1980-89

In 1980, Kansas City Royals superstar George Brett thrilled baseball fans, flirting with a .400 batting average for much of the season. He wound up batting .390 with 24 home runs and 118 RBI, good enough to earn him the American League MVP award. His performance helped the Royals reach the World Series. Despite Brett's .375 batting average, Kansas City lost to Philadelphia in six games as Hall of Famer Steve Carlton won 2 and reliever Tug McGraw saved 2. Nevertheless, sports artist Ted Watts honored Brett after the season by crafting a limited-edition print in his likeness.

A labor dispute marred the '81 season, as a players' strike limited the number of games to fewer than 110. The Cincinnati Reds, who finished that shortened season with the best record in the majors, were ruled ineligible for the postseason when the Powers That Were chose to hold a special divisional playoff series, pitting the teams with the most wins in the first half of the season against those who won the most in the second. The Dodgers accrued more wins than the Reds before the

strike, while Houston led the National League West in wins in the season's second half. The decision made a mockery of the game. When the World Series finally took place, the Dodgers beat the Yankees in six games.

The next season, the Milwaukee Brewers made their only World Series appearance to date, falling to the Cardinals in seven games. In 1983, American League MVP Cal Ripken Jr. led the Orioles to the club's most recent World Series, where the Birds beat the Phillies in six. In the NL that year, Dale Murphy of the Atlanta Braves won his second consecutive MVP award. San Diego got its first taste of World Series baseball in 1984 when the Padres made their first Fall Classic appearance, losing to the Detroit Tigers in five games. The 1985 Series became the Battle of Missouri as the Royals beat the Cardinals in seven. Kansas City's Brett batted .370 in the Series, while Royals right-hander Brett Saberhagen won 2 and posted a 0.50 ERA.

Boston fans suffered yet another postseason disappointment in 1986. The Red Sox finally returned to the World Series, only to lose when the Mets scored eight runs in the last three innings of the seventh and deciding game. Roger Clemens pitched like a mortal in the Series after winning his first Cy Young award and being named AL MVP. In the NL, Mike Schmidt of the Phillies won his third MVP award.

In the 1987 World Series, the Minnesota Twins

Publisher: Ted Watt Art Postcards, #188,570, Oswego, KS • Manufacturer: Not Indicated • Type: Chrome • Postmark: Not Used • Value: $15

Publisher: Minnesota Twins—BRF • Manufacturer: Park Press Inc., Waite Park, MN • Type: Chrome • Postmark: Not Used • Value: $10 Signed

stunned the world when they beat the Cardinals in seven to win their first world championship. Superstar outfielder Kirby Puckett led the Twins with a .357 Series batting average, scored 5 runs and drove in 3, while Dan Gladden chipped in with 7 RBI and Kent Hrbek added 6. Frank Viola was the pitching star, winning 2 games, including the seventh.

The 1988 AL MVP award went to Jose Canseco, who had a fabulous year as he led the Oakland A's to the World Series against the Dodgers. The magic ended there, as the Dodger pitchers—led by Orel Hershiser's 2 wins—kept Canseco and the heavy-hitting A's in check. But there was no stopping the A's in the '89 Series; the club defeated the San Francisco Giants in four straight. Dave Stewart and Mike Moore won 2 games apiece, while Rickey Henderson batted .474, Carney Lansford .438, and Canseco .357 for the winners. The Giants' Kevin Mitchell was the NL MVP that year, while Milwaukee's Robin Yount copped the honor in the AL.

All in all, the 1980s had many positive baseball moments. But for some fans, it wasn't enough to undo the damage wrought by the strike of '81.

1980 MIKE SCHMIDT, Philadelphia Phillies

Many fans consider Phillies superstar Mike Schmidt to be the finest third baseman in major league history. Schmidt played his entire career with the Phils, from 1972 through 1989. His 548 career home runs put him seventh on the all-time list. Schmidt led the National League in home runs eight times—second only to Babe Ruth in career home run titles—and hit 30 or more homers 13 times, a consistency of power surpassed only by Hank Aaron. Three times Schmidt was honored as the NL's MVP—in 1980, '81, and '86. In each of those seasons, he led the NL in home runs, RBI, and slugging percentage. Schmidt smacked 48 home runs and drove in 121 runs, both career highs, in leading the Phillies to the pennant and world championship in 1980. Facing the Royals in the World Series, Schmidt batted .381 in Philadelphia's six-game victory. In the strike-shortened season of '81, he drilled 31 home runs with 91 RBI while compiling a career-best .316 batting average. In his final MVP season, Schmidt slammed 37 home runs and had 119 RBI.

Publisher: Perez-Steele Galleries, Fort Washington, PA • Manufacturer: Not Indicated • Type: Chrome • Postmark: Not Used • Value: $10 Unsigned

As great as Schmidt's hitting prowess was, his fielding was equally superb. He won 10 Gold Glove awards as the NL's finest fielding third baseman. With such impressive statistics, it's no wonder Schmidt was inducted into the Hall of Fame in 1995, his first year of eligibility.

1981 FERNANDO VALENZUELA, Los Angeles Dodgers

Publisher: Los Angeles Dodgers • Manufacturer: Crocker, Los Angeles, CA • Type: Chrome • Postmark: Not Used • Value: $5 Unsigned

Fernando Valenzuela could well be the greatest player Mexico ever sent to the major leagues. Fernando burst onto the baseball scene like a comet in 1981, winning both Rookie of the Year and the Cy Young award as the best pitcher in the National League. With his 13-7 record, Fernando led the league in games started (25), complete games (11), shutouts (8), innings pitched (192), and strikeouts (180). With the players' strike limiting the season to 110 games, Valenzuela's '81 record is even more impressive.

Thanks to the strike, the Dodgers got the chance to play their way into the World Series. Fernando went 1-0 against the Astros in a special division playoff series, 1-1 against the Montreal Expos in the NL Championship Series, and won his only World Series appearance as the Dodgers beat the New York Yankees for the championship.

Valenzuela continued to sparkle for the Dodgers, pitching more than 250 innings per season through 1987 and leading the National League in victories (21) and complete games (20) in '86. Arm trouble began to limit his effectiveness in '88, leading the Dodgers to drop him after 1990. He briefly left the majors, but managed to return and stay until '97 with the Orioles, Phillies, Padres, and Cardinals. At the end of '97, Fernando had 173 wins, 153 losses, an ERA of 3.54, and 2,074 career strikeouts.

Despite his later struggles, Dodger fans will remembered fondly the excitement Fernando created every time he stepped on the mound during his 11 banner

seasons with Los Angeles. He will be remembered as one of the most popular players in Dodgers history, particularly by his fellow Mexican nationals, to whom he was a hero.

1983 CAL RIPKEN JR., Baltimore Orioles

CAL RIPKEN, JR.

Publisher: Baltimore Orioles • Manufacturer: Not Indicated • Type: Chrome Postmark: Not Used • Value: $10–$15

This is the first official postcard of Cal Ripken Jr., published by the Orioles in 1981. Only 21 years old at the time, he was destined for greatness. Ripken came up through the Orioles' minor league system as a third baseman, but manager Earl Weaver soon switched him to shortstop, where he found a comfortable home. Two years after his arrival on the big league scene, Ripken was the American League's MVP, batting .318 and leading the Orioles to the 1983 American League pennant and victory in the world series. Like the immortal Babe Ruth, Ripken is a Maryland native; he grew up less than 30 miles from Baltimore. As a youngster, he saw lots of Orioles action since his father, Cal Sr., was an Orioles coach.

On May 30, 1982, Ripken began a streak of consecutive

games played that would last the better part of 16 seasons, finally ending on September 19, 1998, when he voluntarily took himself out of the lineup. The feat—and his impressive stats—will one day carry him to the Hall of Fame.

1984 RYNE SANDBERG, Chicago Cubs

THE COLLA COLLECTION

Ryne Sandberg

Publisher: Barry Colla, #4494, Santa Clara, CA • Manufacturer: Not Indicated
Type: Chrome • Postmark: Not Used • Value: $3–$5 Unsigned

Although Ryne Sandberg broke into the majors with the Philadelphia Phillies in 1981, it was with the Chicago Cubs that he made his mark as the premier second baseman of the 1980s. In the steal of the century, the Cubs obtained Sandberg and shortstop Larry Bowa for shortstop Ivan DeJesus, who faded into oblivion after three seasons with the Phillies.

In his third season in Chicago, Sandberg was the National League's Most Valuable Player—the Cubs' first MVP since Ernie Banks—in leading his team to the 1984 division title with a .314 batting average. Sandberg also won his first Gold Glove award that year.

While .314 proved to be his highest single-season average, Sandberg remained a consistent hitter, batting below .290 in only one full season thereafter. While his batting remained constant, his power increased until 1990, when he slammed a career- and league-high 40 home runs while driving in 100 runs for the first time. He followed up with 26 home runs and another 100 RBI in '91.

In his career, Sandberg captured nine Gold Glove awards. Three times, he was the NL's leading vote-getter in All-Star balloting. In 1993, Sandberg became the first major leaguer to start nine All-Star games at second base, surpassing the eight starts by Hall of Famers Rod Carew and Nellie Fox. Having retired in 1994, Sandberg is a candidate for Hall of Fame enshrinement in 2000.

1984 GARY CARTER, Montreal Expos

Eleven-time All-Star catcher Gary Carter ranks among the best players of his era. In both 1981 and '84, Gary was named MVP of the All-Star Game. He earned three Gold Gloves and five *Sporting News* Silver Slugger awards in his 19 seasons.

GARY CARTER

Publisher: Montreal Expos • Manufacturer: Not Indicated • Type: Chrome
Postmark: Not Used • Value: $5 Unsigned

Carter signed with the Montreal Expos after being selected in the third round of the June 1972 draft. In 1975, he was Rookie of the Year in the National League, batting .270 with 17 home runs and 68 RBI. Although he never batted .300 during his career, he slammed 30 or more home runs twice and belted 20 or more seven times. Gary socked 31 homers for the Expos in 1977 and hit a career-high 32 in 1985, his first season with the Mets. In his final season with the Expos, 1984, he led the NL with 106 RBI. He had 101 RBI with Montreal in 1980 and 100 and 105 with the Mets in '85 and '86, respectively. Those 105 RBI, along with his 32 home runs, were prime reasons the Mets reached the '86 World Series, which they won.

Carter's total of 2,056 games caught ranks third on the all-time list, trailing only Bob Boone and Carlton Fisk. And his .265 average, 304 home runs, and 1,143 RBI make him a strong candidate for the Hall of Fame.

1984 TONY PEREZ, Cincinnati Reds

Publisher: Bob Hesse, #P16589, Pinellas Park, FL • Manufacturer: Dynacolor Graphics, Miami, FL • Type: Chrome • Postmark: Not Used
Value: $10 Unsigned

Tony Perez was in the twilight of an outstanding career when this Bob Hesse postcard was published in 1984, Tony's first season in Cincinnati since 1976. Although most of his success came with Cincinnati's Big Red Machine in the 1970s, when he played first and third base, Tony recaptured some of that glory in 1985, batting .328 in 50 games as a part-time first baseman for the Reds. It was his highest average in his 23 seasons. Perez retired in 1986 with a career .279 average, ranking as perhaps the greatest Cuban player in major league history. He drove in 101 or more runs seven times in his career. With Cincinnati he had 102 in '67, 122 in '69, 129 in '70, 101 in both '73 and '74, and 109 in '75. His last 100-plus RBI season came with the Boston Red Sox in 1980. Other stops along the Perez trail were Montreal ('77, '78, '79) and Philadelphia ('83). He played his final three seasons back in Cincinnati. Along with his lifetime .279 average, Tony had 379 career home runs and 1,652 RBI.

1984 DAVE WINFIELD, New York Yankees

One of the most gifted all-around athletes in major league history, Dave Winfield didn't spend one day in the minor leagues during his 23-year career. In 1973, as captain of the University of Minnesota baseball team, he won 13 games as a pitcher, batted. 400, and was named MVP in the College World Series. Later that year, after graduation, he joined the San Diego Padres, who had made him their first draft choice. A star basketball player while at Minnesota, Winfield was drafted by both Utah of the ABA and Atlanta of the NBA. And though he didn't play football in college, he was even drafted by the NFL's Minnesota Vikings.

Of Winfield's eight seasons with the Padres, his most successful came in 1978 and '79; he batted .308 both years and drove in a career-high 118 runs in '79. Signing as a free agent with the Yankees in 1981, he enjoyed his best seasons in New York, batting a career-best .340 in 1984 and driving in 100 or more runs for five consecutive seasons (1982–86).

Dave missed the entire '89 season after he underwent back surgery to remove fragments of a herniated disc. After starting the 1990 season with New York, he was traded to the California Angels for pitcher Mike Witt. In Anaheim, he played well enough to be named Comeback Player of the Year by *The Sporting News*.

Signing as a free agent with the Toronto Blue Jays in '92, Winfield helped lead the Blue Jays to the world championship, batting .290 with 26 home runs and 108 RBI in the regular season. He returned to his native Minnesota in '93 and became only the 19th player in history to record 3,000 hits, singling off Oakland's Dennis Eckersley on September 16. He also slammed his

Publisher: TCMA Ltd., Amawalk, NY • Manufacturer: Not Indicated
Type: Chrome • Postmark: Not Used • Value: $5 Unsigned

to record 200 strikeouts in each of his first three years.

Arm injuries and a severe drug problem since have hampered Gooden's career. Repeated violations of baseball's drug policy bought him a suspension for the entire '95 season. Gooden made a comeback of sorts with the Yankees in '96, winning 11 games and losing only 7. An arm injury prevented him from seeing action in the playoffs or World Series as the Yankees won the championship.

Remaining drug free, Gooden joined the Cleveland Indians in 1998, winning 8 and losing 6 with a 3.76 ERA. Despite his many problems, Dwight has nearly 200 victories, winning almost twice as many games as he has lost. He always will be remembered as one of the finest young pitchers in baseball history, a star whose brightness dimmed far too soon.

Publisher: TCMA Ltd., Amawalk, NY • Manufacturer: Not Indicated •
Type: Chrome • Postmark: Not Used • Value: $5 Unsigned

450th home run that season, off California's Russ Springer. Those exploits put Winfield in esteemed company; only Hall of Fame legends Hank Aaron, Willie Mays, Stan Musial, and Carl Yastrzemski, plus HOFer-in-waiting Eddie Murray, reached both of those marks. There's little doubt that 12-time All-Star and super-athlete Dave Winfield will soon be enshrined at Cooperstown himself.

1985 DWIGHT GOODEN, New York Mets

Dwight Gooden exploded across the baseball landscape like a shooting star, parlaying a blazing fastball into instant stardom with the New York Mets in 1984. In his rookie season, the 19-year-old "Doc" won 17 games and led the majors in strikeouts with 276. He was even better in '85, topping the National League with 24 wins, a 1.53 ERA, 268 strikeouts, and 16 complete games; the performance made him the youngest man ever to win a Cy Young award. Gooden's record slipped to 17-6 in '86, but he managed 200 strikeouts, becoming the first pitcher in history

Publisher: Bob Hesse, #P16588, Pinellas Park, FL • Manufacturer: Dynacolor Graphics, Miami, FL • Type: Chrome • Postmark: Not Used
Value: $10 Unsigned

1985 DAVE PARKER, Cincinnati Reds

Many felt that Dave Parker's career was pretty much over when he joined the Cincinnati Reds after 11 successful seasons with the Pittsburgh Pirates. The Cobra had won back-to-back batting titles in Pittsburgh, hitting .338 in 1977 and .334 in '78. In the latter season, he also slammed 30 home runs, drove in 117 runs, and was named NL MVP. But his numbers dropped in the 1980s, and his retirement seemed imminent.

Parker surprised everyone in '84, hitting 16 home runs and driving in 94 runs. He was even better in '85 when he batted .312, blasted 34 homers, and led the NL with 125 RBI, a personal high.

Parker finally concluded his career in 1991 with a lifetime batting average of .290 to go with 339 home runs and 1,493 RBI.

The photo on this beautiful color postcard was taken by sports photographer Bob Hesse during Parker's Cincinnati stint at the Reds' Tampa training facility.

1985 WADE BOGGS, Boston Red Sox

Since he arrived in the major leagues in 1982, Wade Boggs has seldom batted below .300. The first time was his last season with the Red Sox, 1992, when he hit a mediocre .259. Joining the Yankees as a free agent in '93, Boggs promptly returned to normal, hitting .302 and proving his career was far from over. He remained with the Yankees through the '97 season, batting .342, .324, .311, and .292 in his remaining four seasons. In 1998, Boggs moved closer to his home, signing with the expansion Tampa Bay Devil Rays for their inaugural season and batting a respectable .280. His performance guaranteed him another season in '99, when he surpassed the 3,000 hit mark.

Boggs has proven to be one of the great hitters of modern times, posting a career average of .329, a mark that—if sustained—will assure his induction into the Hall of Fame. On four occasions, Boggs had the highest batting average in the majors, his career best being the .368 mark he compiled in 1985. Never a power hitter, Boggs posted double-digit home run totals only twice, including a career-high 24 in 1987, when he also had a career-best 89 RBI. A true hitting machine, Boggs has a .321 batting average in 12 All-Star Games. He earned a world championship ring with the Yankees in 1996—after coming painfully close with the Red Sox in '86.

Publisher: Sandpiper Studios, Winterhaven, FL • Manufacturer: Not Indicated
Type: Chrome • Postmark: Not Used • Value: $10 Unsigned

Publisher: Chicago White Sox • Manufacturer: Not Indicated
Type: Chrome • Postmark: Not Used • Value: $5 Unsigned

1985 CARLTON FISK, Chicago White Sox

Carlton "Pudge" Fisk was an exceptional catcher for more than 20 seasons, almost equally divided between the Boston Red Sox and Chicago White Sox. A feared offensive threat, he slammed a career-high 37 home runs and drove in a career-best 107 runs for the White Sox in 1985. And who can forget his unparalleled moment with the Red Sox in the 1975 World Series, when his dramatic sixth-game home run in the bottom of the 12th inning gave Boston a 7-6 win. Even though the Sox lost the seventh game, Fisk's homer ranks as one of the most exciting events in World Series history.

Fisk also was outstanding defensively—and surprisingly speedy for a catcher, stealing 17 bases in his blockbuster '85 season. Batting average–wise, his two best seasons came with the Red Sox, in 1975 when he batted .331 in 79 games and in '77 when he hit .315 with 26 home runs and 102 RBI. Had he not become eligible for the Hall of Fame in the same year as George Brett, Nolan Ryan, and Robin Yount, he probably would have been enshrined in 1999. As it is, it should be just a matter of time before he takes his rightful place among the baseball immortals at Cooperstown.

1985 DON MATTINGLY, New York Yankees

Before a severe back injury began to hamper his career in 1990, Yankees captain Don Mattingly was the finest first baseman in baseball. He could hit for average with power *and* field his position to near perfection. In his first full season with the Yankees in 1984, Mattingly won the American League batting title with a .343 average; he also hit 23 home runs and drove in 110 runs. In 1985, he was the AL MVP, batting .324 with 35 home runs and 145 RBI, both career highs. He posted a career-best .352 batting average in '86. His average topped .300 for six consecutive seasons in all, putting him in the company of Yankee luminaries Earle Combs, Bill Dickey, Joe DiMaggio, Lou Gehrig, and Babe Ruth.

Mattingly was on a sure path to join those men in Cooperstown until his back betrayed him. Prior to the injury, he averaged 25 home runs, 114 RBI, and a .327 batting average. In 1990, the pain was so bad he was able to play in only 102 games, batting a career-low .256. From that low point, Mattingly slowly worked his

Publisher: New York Yankees • Manufacturer: Not Indicated
Type: Chrome • Postmark: Not Used • Value: $5 Unsigned

way back, hitting .288, .287, .291, .304, and .288 over his last five seasons. His power hitting never fully returned, though, as he averaged 10 home runs and 64 RBI from 1990–95. Though his numbers were no longer the stuff of legends, Mattingly remained a valued contributor and leader for the Yankees.

1985 PHIL NIEKRO, New York Yankees

Publisher: TCMA Ltd., #NY 85-15, Amawalk, NY • Manufacturer: Not Indicated • Type: Chrome • Postmark: Not Used • Value: $5 Unsigned

It's strange to see knuckleballing Hall of Famer Phil Niekro in Yankee pinstripes, because most fans associate him with a Braves uniform. But New York was one of the final stops in his remarkable 24-year career. This 1985 team-issued postcard cites Niekro's '84 stats, which show a record of 16 wins, 8 losses, and an ERA of 3.09. He won 16 games again in '85 before joining Cleveland in '86, where he compiled an 11-11 record. He concluded his career in '87 with a farewell tour, bouncing from Cleveland to Toronto and back to Atlanta for his final game. It's fitting that his career ended "at home."

Actually, when Niekro joined the big leagues in 1964,

the Braves were still in Milwaukee. He came up as a reliever and remained in that role until 1967, the Braves' second season in Atlanta. He became a starter in '67, and the rest is history. He won 20 or more games in three seasons, and retired with 318 career victories. No pitcher in history has used the knuckleball with greater success— though Phil's brother, Joe, did well enough. A knuckleballing star in his own right, Joe won 221 games over 22 seasons, making the Niekros the winningest brother combination in history with 539 career victories.

1986 ROGER CLEMENS, Boston Red Sox

"Rocket" Roger Clemens shot into the major leagues like his nickname. He joined the Boston Red Sox in 1984 with a supersonic fastball and immediately established himself as one of baseball's great pitchers. Fifteen years later, he has more than 200 wins and an unprecedented five Cy Young awards to prove his greatness. Roger's first Cy Young came in 1986, as he led the Red Sox to the American League pennant with a 24-4 record. His second Cy Young came in 1990, when he

Publisher: Boston Red Sox • Manufacturer: Mini Pics Sports Action, Boston, MA • Type: Chrome • Postmark: Not Used • Value: $5–$7 Unsigned

went 21-6 and compiled a career-best 1.93 ERA. He won again the following year on the strength of an 18-10 record and 2.62 ERA.

Shoulder trouble began to plague Clemens soon after, and he spent a great deal of time on the disabled list in '94 and '95. Believing Clemens' best days were behind him after 13 years, the Red Sox let him go as a free agent. He signed with the Toronto Blue Jays before the 1997 season. He promptly became the first American Leaguer since Hal Newhouser to win pitching's triple crown, leading the league with 21 wins, 292 strikeouts, and a 2.05 ERA. The performance earned Clemens his fourth Cy Young award. In 1998, he became the first AL hurler since Lefty Grove to take the crown in consecutive years, tying David Cone and Rick Helling with a league-leading 20 wins and standing alone at the top with 271 strikeouts and a 2.65 ERA. His fifth Cy Young came by unanimous vote.

Exhibiting remarkable control for a fastball pitcher, Clemens had a strikeout-to-walk ratio of better than 3:1 with 3,153 Ks to only 1,012 walks heading into the '99 season. Prior to the '98 season, "Rocket" led all active pitchers in wins (233), strikeouts (3,153), and career shutouts (44). Clemens' .644 winning percentage is second best among active pitchers. The Rocket will undoubtedly be elected to the Hall of Fame the required five years after his career ends.

1987 MARK MCGWIRE, Oakland A's

In Mark McGwire's first full season in the major leagues, he gave a portent of things to come, slamming an American League–leading 49 home runs and driving in 118 runs. The Oakland Athletic was a unanimous choice as American League Rookie of the Year.

The 49-homer total marked his career high with the A's through the mid-'90s. After a 42-homer, 104-RBI performance in 1992, McGwire developed a serious heel injury that limited his play in 1993 and '94. He came back in '95 to blast 39 homers, then socked 52 dingers in '96 while driving in 113 runs. The home runs kept coming in 1997, when he hit 34 for Oakland in two-thirds of a season before he was traded to the Cardinals. With St. Louis, of course, McGwire made history in 1998 with his stunning 70-homer season.

1987 OZZIE SMITH, St. Louis Cardinals

Known as the "Wizard of Oz," Cardinals shortstop Ozzie Smith was one of the finest defensive players in baseball history. A crowd-pleasing, acrobatic performer, Smith used to take his position in the field with a standing somersault.

Ozzie broke into the majors with the Padres in 1978. His rookie .258 batting average was his highest in four

Publisher: Barry Colla, #5688, Santa Clara, CA • Manufacturer: Not Indicated
Type: Chrome • Postmark: Not Used • Value: $10 Unsigned

Publisher: Barry Colla, #10189, Santa Clara, CA • Manufacturer: Not Indicated
Type: Chrome • Postmark: Not Used • Value: $5 Unsigned

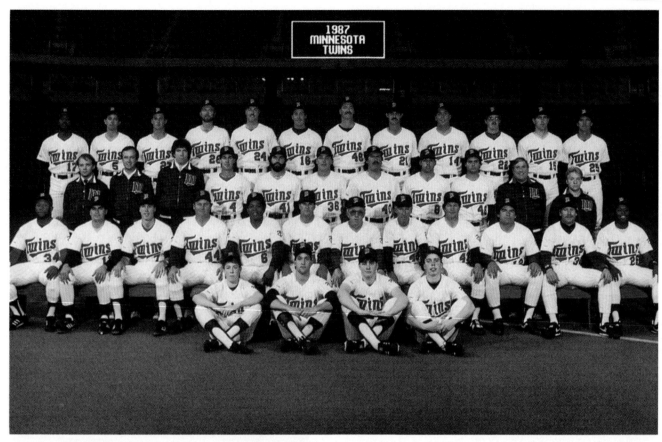

Publisher: Minnesota Twins—BRF • Manufacturer: Park Press Inc., Waite Park, MN • Type: Chrome • Postmark: Not Used • Value: $10

seasons in San Diego. On February 11, 1982, Ozzie was dealt to St. Louis for shortstop Garry Templeton in a deal that proved good for both teams. Never a prolific batter, Smith did manage a career-high .303 batting average in 1987, along with a personal-high 75 RBI. In the field, though, he had no peers, winning Gold Glove awards every year from 1980–92. Smith was named to the National League All-Star team 14 times, including 11 consecutive seasons from 1982–92. With such dominance at his position, there's little doubt he should be enshrined in the Hall of Fame. The only question is whether he'll perform his trademark flip during the induction ceremony.

1987 MINNESOTA TWINS

The Minnesota Twins won their first world championship in 1987, defeating the St. Louis Cardinals in a seven-game thriller. With rookie manager Tom Kelly making all the right moves, the Twins won the American League West title with an 85-77 record. In the American League Championship Series, they stunned the Detroit Tigers, a team that finished the year with 98 victories but lost four games to one in the playoffs.

The Twins were led by outfielder Kirby Puckett, who batted .332 while driving in 99 runs. Gary Gaetti was the Twins' RBI leader with 109 and also led AL third

baseman in putouts with 134. The pitching was led by Frank Viola, who won 17 against 10 losses, and Bert Blyleven, who was 15-12. But perhaps the real pitching hero was reliever Jeff Reardon, who saved 31 games during the season. He saved two more in the ALCS and another in the World Series against St. Louis. Reardon also won a game in the ALCS, while Blyleven notched a pair and Viola won the other. In the World Series, Viola won 2, Blyleven 1, and reliever Dan Schatzeder 1. All of those wins came in Minnesota. Throughout the Series, both the Twins and Cardinals won all of their home games.

1987 KIRBY PUCKETT, Minnesota Twins

Kirby Puckett ranks with Hall of Famers Harmon Killebrew and Rod Carew as the best and most popular players in Minnesota Twins history. Beloved by fans and players alike, Puckett enjoyed a brilliant career that was cut short when a vision ailment forced his retirement in 1995.

Puckett was drafted from Triton Junior College in his native Illinois in the third round of the 1982 free agent draft. He became an instant star with Elizabethton in the Appalachian League, batting .382. Joining the Twins in 1984, Kirby batted .296 his rookie year; he got even

Publisher: Minnesota Twins—BRF • Manufacturer: Park Press Inc., Waite Park, MN • Type: Chrome • Postmark: Not Used • Value: $5–$7 Unsigned

better with time, as his career .318 average indicates. In 1987, he led the Twins to the American League pennant and their first world championship, hitting .332 during the regular season and .357 during the World Series against St. Louis. In '88, Kirby batted a career-high .356 with 24 home runs and a career-best 121 RBI. He may not have been a monster home run hitter, but Puckett packed surprising power on his 5-foot 9-inch, 215-pound frame, hitting 31 home runs in 1986 and drilling 22 or better three other times. Puckett matched his plate prowess with solid defensive play, winning six Gold Glove awards as the Twins' center fielder. Like Killebrew and Carew, Puckett should be enshrined in the Hall of Fame, probably during his first year of eligibility in 2001.

1988 JOSE CANSECO, Oakland A's

The 1988 baseball season belonged to Jose Canseco. Seldom in the sport's history has one player so dominated the game in so many aspects. Canseco led the majors in home runs and RBI with 42 and 124, respectively, while posting a career-high .307 average. He also became the first player in history to hit 40 home runs and steal 40 bases in a single season. He was the unanimous choice of the Baseball Writers Association as American League MVP and was honored by *The Sporting News* and the Associated Press as well.

Jose was a star from the moment he donned an Oakland A's uniform. Called up from Tacoma late in the '85 season, he batted .302 with 5 homers and 13 RBI in just 29 games. In '86, he was named the American League's Rookie of the Year after slamming 33 home runs and driving in 117 runs while batting .240. He raised his average to .257 in '87 while belting 31 home runs with 113 RBI. Then came his amazing 1988 season.

Unfortunately, serious injury problems have hampered his career ever since. He missed the first half of

Publisher: Barry Colla, Santa Clara, CA • Manufacturer: Not Indicated Type: Chrome • Postmark: Not Used • Value: $5–$7 Unsigned

the '89 season with a fractured hand that required surgery, but still managed 17 home runs and 57 RBI in 65 games. In '90 and '91, he blasted 37 and 44 home runs while driving in 101 and 122 runs. In 1992, he began to tour the AL, stopping in Texas and Boston, where chronic back problems curtailed his activities. Not even a return to Oakland in '97 could spark a return to form. Finally, in 1998, Canseco exploded with the Blue Jays, knocking 46 home runs with 107 RBI while hitting just .237, proving once again that a healthy Jose Canseco is one of the game's best. In 1999, Canseco moved to Tampa and began to post All-Star numbers until a back injury put him back on the disabled list.

1988 OREL HERSHISER, Los Angeles Dodgers

Publisher: Los Angeles Dodgers • Manufacturer: Not Indicated
Type: Chrome • Postmark: Not Used • Value: $5 Unsigned

Right-hander Orel Hershiser had a dream year in 1988. His 59 consecutive scoreless innings broke Don Drysdale's major league record. His 23 wins were the most for any Dodger since Sandy Koufax won 27 in 1966. After winning the National League Cy Young award by

unanimous vote, he led the Dodgers to the world championship. Hershiser was named MVP of the NL Championship Series against the New York Mets and of the World Series against the Oakland A's. Orel won the Series' fifth and deciding game, hurling a complete-game shutout. It was his second complete-game win of the Series. Over 18 brilliant innings, Hershiser gave up only 7 hits while striking out 17 batters and compiling a 1.00 ERA.

After going 15-15 in 1989, Hershiser sustained a right shoulder injury that eventually required surgery. He missed nearly the entire 1990 season, going 1-1 in four April appearances. He returned in 1991 to post a 7-2 record, earning Comeback Player of the Year honors. Three losing seasons followed, prompting the Dodgers to make Hershiser a free agent. Signing with the Cleveland Indians, he resurrected his career. In three seasons with the Tribe, he won 16, 15, and 14 games. In the '95 AL Championship Series against Seattle, Hershiser went 2-0, becoming the first player to win the Championship Series MVP award in both leagues. His run of postseason excellence ended in the '97 World Series against Florida, when he was tagged with two losses as Cleveland lost in seven games.

Orel returned to the NL in '98 with the San Francisco Giants, winning 11 games to give him 190 career wins. He joined the New York Mets in '99, poised to reach the 200-win level. A model citizen off the field, Orel frequently signs his autographs with a biblical quote.

1988 WILL CLARK, San Francisco Giants

Will "The Thrill" Clark began his major league career with a bang. On April 8, 1986, in his first at-bat for the San Francisco Giants, he homered off the legendary Nolan Ryan at the Houston Astrodome. With a debut like that, what do you do for an encore? Obviously, Clark could not duplicate that feat on a regular basis, but he has had an outstanding major league career, coming into the '99 season with a .302 career batting average.

After a brilliant college career, Clark was the second player chosen in the June '85 draft. After just one season in the minors with Fresno, he batted .287 his first year with the Giants. In 1988, his 109 RBI led the National League; he drove in 111 runs the following season while compiling a career-high .333 batting average. His best RBI mark came with the Giants in 1991, when he drove in 116 runs.

Although injuries have hampered Clark's career, he has still managed 253 homers through '98, with his 35 with the Giants in '87 a career best. After five years with the Texas Rangers, where he batted .329 in 1994 and .326 in '97, Clark took his bat to Baltimore for the 1999 season.

Publisher: Making Waves, Littleton, CO • Manufacturer: Not Indicated
Type: Chrome • Postmark: Not Used • Value: $5–$8 Unsigned

1989 ROBIN YOUNT, Milwaukee Brewers

Robin Yount was arguably the finest all-around player in Milwaukee Brewers history. Affectionately called "The Kid" when he joined the Brewers in 1974 as an 18-year-old rookie, Yount became known as "The Franchise" in his later years. Yount was the Brewers' shortstop from 1974 through 1984, when he moved to center field and continued to excel.

In his 20 years with the Brewers, Yount was twice named American League MVP—in 1982 and 1989. In his first MVP season, he posted career highs in batting average (.331), hits (210), home runs (29), and RBI (114) as he led the Brewers to their only American League pennant. Incidentally, he also won the Gold Glove award for his defensive play. Yount sizzled in the '82 World Series, batting .414 with 6 RBI, but it wasn't enough to stop the Cardinals, who beat Milwaukee in seven games. In his second MVP year, Yount batted .318 with 21 homers and 103 RBI.

Yount concluded his career after the 1993 season with 3,142 career hits, 15th best in baseball history. He is one of only three players to record at least 3,000 hits, 200 home runs, 200 stolen bases, and 100 triples; the others are Willie Mays and George Brett. Yount's 2,856 games with one team place him in similarly rare company; only Carl Yatrzemski, Stan Musial, and Brooks Robinson have more. And Yount's feat of winning MVP awards at two positions has been matched only by Musial and Hank Greenberg.

Considering the high company that Yount's statistics put him in, it's only fitting that he joined his peers in the Hall of Fame in 1999, his first year of eligibility.

Publisher: Barry Colla, Santa Clara, CA • Manufacturer: Not Indicated
Type: Chrome • Postmark: Not Used • Value: $5–$8 Unsigned

1990-99

When time has passed and history recalls the 1990s, it will reveal a decade of rising salaries, labor unrest, unfettered growth in the sport, and the return of the home run. No decade—including the hitter-happy 1930s—had more offense. And as baseball expanded to Colorado, Florida, Arizona, and Tampa Bay, the infusion of cash and the thinning of the talent pool pushed salaries to an average of $1.7 million per player.

The strike of 1994, which canceled the World Series for the first time since 1904, nearly destroyed the game as fans stayed away in droves. But two events helped bring some of those disillusioned fans back. The first came in 1995, when Cal Ripken Jr. of the Orioles broke Lou Gehrig's record of 2,130 consecutive games played. The second occurred during the 1998 season, when the home run race between Mark McGwire and Sammy Sosa stimulated interest in the sport not seen for years. McGwire and Sosa each broke Roger Maris' 37-year-old single-season record of 61 homers with 70 and 66, respectively.

Baseball also went through several curious cycles. The small-market Cincinnati Reds and Minnesota Twins won the decade's first two championships. Then, the Toronto Blue Jays were the dominant team, winning in

Now we've got pitching so good it's scary.

Publisher: Arizona Diamondbacks • Manufacturer: Not Indicated
Type: Chrome • Postmark: Not Used • Value: $5–$8 Unsigned

1992 and '93. But the marketplace quickly changed. The opening of beautiful, retro-style Oriole Park at Camden Yards in 1992 led to a rash of new stadiums—and new revenues—for ballclubs. The Cleveland Indians, baseball's worst team for 40 years, built a new park and with it—thanks to sellouts every night—a club that reached the World Series in 1995 and '97. Team payrolls jumped to more than $50 million by the middle of the decade and approached $90 million by the end of the century. When the Orioles signed free-agent slugger Albert Belle after the 1998 season, he became the sport's all-time highest-paid player at just under $12 million per season.

The emphasis on dollars changed professional baseball, perhaps irrevocably. This became apparent in 1997, when the Florida Marlins became the fastest expansion team in any sport to win a championship. The Marlins essentially bought their World Series victory, cobbling together a team of high-priced veterans, almost all of whom were sold off before the next season. The newer Tampa Bay Devil Rays and Arizona Diamondbacks hadn't reached quite the same level of spending by the end of the decade, but were hardly miserly, offering fat contracts to both aging stars like Devon White, Wade Boggs, Fred

Tropicana Field – Home of the Tampa Bay Devil Rays

Publisher: Tampa Bay Devil Rays • Manufacturer: Not Indicated • Type: Chrome • Postmark: Not Used • Value: $5

McGriff, and Randy Johnson, and to promising youngsters like Travis Lee.

Besides providing an infusion of cash, the new, smaller parks also led to a revival of offense. Home runs per game climbed to more than 2.02 each year from 1994. Expansion and the five-man rotation thinned pitching staffs, and the likelihood of seeing another 300-game winner almost evaporated. Each year from the '94 strike season, at least one player was on pace to break Maris' record. When the record was finally broken in 1998, four players—McGwire, Sosa, Ken Griffey Jr., and Greg Vaughn—had at least 50 homers. Before Cecil Fielder hit 51 in 1990, no one had reached the 50 mark since George Foster in 1977.

Few decades offered so many glimpses at greatness. Nolan Ryan, George Brett, Robin Yount, Ozzie Smith, Paul Molitor, Dave Winfield, Eddie Murray, Carlton Fisk, Kirby Puckett, and Joe Carter—all future Hall of Famers—retired after great careers. Greg Maddux, Cal Ripken Jr., Tony Gwynn, Barry Bonds, Mark McGwire, and Roger Clemens continued their way toward the Hall. And young stars Ken Griffey Jr., Frank Thomas, Sammy Sosa, Juan Gonzalez, Mike Mussina, and Alex Rodriguez got a jump-start on careers that pointed them toward Cooperstown.

The decade also saw the return to dominance of the New York Yankees. In 1996, the Yankees won the World Series for the first time since 1978. They won again in 1998, posting one of the greatest seasons of all time. The Yankees went 114-48 during the regular season and 11-2 in the postseason. They swept the Padres in the World Series, giving them a 125-50 overall record, the best in history.

But the decade's winningest team was the Atlanta Braves. The club was a perennial title contender, reaching the postseason every year since 1991. Despite having arguably the greatest pitching staff in history for most of the decade—with Greg Maddux, Tom Glavine, and John Smoltz winning the Cy Young award each year from 1991 to '96—the Braves' only World Series victory came in 1995, when they defeated the Indians in a thrilling Fall Classic. Otherwise, their failure in the postseason was making them into the Buffalo Bills of pro baseball by the turn of the century.

1990 CURT SCHILLING, Baltimore Orioles

Publisher: Baltimore Orioles • Manufacturer: Not Indicated
Type: Black & White • Postmark: Not Used • Value: $5

The major league strikeout leader in 1997 and '98 was a baseball late bloomer. Originally signed by the Boston Red Sox in 1986, Curt Schilling was traded to the Orioles with Brady Anderson in 1988 and spent three years shuttling between the majors and minors. He was then sent to Houston for one year before going to the Phillies in 1992. There, he won 14 games his first season, although an assortment of injuries over the next three seasons made him consider retirement. But in 1997, at age 30, he came back with a 17-11 record and an NL-leading 319 strikeouts, 10th best all time. He once again led the league with 300 strikeouts in 1998, averaging nearly eight innings per start.

This postcard of Schilling was produced by the Orioles in '89, long before he established himself as one of the most durable, effective pitchers in the game.

1991 RICKEY HENDERSON, Oakland A's

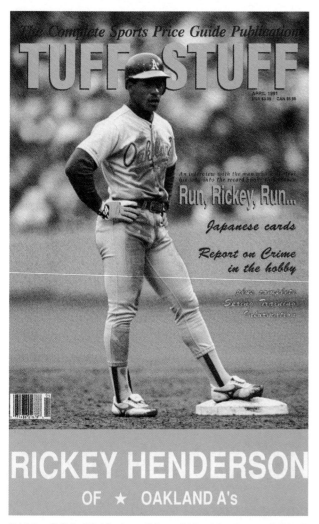

Publisher: Tuff Stuff Publications, Richmond, VA • Manufacturer: Tuff Stuff
Type: Chrome • Postmark: Not Used • Value: $10

This postcard, reproducing the cover of the April 1991 issue of *Tuff Stuff,* shows baseball's all-time stolen bases leader after having pilfered another base. It's appropriate Henderson was the cover boy on *Tuff Stuff's* baseball issue in '91. That's the year he set the all-time stolen base record, breaking Hall of Famer Lou Brock's mark of 938.

Henderson was in the twilight of his career in 1999, but his legacy will last. Other than being the all-time stolen base king and holding the single-season mark with 130 in 1982, he is arguably the game's greatest leadoff hitter and the player responsible for ushering in the 1980s era of speed and defense. Twelve times he has been a league leader in steals. But he also has more homers than any leadoff man in history and has topped 100 runs 13 times. He was the American League MVP in 1990.

When he signed with the Mets in 1999 after his fourth stint with Oakland, Rickey was 40 years old and his legs

had 20 seasons in the big leagues. But he showed no signs of slowing down. In 1998, he stole 66 bases, succeeding 84 percent of the time.

1991 TOM GLAVINE, Atlanta Braves

Publisher: Atlanta Braves • Manufacturer: Barry Colla, Santa Clara, CA
Type: Chrome • Postmark: Not Used • Value: $5–$8 Unsigned

This quiet, reliable left-hander was largely responsible for the Braves being the winningest team of the 1990s. He posted double-digit win totals each year since 1989, including a career-best 22-6 in 1993. Four times in the '90s he led the National League in victories. He entered 1999 with a 173-105 record. His ERA also dropped each year from 1994–1998.

Interestingly, Glavine was such a fine athlete at Billerica High School in Massachusetts, where he excelled in baseball and hockey, that in 1984 he was the Braves' second-round draft pick and the fourth-round selection of the Los Angeles Kings in the National Hockey League draft. Glavine likes to joke that if he'd played hockey, some guy named Gretzky would not have been such a great center. That was Glavine's position.

1991 DENNIS MARTINEZ, Montreal Expos

Publisher: Barry Colla, #6793, Santa Clara, CA • Manufacturer: Not Indicated
Type: Chrome • Postmark: Not Used • Value: $5

Right-hander Dennis Martinez is a national hero in his native Nicaragua, where he earned the nickname "El Presidente." He's one of only seven players to win 100 or more games in each of the American and National leagues. He finished a 23-year career with a 245-193 record. But his career almost ended prematurely. Martinez battled alcoholism at his peak, costing him a chance at 300 victories. His career—and life—was saved when he was traded to Montreal in 1986. There he overcame his addiction and won at least 10 games per year for the Expos and Indians over the next nine seasons. He closed out his career with the Mariners in 1997 and the Braves in 1998, where he worked as a reliever and spot starter, passing Juan Marichal as the winningest Latin American pitcher in major league history. Above, Martinez is pictured in the uniform he wore while he turned his life around.

1991 NOLAN RYAN, Texas Rangers

Although records are purportedly made to be broken, right-hander Nolan Ryan's seven no-hitters and 5,714 career strikeouts may last forever. As a tribute to his spectacular 27-year career, Ryan was elected to the Hall of Fame in 1999 on 98 percent of the ballots, second-highest behind former Mets teammate Tom Seaver.

Although he was blessed with a 100-mph fastball and one of the meanest, nastiest curveballs in history, it was an inner fire and stubbornness that kept Ryan going. He began his career in 1966 with the Mets, where his lack of control kept him languishing in the bullpen and as a spot starter. Ironically, his only championship came in 1969, even though he wasn't an integral part of the great Mets pitching staff.

When Ryan was traded to the Angels in 1971 for veteran third baseman Jim Fregosi, everyone felt the Angels had been fleeced. But Ryan won 19, 21, and 22 games over the next three seasons while leading the American League in strikeouts—including a record 383 in 1973. He signed with his hometown Astros in 1980,

Publisher: Barry Colla, #6792, Santa Clara, CA • Manufacturer: Not Indicated
Type: Chrome • Postmark: Not Used • Value: $5–$8 Unsigned

becoming baseball's first $1 million-a-year player, and won the National League ERA crown in 1981.

What perplexes historians—and physicians—is how Ryan kept getting better with age. Some batters attributed it to his throwing a scuffed ball. But when he pitched his last no-hitter, against Toronto in 1991, he struck out 16 and was throwing in the mid-90s in the ninth inning. After age 29, he won 202 games and struck out 3,629. From age 35 to the end of his career, batters hit just .202 off him. Ryan pitched four no-hitters for the Angels, one for the Astros, and two for his last team, the Texas Rangers.

Ryan signed with the Rangers in 1989 and promptly fanned 301 batters at age 42. When he retired after the 1993 season, he had led his league in strikeouts 11 times and held or tied 53 records, including the highest strikeout-per-9-innings ratio at 9.42, Yet his career record is 324-292.

1991 GEORGE BRETT, Kansas City Royals

Publisher: Tuff Stuff Publications, Richmond, VA • Manufacturer: Tuff Stuff
Type: Chrome • Postmark: Not Used • Value: $10–$15

One of the great natural hitters, George Brett retired with a .305 average and 3,154 hits. He won batting titles in 1976, 1980, and 1990—the only player to win the Silver Bat in three decades. He is also the only player to collect 3,000 hits, 300 homers, 600 doubles, 100 triples, and 200 stolen bases. His stellar 20-year career was winding down when he appeared on the June 1991 cover of *Tuff Stuff* magazine.

Brett was no mere singles hitter. His picture-perfect stroke helped him lead the league in doubles twice, in triples three times, and in slugging average three times. He hit 20 or more homers eight times. He was voted into the Hall of Fame on his first ballot in 1999, sharing the honor with Nolan Ryan and Robin Yount.

A fiery competitor, Brett became known for clutch homers. He hit three in game 3 of the 1978 American League Championship Series against the Yankees. He hit a three-run blast off the Yankees' Goose Gossage in Game 3 of the 1980 ALCS to clinch the pennant. He had three homers in the exciting 1985 ALCS in which the Royals beat the Blue Jays in seven games before winning Brett's only World Series title. But his most famous homer was one that was nullified.

In 1983, Brett hit a monstrous two-run, two-out, ninth-inning homer off Gossage at Yankee Stadium. New York manager Billy Martin protested that the pine tar on Brett's bat had exceeded the legal length, and umpire Joe Brinkman called Brett out. He went berserk, charging out of the dugout in a screaming, cussing, gyrating frenzy that remains a video favorite. Kansas City won an appeal, and the final four outs of the game had to be replayed, with Brett's "Pine Tar Episode" homer standing for the ages.

1992 GREG MADDUX, Chicago Cubs

Right-hander Greg Maddux has four Cy Young awards and has earned a rightful place among the game's all-time best. In 1995, his 1.63 ERA made him the first pitcher since Walter Johnson in 1919 to have back-to-back seasons with an ERA under 1.70.

At just 6 feet and 175 pounds and lacking a blazing fastball or knee-buckling breaking pitch, Maddux has relied on remarkable control and the ability to outsmart hitters. Throughout the 1990s, he changed speeds so well that hitters rarely saw the same pitch twice in a game. And because he was always throwing strikes and getting ahead in the count, hitters came up swinging—and often sat right back down.

Signed originally by the Cubs out of Valley High in Las Vegas, Maddux became the youngest Cub in history to play in a major league game in 1986, at age 20. (Maddux is about that age in the postcard illustrated on p. 181). He won his first Cy Young award with the Cubs in 1992, going

GREG MADDUX

Canon **CHICAGO**

Publisher: Chicago Cubs/Cannon • Manufacturer: Not Indicated
Type: Black & White • Postmark: Not Used • Value: $5–$8 Unsigned

Publisher: Barry Colla, #2093, Santa Clara, CA • Manufacturer: Not Indicated
Type: Chrome • Postmark: Not Used • Value: $5

20-11 with a 2.18 ERA. He then signed with the Braves as a free agent and won the next three Cy Young awards— making him the first pitcher to capture four in a row.

Although Maddux has won 20 games only twice, he entered 1999 with a 202-107 record in 13 seasons. At age 33, he was in range of getting 300 career victories. But that doesn't matter. If Maddux were to walk away from the game today, his place in Cooperstown would be assured.

1993 JOE CARTER, Toronto Blue Jays

One of the game's steadiest performers, Joe Carter finished his career in 1998 with 2,184 hits, a .259 average, 396 home runs, and 1,445 RBI. He drove in at least 102 runs in 10 of 12 seasons between 1986 and 1997, though his 121 RBI for Cleveland in 1986 was the only time he led the league.

Carter came up with the Cubs and established himself as an All-Star in six years with the Indians. After being traded to San Diego in 1990, he was then sent to Toronto in 1991, becoming an important part of the Blue Jays teams that won world championships in 1992 and '93. His game-winning home run in the bottom of the ninth inning of Game 6 of the 1993 series off Mitch Williams of the Phillies gave Toronto its second consecutive crown.

1993 JOHN OLERUD, Toronto Blue Jays

One of those rare players who went directly from college to the majors, Olerud won the American League batting title with a .363 average in 1993. He also had 200 hits, 24 home runs, and 107 RBI in helping the Blue Jays to their second world championship. But his numbers dropped considerably over the next three years, bottoming out with a .274 average in 1996. He was traded in 1997 to the Mets, where, in his second year in 1998, he challenged for the batting title by hitting .354, second to Colorado's Larry Walker by one point.

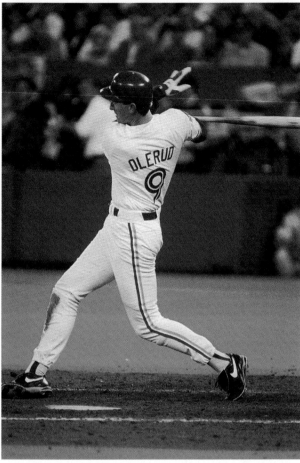

Publisher: Barry Colla, #5693, Berkeley, CA • Manufacturer: Not Indicated
Type: Chrome • Postmark: Not Used • Value: $5

1993 BARRY BONDS, San Francisco Giants

The similarity between Barry Bonds and Ken Griffey Jr. is truly remarkable. Both had fathers who were stars in the big leagues and who taught them the elements of the game. Both are outstanding players on offense and defense, and both are certainties for the Hall of Fame.

Bonds was an all-America selection at Arizona State before he signed with the Pittsburgh Pirates in 1985. He got off to a slow start with the Pirates in 1986, his first major league season, batting just .223 in 113 games. However, by 1990, he was the most valuable player in the National League, an honor he won two other times (1992 and 1993, his first season after signing with the Giants).

Bonds carries a .290 lifetime batting average into the 1999 season and is the first player to have 400 homers and 400 steals in his career. He's an 11-time Gold Glove winner, and at age 34, has a chance at 3,000 career hits. He entered 1999 with 1,917 hits.

Publisher: San Francisco Giants • Manufacturer: Not Indicated
Type: Chrome • Postmark: Not Used • Value: $5

THE COLLA COLLECTION

Darren Daulton

Publisher: Barry Colla, #3494, Santa Clara, CA • Manufacturer: Not Indicated

Type: Chrome • Postmark: Not Used • Value: $5

1993 DARREN DAULTON,
Philadelphia Phillies

Despite serious shoulder and knee injuries, courageous catcher Darren Daulton managed to play 14 big-league seasons, with 1992 and '93 being his best. In 1992, his 109 RBI made him just the fourth catcher to lead that category. In '93, he drove in 105 runs to help carry the Phillies to the National League pennant.

Traded to the Florida Marlins late in the '97 season, Daulton was able to enjoy his only world championship. It was a fine way to end a career that began in 1980 and saw many personal and professional setbacks. Early in his career, he shuttled between the Phillies and the minors for most of four seasons. His progress always seemed to be hampered by injury or inconsistency. Then, in 1991, as he was establishing himself as one of the game's best receivers, he was involved a serious automobile accident that almost ended his career.

Booed and sneered at by Philly fans in the late 1980s, he became a beloved figure after the auto acci-

dent. When he was traded to the Marlins as part of the Phillies' rebuilding effort, fans cheered the move, saying the ballclub owed it to Daulton so he could get a World Series ring.

1993 ANDRES GALARRAGA,
Colorado Rockies

THE COLLA COLLECTION

Andres Galarraga

Publisher: Barry Colla, #3594, Santa Clara, CA • Manufacturer: Not Indicated

Type: Chrome • Postmark: Not Used • Value: $5

Arguably the best Venezuelan player since Hall of Famer Luis Aparicio, Andres Galarraga fought injuries and a career-threatening slump to become one of the decade's top offensive players.

Signed out of a Caracas high school by the Montreal Expos in 1979 at age 18, Galarraga earned the nickname "The Big Cat" for his remarkable agility around first base. In his second full season, in 1987, he batted .305, then followed by hitting .302 in 1989 and leading the National League in hits.

Then he suddenly stopped hitting. He labored with the Expos for three more years, falling to .219 with just nine home runs and 33 RBI in 1991. He was traded to the Cardinals in 1992, when batting coach Don Baylor found a flaw in his swing and changed his stance. "The Big Cat" batted .243 while missing one-third of the season with a broken wrist.

When the expansion Colorado Rockies began play in 1993, Baylor was named manager and signed Galarraga as a free agent. The move paid immediate dividends. Galarraga became the first player on an expansion team to win a batting title, hitting .370. In 1996, he led the NL with 47 homers and 150 RBI; he again led the NL in RBI in 1997.

Called a product of the light air in Colorado's Coors Field, where it's 66 percent easier to hit a home run than in any other park, Galarraga signed with the Braves as a free agent in 1998. There, at age 38, he batted .305 with 44 homers and 121 RBI and silenced a lot of critics.

Nicknamed "The Big Hurt" because he has been destroying American League pitching since he broke in with the White Sox in 1991, Frank Thomas established himself as one of the game's most productive sluggers in the 1990s. Until 1998, when he slumped to .265, he had never batted below .308. He was the American League MVP in 1993 and '94, and he combined the rare ability to hit for power and average, making him a triple-crown threat each year. He was the AL batting champ in 1997, challenged for the title in '94 and '96, and averaged 32 home runs and 107 RBI in his first nine seasons.

A scholarship football player at Auburn, Thomas was also a baseball all-America selection. The 6-foot-5, 270-pound designated hitter/first baseman has few holes in his strike zone. There's virtually nowhere to pitch him. And while he had an off year in 1998, the truth remains that he still hit 30 homers and drove in 110 runs, maintaining a pace that will likely get him into the Hall of Fame.

1993 FRANK THOMAS, Chicago White Sox

Publisher: Barry Colla, #7092, Santa Clara, CA • Manufacturer: Not Indicated
Type: Chrome • Postmark: Not Used • Value: $5

1994 PAUL MOLITOR, Toronto Blue Jays

Publisher: Barry Colla • Manufacturer: Not Indicated • Type: Chrome
Postmark: Not Used • Value: $5–$8 Unsigned

With a .306 career average and 3,319 hits, Paul Molitor ranks among the best hitters in modern baseball—an amazing feat considering he was on the disabled list 12 times in 21 years. He essentially missed three full seasons. Injuries forced him to be a designated hitter most of his career.

But Molitor simply got better with age. He had 1,975 hits after age 30, leading the American League with 225 hits in 1996, when he was 40 years old. Although he never won a batting title, he hit better than .300 12 times, led the league in hits three times and in runs three times, and stole 504 career bases.

Molitor spent 15 years with the Milwaukee Brewers, helping the team reach the World Series in 1982. He signed with Toronto in 1993 and promptly won his first World Series ring. After three seasons, he joined his hometown Minnesota Twins, where he played three more years before retiring as one of the best players of the modern generation.

The 1997 National League season belonged to strong-armed Rockies outfielder Larry Walker, who was an overwhelming choice for MVP on the strength of a .366 batting average, a league-leading 49 home runs, 130 RBI, and 409 total bases. Add to that his third Gold Glove award and personal-best 33 stolen bases, and it's easy to see why he received 22 of the 28 first-place votes.

A native of Maple Ridge, British Columbia, Walker has already established himself as the finest player from Canada. Originally signed by the Montreal Expos—whose uniform he wears on this postcard—he batted .322 with a league-high 44 doubles in 1994. He signed with the Rockies in 1995 and has seen his production soar. But injuries plagued him in 1996 and '98.

Still, Walker's .363 average in '98 captured the batting title and made him, Tony Gwynn, and Wade Boggs the only players to have back-to-back seasons hitting at least .360.

1994 LARRY WALKER, Montreal Expos

Publisher: Montreal Expos/PetroCanada • Manufacturer: Not Indicated
Type: Chrome • Postmark: Not Used • Value: $5

1995 WALTER JOHNSON, Washington Senators

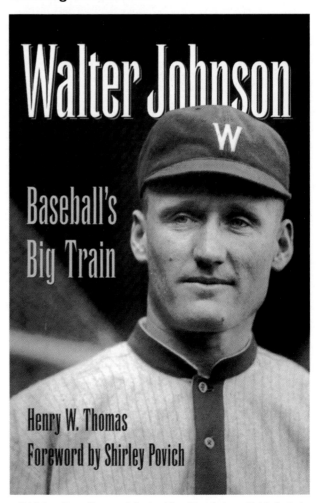

Publisher: Henry Thomas, Arlington, VA • Manufacturer: Not Indicated
Type: Chrome • Postmark: Not Used • Value: $5

Walter Johnson, Baseball's Big Train is one of the most thorough baseball biographies you'll find. Lovingly compiled by Walter's grandson, Henry W. Thomas, the book meticulously chronicles the quiet, dignified life of the great Washington Senators pitcher.

Although Thomas had remarkable family archives at his disposal, he spent most of his research time at the Library of Congress and interviewing people who knew his grandfather. The project took 10 years to complete. The writer was only 8 months old when his grandfather died in 1946, so he relied on testimonies from his mother and countless others, such as the late *Washington Post* columnist Shirley Povich, who covered "The Big Train" during his later years with the Senators.

"I searched for negative comments as well as the positive because I wanted this to be an honest look at his life," Thomas said. "Amazingly, I couldn't find any [negatives]. He was loved by everyone who came in contact with him, even his opponents. He was truly a remarkable person."

In support of the book (available by writing to 2810 Lorcom Lane, Arlington, Va. 22207), the publisher, F.P. Burke, issued the postcard pictured here.

1996 JOHN SMOLTZ, Atlanta Braves

John Smoltz

Publisher: Barry Colla, Berkeley, CA • Manufacturer: Not Indicated
Type: Chrome • Postmark: Not Used • Value: $5

The Atlanta Braves have had the best pitching in baseball during the 1990s, and ultracompetitive John Smoltz is one of the reasons. His hard slider and mid-90s fastball have helped him win 10 or more games in nine of his first 10 full seasons in the big leagues, including a 24-8 record in 1996 that earned him the Cy Young award. In '97, Smoltz's 241 strikeouts made him the first Braves pitcher to record 200 or more strikeouts four times. A great performer in big games, he recovered from arm surgery to go 17-3 with a 2.90 ERA in 1998, showing that at age 32 and with 146 victories, he might have a chance at the Hall of Fame.

1996 MIKE MUSSINA, Baltimore Orioles

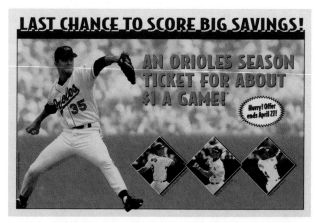

Publisher: Comcast/HTS, Baltimore, MD • Manufacturer: Not Indicated
Type: Chrome • Postmark: Not Used • Value: $5–$8

Right-hander Mike Mussina entered 1999 with a 118-59 record and .667 winning percentage, the best percentage among active pitchers. He's also a three-time Gold Glove winner. But the most games he has ever won in a season is 19—accomplished in 1995 and '96—because injuries and spells of inconsistency have plagued him. Just 29, the former Stanford All-American is arguably the best right-hander in the American League behind Roger Clemens. His assortment of fastball, curveball, circle changeup, and knuckle-curve makes him one of today's nastiest pitchers. He's also a fierce competitor, rarely losing a big game.

60 Years of Padres Baseball

Ted Williams & Tony Gwynn

Publisher: San Diego Padres • Manufacturer: Not Indicated • Type: Chrome
Postmark: Not Used • Value: $10–$15

1996 TONY GWYNN, San Diego Padres

Baseball has not seen a hitter like Tony Gwynn since Stan Musial. Gwynn entered 1999 with a .339 batting average and only 72 hits shy of 3,000. He had eight batting titles, including four in a row from 1994–97, and no player had more hits in the 1990s.

Gwynn has flirted with becoming the first batter since Ted Williams in 1941 to bat .400. The strike of 1994 stopped him at .394 after 106 games. Gwynn has said that year was his best—and last—chance at the historic mark. Several ill-timed injuries have cost him chances at more batting titles or a run at .400, but Gwynn has set such a lofty standard with his hitting that batting .321 in 1998 was considered a slump. He had batted .353 or better for each of the previous five seasons.

This postcard, published by the Padres in conjunction with San Diego's 60th anniversary of professional baseball, pictures the two greatest hitters in the city's history. Ted Williams was born in San Diego and played with the Padres of the Pacific Coast League before he signed with the Boston Red Sox organization in 1938.

1996 ROBIN VENTURA, Chicago White Sox

After a fabulous college career at Oklahoma State, where he had a 58-game hitting streak and was named *Baseball America*'s 1980s College Player of the Decade, Ventura became one of the majors' steadiest performers in the 1990s. He won four Gold Gloves, and while his career .274 average entering 1999 doesn't belie his offensive skills, he is one of the game's smartest hitters, constantly making adjustments to pitchers and game situations. He is one of only 10 players to hit two grand slams in one game, accomplishing the feat Sept. 4, 1995, at Texas.

Publisher: Chicago White Sox • Manufacturer: Not Indicated
Type: Chrome • Postmark: Not Used • Value: $5

Publisher: Los Angeles Dodgers/David Sunflower Seeds, #5794

Manufacturer: Not Indicated • Type: Chrome • Postmark: Not Used

Value: $5

1997 CHAN HO PARK, Los Angeles Dodgers

Chan Ho Park became the first Korean to play in the major leagues when he debuted with the Los Angeles Dodgers on April 8, 1994, in a relief role in the ninth inning against the Atlanta Braves.

Used as both as a starter and reliever since, Park enjoyed his best season in 1997, when he tied teammate Hideo Nomo—the major leagues' first Japanese player in a generation—for most wins by a Dodger with 14. He followed with 15 victories in 1998, leading the team in wins, ERA, games started, innings pitched, and strikeouts. Not bad for a guy who turned just 25 midway through the season. Unfortunately, Park got off to a slow start in 1999, raising questions about his consistency.

1997 MIKE PIAZZA, Los Angeles Dodgers

Since going 3-for-3 in his major league debut in 1992, Mike Piazza has not stopped hitting. He carried a .333 lifetime batting average with 200 homers and 644 RBI into the 1999 season.

Selected by the Dodgers in the 62nd round in 1988 as a favor to then manager Tommy Lasorda, Piazza proved that unheralded players can become superstars. He played winter ball and worked out diligently, forcing his way through the Dodgers' system. When he made the team for good in 1993, he became the National League's Rookie of the Year.

Piazza has since become a regular 30-homer, 100-RBI player—and a regular member of the All-Star team. He was runner-up for MVP in 1996 and '97. But more impressive was his batting average. Slow, aching, battered catchers are not supposed to chase batting titles. But Piazza defied logic and history and hit .346 in 1995 and .362 in 1997—the later ranking as his best season and the best single-season average ever by a catcher. Piazza also racked up 40 homers and 124 RBI.

Publisher: Los Angeles Dodgers, #10193 • Manufacturer: Not Indicated

Type: Chrome • Postmark: Not Used • Value: $5–$8

In the middle of a salary dispute with the Dodgers in 1998, Piazza was sent to the Marlins in a blockbuster trade. Two weeks later, he was shipped to the Mets, who signed him in the off-season to a $91 million contract. Despite all the moving, he still batted .328 with 23 homers and 76 RBI. At age 30, his sore knees weren't ready to concede yet.

1997 JIM THOME, Cleveland Indians

This big first baseman has developed into one of today's best run-producers, becoming an MVP candidate and a steady 30-homer, 100-RBI man. A notorious low fastball hitter with a lively bat, Thome hit 38 homers in 1996 and 40 in 1997. A broken hand caused him to miss a chunk of the 1998 season, but he still hit 30 homers and drove in 85 runs.

Only 28 years old heading into the '99 season, Thome is a major star in Cleveland. His name is becoming known elsewhere, too; in 1999, he was elected the American League's All-Star first baseman. As his popularity grows, so does demand for him as a spokesman, as this postcard endorsing Buick automobiles attests.

Publisher: Northern Ohio Buick Dealers, Cleveland, Ohio • Manufacturer: Not Indicated • Type: Chrome • Postmark: Not Used • Value: $10

THE COLLA COLLECTION

Ken Griffey, Jr.

Publisher: Barry Colla • Manufacturer: Not Indicated • Type: Chrome Postmark: Not Used • Value: $5–$8

1997 KEN GRIFFEY JR., Seattle Mariners

Ken Griffey Jr. is inarguably the best player of his generation. He was an All-Star in each of his first 11 big-league seasons. By the start of 1999, he had 350 career homers and had won the American League home run title three times, with 40 in strike-shortened 1994 and with 56 each in 1997 and '98. He also had nine consecutive Gold Gloves. The only thing keeping him from Cooperstown is time.

Griffey's success is no surprise. The first player taken in the 1987 draft, he is the son of former big-leaguer Ken Griffey, a brilliant hitter who spent the best years of his career with Cincinnati's Big Red Machine. Junior was so good at baseball as a kid that it seemed robotic to him. He once went through an entire Little League season without making an out. He played less than one full season in the minors. And once he reached the majors, he became the sport's biggest draw.

In 1997, he became just the 13th player to earn a unanimous selection as MVP. As the century came to a close, he was just 30 years old. Statistician Bill James

Publisher: Florida Marlins/NationsBank, Fort Lauderdale, FL • Manufacturer: Not Indicated • Type: Chrome • Postmark: Not Used • Value: $5–$8

said Griffey has a 45 percent chance of breaking Hank Aaron's all-time record of 755 home runs. This much is certain: Griffey is a bona fide Hall of Famer. The only question is, what records will he set before his career finally comes to a close?

1997 FLORIDA MARLINS

Just five seasons after their birth, the Marlins became the fastest expansion team to win a championship when they shocked Cleveland in a thrilling seven-game World Series. This postcard was published to promote the team's Fan Fest in early 1998, an event designed to celebrate the world championship and sell tickets for the '98 season. Attending fans were able to have their pictures taken with the 1997 World Series trophy. But enthusiasm for the team was quickly lost. Claiming they had lost $30 million despite winning the championship, the Marlins gutted their team of high-priced stars like Kevin Brown, Bobby Bonilla, Moises Alou, Robb Nen, and Charles Johnson, trimming their payroll from $52.45 million to $19.1 million. The team lost 108 games in 1998, the most of any team following a championship season.

1997 IVAN RODRIGUEZ, Texas Rangers

1997 NELLIE FOX, Washington Senators

Publisher: Texas Rangers • Manufacturer: Not Indicated
Type: Chrome • Postmark: Not Used • Value: $5

Publisher: Washington Baseball Historical Society • Manufacturer: George
Brace, Chicago, IL • Type: Chrome • Postmark: No. Va., April 15, 1998
Value: $5

Only 27 years old entering the 1999 season, Ivan "Pudge" Rodriguez was already one of the all-time great catchers. Winner of seven straight Gold Gloves, he had developed into a steady .300 hitter with the ability to hit 20 homers while driving in 90 runs.

But it's his remarkable defense that has made him a mainstay since he broke into the bigs at age 19 in 1991. Pudge threw out 53 percent of attempted base stealers in 1998, and his snap pickoff throws to bases often catch runners napping. He has been the American League's All-Star starter at catcher every year since 1993, playing the position at such a level that he evokes memories of guys named Cochrane, Dickey, and Bench.

In 1996, Tom Holster and a group of rabid Washington Senators fans formed the Washington Baseball Historical Society, a fan club to perpetuate the memory of major league baseball in Washington. Although the city's diamond has been dormant since 1971, when the expansion Senators left for Texas, Holster has been the driving force behind two well-attended memorabilia shows in Washington that hosted many former Senators, including a reunion of the 1969 team that included Ted Williams, the team's manager. This color postcard of Senators coach Nellie Fox, featuring the brilliant photography of George Brace, was sent to the more than 450 members of the WBHS as a reminder to renew club membership. Fox, one of the game's all-time great second basemen, was elected to the Hall of Fame in 1997. For more information on the Washington Senators Historical Society, contact Holster at P.O. Box 223661, Chantilly, Va. 20153. Dues are only $12 per year.

1997 PAUL O'NEILL, New York Yankees

Since he joined the Yankees in 1993, outfielder Paul O'Neill has quietly developed into one of the game's steadiest players. Although he showed signs of brilliance with the Cincinnati Reds, where he was an integral part of the 1990 world championship team, O'Neill was erratic. In six seasons with the Reds, he averaged .259 at the plate, and was perhaps most famous for being a direct descendant of writer Mark Twain. It wasn't until the volatile and intense O'Neill reached New York that he became a star. Through 1998, O'Neill had never batted below .300 with New York. A fine defensive outfielder with a terrific arm, O'Neill played 235 consecutive errorless games before his streak ended during the '97 season.

PAUL O'NEILL

Publisher: New York Yankees • Manufacturer: Not Indicated
Type: Chrome • Postmark: Not Used • Value: $5

1998 CAL RIPKEN JR., Baltimore Orioles

In a year in which some of the most hallowed records in the game were broken, Cal Ripken Jr. brought to conclusion a standard that may never be approached: his 2,632 consecutive games played. Ripken voluntarily brought "The Streak" to an end on Sept. 20, 1998.

The marvel of Ripken's record is the stubborn, iron-fisted manner in which he went about his job. "The Streak" began May 30, 1982, and for the next five years—covering 8,243 innings—he didn't miss a single inning. Only four times during the 16 years of "The Streak" did he come close to missing a game. And not once did he play as a substitute or designated hitter to keep "The Streak" going. Each game was a start at shortstop or third base.

Ripken's career covers 20 pages in the Orioles' media guide. Among his accomplishments are most home runs by a shortstop, being the American League Rookie of the Year in 1982, MVP in 1983 and '91, and an All-Star every year from 1983 to '98. But the records Ripken is most proud of are for his defense. Surprising as it may seem, he is statistically the greatest fielding shortstop of all time. He holds or shares 12 big-league or AL fielding records. In 1990, his .996 fielding percentage (three errors in 677 chances) was the highest of any shortstop

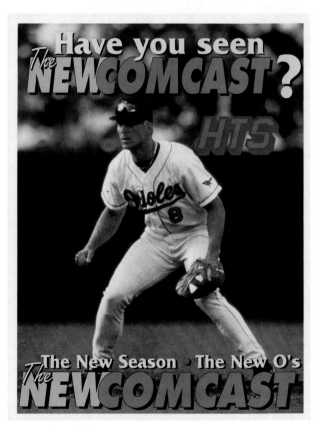

Publisher: Comcast, Baltimore, MD • Manufacturer: Not Indicated
Type: Chrome • Postmark: Not Used • Value: $5–$10

in history. And yet, he did not win the Gold Glove; it went to Chicago's Ozzie Guillen, who had 17 errors.

"I'm embarrassed for my peers," said then Texas Rangers manager Bobby Valentine when Ripken didn't win the Gold Glove. From that year forward, the award was more carefully chosen and scrutinized by the managers and coaches who make the selections.

But it was 1995 when Ripken had his biggest impact on the game. With baseball coming off the strike of 1994—the game's most destructive period since the 1919 Black Sox Scandal—Ripken's final games toward breaking Lou Gehrig's consecutive-games-played record revived the sport. Ripken, who had spent years fighting the association "The Streak" had tagged to his career, understood that baseball was ailing and that breaking Gehrig's mark of 2,130 games would help heal the sport. On Sept. 6, 1995, the world helped him celebrate breaking the record when he played in consecutive game No. 2,131 against the Angels.

Baseball's recovery was underway.

1998 KEVIN BROWN, San Diego Padres

Publisher: San Diego Padres • Manufacturer: Not Indicated • Type: Chrome
Postmark: Not Used • Value: $5

The highest-paid pitcher in history personifies the title of the radio and television Western *Have Gun, Will Travel*. After the 1998 season, Brown signed a seven-year, $105 million contract with the Los Angeles Dodgers, his fifth team in six years. In '97, he helped lead the Florida Marlins to the world championship and was then the driving force in getting the San Diego Padres to the series in 1998.

Brown was originally signed by the Texas Rangers after an all-America career at Georgia Tech. He won his first big-league game in 1986 and stayed with the Rangers until 1994, leaving for the Orioles for one year.

But until he joined the Marlins in 1996, Brown was an inconsistent pitcher with an erratic personality. His inability to win games confounded most everyone. His hard, sinking fastball was almost impossible to hit. His best year in Texas was 1992, when his 21 wins tied for the league lead. But for the most part, he was barely a .500 pitcher. He won just 10 games for the Orioles in 1995, despite a 3.60 ERA. Along the way, he infuriated teammates with cold stares when they made errors behind him.

When he signed with the Marlins, he suddenly became one of baseball's most dominant pitchers. He won 17 games in 1996 and had a 1.89 ERA. He won 16 in leading them to the championship in '97. Traded to the Padres as part of a salary purge, he added a split-fingered fastball and went 18-7 with a 2.38 ERA in '98. In free agency, Brown became the subject of one of the most intense bidding wars in baseball history, which made him baseball's first $100-million player.

1998 JUAN GONZALEZ, Texas Rangers

By the time he was 30 years old in 1999, Juan Gonzalez was established as one of the great sluggers of all time and the best to come out of Latin America. He was a two-time American League home run champion, winner of the MVP award in 1996 and 1998, and the best RBI man in baseball.

His career began with enormous expectations, and he has lived up to them. In 1992, at age 22, he became the seventh-youngest home run champion when he led the AL with 43. A year later, he slugged 46 to win the home run title again. By the time he was 24, only Eddie Mathews, Mel Ott, Ken Griffey Jr., Frank Robinson, and Mickey Mantle had more homers at such an early age, thus beginning Gonzalez's assault on the record books in ways that lead directly to the Hall of Fame.

Always a great clutch hitter, he developed into a great situational hitter. During the 1996 season, in which Gonzalez led the once lowly Rangers to the playoffs for the first time, he batted .314 with 47 home runs and 144 RBI. In 1998, he had one of the great seasons in history,

JUAN GONZALEZ • OF

DR PEPPER BOTTLING
COMPANY OF TEXAS

RANGERS

Publisher: Texas Rangers • Manufacturer: Not Indicated • Type: Chrome
Postmark: Not Used • Value: $5

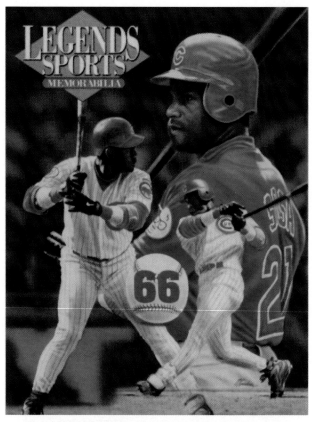

Publisher: Legends Magazine • Manufacturer: Not Indicated
Type: Chrome • Postmark: Not Used • Value: $5

batting .318 with 50 doubles, 45 homers, and 157 RBI.

A personable and likable player who grew up in a poor section of Puerto Rico, Gonzalez has always spent time signing autographs, doing charity work, and visiting with kids in hospitals and schools. In an era when some of the best players in baseball came from Latin America, none was more popular than Gonzalez, whose 301 career homers entering 1999 put him on a fast track to Cooperstown.

1998 SAMMY SOSA, Chicago Cubs

Through hard work and determination, Cubs outfielder Sammy Sosa has worked his way to being one of the game's top talents. He was the National League's MVP in 1998, batting .308 with 66 home runs and 158 RBI. While Mark McGwire of the Cardinals won the home run title, it was their joint pursuit of Roger Maris' single-

season record of 61 that drove interest in baseball to heights not seen in decades.

The happy-go-lucky Sosa was just 15 years old when he was signed by the Texas Rangers out of the Dominican Republic in 1985. He reached the majors in 1989, but scouts felt he was too undisciplined as a hitter to become a big-league star. He was traded to the White Sox during the 1989 pennant drive as part of a package for hitter Harold Baines. Sosa was sent to the Cubs in 1992 for pitcher Ken Patterson and washed-up outfielder George Bell.

In 1993, his second year with the Cubs, it all began to click for Sammy. Only 24 years old, he hit 33 homers and drove in 93 runs. Steady progress followed. He batted .300 in 1994, and in '95 he became the first Cub to lead the team in homers and stolen bases three years in a row. Slowly but assertively, Sosa was becoming a five-tool talent. He learned to work pitch counts and blasted 40 homers in 1996 and 36 in 1997.

But no one—not even Sosa—could have predicted that he would bash 66 in 1998. At age 30, he was still developing his game. Time will reveal Sosa's place in baseball's annals.

Publisher: Leroy Neiman • Manufacturer: Not Indicated • Type: Chrome
Postmark: Not Used • Value: $10

1999 MARK McGWIRE, St. Louis Cardinals

As Babe Ruth and his home runs were credited with saving baseball after the "Black Sox Scandal" erupted in 1920, the 1998 home run chase by Mark McGwire and Sammy Sosa of the Cubs restored the faith of fans alienated by the 1994 players' strike.

McGwire didn't simply break Roger Maris' 37-year-old single-season record of 61 home runs. He shattered it, swatting a remarkable 70. But it was not an easy journey for the big, likable first baseman. Sosa hit a record 20 homers in June to put the heat on McGwire. It was not until the final weekend, when Big Mac hit four homers—including two in the last game of the season—that he escaped with the home run crown.

McGwire broke Maris' record Sept. 8, 1998, with a fourth-inning homer off the Cubs' Steve Trachsel. It was only fitting that Sosa and the Cubs were in St. Louis that night. One of the memorable, game-stopping moments of celebration was provided by Sosa, who rushed in from right field to hug McGwire.

Despite injuries that essentially took three years off his career, McGwire entered 1999 with 457 homers in just 13 years. That translated to an all-time best of one home run every 11.23 at-bats. He's the only player to hit 50 or more homers in three straight seasons and, at age 35, seemed on the cusp of reaching the Hall of Fame.

ALPHABETICAL INDEX OF POSTCARD SUBJECTS

Note: **boldface** *indicates illustration*

INDEX OF ILLUSTRATIONS BY TEAM

Ron Menchine, Voice of the Senators

Publisher: Ron Menchine • Manufacturer: Mitchell Color Cards, Petosky, MI • Type: Chrome • Postmark: Not Used • Value: Priceless

ABOUT THE AUTHOR

An Autobiographical Essay
By Ron Menchine

I fell in love with baseball and ballparks the first time my father and grandfather took me to a game at Oriole Park in Baltimore. The year was 1939. I was 5 years old, and baseball was celebrating its 100th anniversary. The Orioles were an International League team, a minor league farm club for the Cleveland Indians, playing in a ballpark that had been built in 1914 for the Baltimore Terrapins of the Federal League.

A few years later, my aunt Grace visited New York City. Knowing my interest in baseball, she sent me a postcard of Yankee Stadium. Fascinated with the architecture, I began to write major and minor league teams asking for pictures of their stadiums. Many of them responded by sending postcards. In the late 1940s, I started writing major league players to ask for autographs, and nearly all of them replied with postcards. In those days before Baltimore had a major league team, I adopted the Orioles' affiliate, the Indians, as my favorite. Postcards sent to me by Indians greats like Mike Garcia, Bob Lemon, Bob Feller, Early Wynn, and Al Rosen remain prized possessions to this day. I'll never forget the thrill of receiving an autographed postcard from my boyhood hero, Lou Boudreau, in 1949.

I spent four delightful college years at the University of Maryland, where I laid the foundation for my future career by broadcasting Terrapin sporting events on campus radio station WMUC. While in college, I met three outstanding announcers who befriended me and greatly influenced my work: Bob Wolff, voice of the Washington Senators; Ernie Harwell, voice of the Orioles; and Jim Simpson, who announced NBC's Baseball Game of the Week. Each one stressed that there is no substitute for thorough preparation. It's a lesson I have always lived by and continue to pass on to this day.

While I was at Maryland, Ernie and Bob were kind enough to make arrangements for me to tape-record games at Memorial Stadium in Baltimore and Griffith Stadium in Washington, D.C. It was my dream to one day broadcast big-league baseball myself. That dream became a reality in 1969, when I was named "Voice of the Senators." For three glorious years, I chronicled the team's games on radio. When owner Bob Short moved the team to Texas following the 1971 season, I was devastated. I'm still waiting for baseball to return to the nation's capital.

But the memories of my stint with the team will be with me forever. Pitching coach Sid Hudson introduced me to the finest restaurants in American League cities, while I introduced Midwest natives Del Unser and Bernie Allen to Maryland's hardshell crabs. On charter flights, I talked baseball with Hall of Famers Ted Williams and Nellie Fox, and discussed finance with Jim Hannan, who went on to become a successful Washington stockbroker. I learned about snowmobiling from ace pitcher Dick Bosman, who owned a snowmobile franchise in his native Wisconsin. I came to know Frank Howard, one of the nicest guys in baseball and the most powerful slugger I ever saw. I enjoyed the antics of Eddie Brinkman, Jim French, and Tim Cullen, the team comedians who always seemed to make Howard the butt of their jokes. And I laughed when pitcher Joe Grzenda, whose arm troubles led him to spend many years riding minor league buses, told me what he would do if he stayed in the majors long enough to qualify for a pension. "If I ever get my four years in," he said, "I'm going to buy a bus and burn it." With the help of two seasons of more than 40 appearances as a reliever for the Senators, Joe eventually earned his pension, but he never did buy that bus.

As I traveled the country with the Senators, I was able to meet many top postcard collectors who helped me enhance my collection greatly and who became good friends. People like John Sullivan in Chicago, Frank Nagy in Detroit, Dick Dobbins in Oakland, and Buck Barker in St. Louis, who unfortunately are now deceased. People like Ed Budnick in Detroit, Ray Medeiros in Los Angeles, Pat Quinn and Jim Rowe in Chicago, George Tinker in Richmond, and many others.

Closer to home, retired Air Force major Mel Bailey and his late wife Marty hosted many collector gatherings and provided numerous fine meals. Today, Mel resides in Riverside, Calif., where he photographs nearly all major league players as he has for 30 years. His photos have graced the covers of many national publications. No matter how obscure the player, chances are Mel has captured him on film.

I'd be remiss if I didn't take the opportunity to thank my fellow Senators broadcasters, Shelby Whitfield and Tony Roberts, and Washington writers George Minot, Russ White, and the late Merrell Whittlesey, who frequently accompanied me on my jaunts to antique shops and flea markets where many of the items seen in this book turned up. More than 300 postcards are pictured in these pages, but many others appear in my first book, *A Picture Postcard History of Baseball*. Autographed copies are available directly from me for $15 including postage. Write Ron Menchine, P.O. Box 1, Long Green, Md. 21092.

HUGGINS
SECOND BASEMAN PAR EX GELLENGE